Starting Your Subchapter "S" Corporation

How to Build a Business the Right Way

Arnold S. Goldstein

JOHN WILEY & SONS
New York • Chichester • Brisbane • Toronto • Singapore

ISBN 0-471-60604-9
ISBN 0-471-60602-2 (pbk.)

Printed in the United States of America

10 9 8 7 6 5 4 3 2 1

PREFACE

Tens of thousands of businesses are electing to take advantage of what is known as the S Corporation or "S-Chapter Corporation" as it is often called. The S Corporation has become particularly popular since the passage of the 1986 Tax Reform Act, because for the first time individuals are taxed at a lower rate than are corporations. And that is only one major advantage of an S Corporation: Only this form of business organization offers you both the advantages of the lowest possible tax coupled with the limited liability and other benefits of a regular corporation. This book is in response to the numerous requests for a practical guide to S Corporations.

If your business is presently operated as a regular corporation, you will find all the needed information to quickly and conveniently convert it to an S Corporation. Conversely if you are planning to start a new business or presently operate an existing business under a proprietorship or partnership form of organization, this guide will help you set up an S Corporation by guiding you through the process of incorporating a regular corporation, which is a first step towards an S Corporation.

While the S Corporation offers many tax benefits there are also several disadvantages to an S Corporation and therefore you should carefully review the pros and cons before deciding to become an S Corporation. Further, not all corporations can qualify for S Corporation status. For these reasons you should have your situation carefully analyzed by a qualified accountant or tax attorney if there is any question whether an S Corporation can best serve your needs.

Within this guide you will find both the information you need to determine how an S Corporation functions, and what you must do to properly administer it and take advantage of its several significant benefits. You will also find forms you need to convert your present corporation to an S Corporation, maintain your corporate records in full legal compliance, and protect yourself, your corporation, and other shareholders with essential agreements.

This book will also answer your critical questions and many more in a clear, straightforward manner.

Setting up your own S Corporation is not as difficult as you might imagine. You will discover that as you read these pages and gain the knowledge you need.

Arnold S. Goldstein

Chestnut Hill, Massachusetts
January 1988

ABOUT THE AUTHOR

Arnold S. Goldstein is a senior partner in the Boston law firm of Meyers, Goldstein & Kosberg where he specializes in corporate law. He is also a professor at Northeastern University where he teaches management and law.

A popular writer on management topics, his prior books include the complete Guide to Buying and Selling a Business (John Wiley & Sons) and Starting on a Shoestring (John Wiley & Sons).

Mr. Goldstein holds the degrees of Bachelor of Science, Master of Business Administration, Doctor of Jurisprudence, and Master of Laws, and is a member of the Massachusetts and Federal Bars and numerous professional and civic organizations.

CONTENTS

CONTENTS

CHOOSING THE FORM OF ORGANIZATION

1

OVERVIEW

Most people when starting a business consider the various types of business organization available to them. An individual venturing into business has the choice of operating his business as a sole proprietorship or corporation. If two or more people are going into business together they also have a choice—a partnership or corporation form of organization.

Whether to incorporate or to conduct a business in some other form—a sole proprietorship or a partnership—involves many considerations. If you are currently doing business you will have the demands on your time of running a business which often prevents you from taking time out to carefully consider your options, assess your situation and plan. Even if you are not yet in business, but planning to start a new enterprise, do not rush into business without first carefully considering the best form of organization. Many factors go into the decision for selecting the best structure of a business enterprise. Some of the more important factors in determining what type of business entity you should use include:

1. Liability and personal exposure.
2. Costs including filing fees.
3. Management structure and whether it needs to be centralized or dispersed.
4. The available methods of raising capital.
5. The ability to attract and keep key personnel through various fringe benefits or participations such as stock options.
6. Tax considerations.

The three basic forms of business entity—individual or sole proprietorship, partnership, and corporation—each offer their own unique advantages and disadvantages.

SOLE PROPRIETORSHIPS

A sole proprietorship is a business that is owned by an individual who is solely responsible for all aspects of the business. The owner is personally responsible for all debts of the business even in excess of the amount invested.

When an individual forms a business and operates it in his or her own name (or a trade name), that person runs the risk of having all of his or her personal assets exposed to creditors of the business. So, for example, if an employee accidentally injures a customer or some other person, the owner of the business stands liable for the injury. Even if there is insurance coverage, the possibility always exists that liability may exceed the coverage provided by the policy.

Other drawbacks exist. If the sole proprietor becomes ill or dies, the business he or she has developed immediately loses much of its value. Moreover, the business terminates with the death of the proprietor creating added problems in disposing of it.

The advantages of a sole proprietorship include:

1. Low start up costs since legal and filing fees are at a minimum. However, many states and cities require at least a filing with the county clerk especially if a fictitious business name is adopted.
2. Greatest freedom from regulation.
3. Owner is in direct control.
4. Minimum working capital requirements.
5. Tax advantages to owners of small businesses.
6. All profits inure to the owner.

The disadvantages include:

1. Unlimited liability. The proprietor is responsible for the full amount of business debts no matter how incurred, which means that his personal property may be taken to cover debts of the business.
2. Unstable business life, since the sole owner's death or illness would terminate the business.
3. Difficulty in raising capital and in obtaining long-term financing.

PARTNERSHIPS

A partnership is a legal entity that is jointly owned by two or more individuals (although in some cases partners may also be corporations or other entities). As in the sole proprietorship, the owners are personally liable for all debts of the firm unless a special type of partnership, the limited partnership, is set up. Limited partnerships are very complex legal structures, and still must have at least one partner who has unlimited liability. Even partnership agreements for regular partnerships can be quite complex.

The partnership shares many of the benefits and drawbacks of the sole proprietorship. Each partner is personally liable for all of the business debts. The partnership relation comes to an end whenever any partner decides he or she no longer wants to be part of the business or if a partner dies.

Other drawbacks include the difficulty of obtaining new partners, particularly if they do not share profits on an equal basis.

As in the case of the sole proprietorship, the partnership is not a taxable entity. Its profits, gains, losses, and credits "pass through" to its partners.

The advantages of a partnership include:

1. Ease of formation (although more complicated than the sole proprietorship).

2. Low start up costs, especially since there usually are fewer filing fees and franchise taxes.

3. Limited outside regulation, unless the type of business itself is one that is in a regulated industry.

4. Broader management base than a sole proprietorship and a more flexible management structure than the corporation.

5. Possible tax advantages, since it avoids the double taxation of corporations, and because income can be taxed at personal income rates. Naturally, the personal income situations of the partners could also make this a disadvantage.

6. Additional sources of capital, and leverage by adding limited and special partners.

7. Each partner can bind all of the co-partners, and, in the absence of restrictions in the partnership agreement, may terminate the partnership.

8. The duration of the entity can be limited to a stated time, or can continue indefinitely by amendment.

The disadvantages of a partnership include:

1. Unlimited liability of at least one partner and except in limited partnership situations all the partners have unlimited liability. The personal assets of each of the general partners are available to satisfy partnership debts.

2. The life of a partnership is unstable since changing partners by adding new ones or by death or departure of partners causes the partnership to terminate.

3. Obtaining large sums of capital is relatively difficult as the financing cannot be obtained from the public through a stock offering.

4. The acts of just one partner, even unauthorized acts in many cases, bind all the partners.

5. An individual partnership interest cannot be easily sold or disposed of.

6. Most tax supported fringe benefits like pension and profit-sharing arrangements available only to corporations are unavailable to partnerships.

CORPORATIONS

A corporation is a business that is formed and authorized by law to act as a single entity, although it is constituted and owned by one or more persons. It is legally endowed with rights and responsibilities and has a life of its own independent of the owners and operators. It has been defined by the United States Supreme Court as "an artificial being, invisible, intangible and existing only in contemplation of the law."

The most significant feature of a corporation is its ability to shield its shareholders from personal liability. The shareholder is not liable for the debts of the business. Except in cases of fraud, the share-holders maximum risk is the amount of money he or she invests in it.

Second, the corporate form of organization also makes it easier to attract additional investors.

Third, the corporation has perpetual life. The death or disability of a shareholder has no effect on the continued existence of the corporation.

The advantages of a corporation include:

1. Limited liability, that is the owners are liable for debts and obligations of the corporation only to the extent of their investment in the corporation, with the exception that they can be

personally liable for certain types of taxes such as payroll taxes which have been withheld from the employees pay checks but not paid over to the Internal Revenue Service and state sales taxes. If the business fails or loses a lawsuit the general creditors cannot attach the owners homes, cars and other personal property.

2. Capital can be raised more easily than in other forms of ownership. This does not mean, however, that a new corporation can easily sell stock. In the first place the sale of stock is highly regulated by both Federal and state governments and obtaining bank loans for a fledgling business may be no easier for a new corporation than for a partnership or proprietorship.

3. Ownership is more easily transferable and this includes transferring shares to family members as gifts or otherwise as well as selling your interest to some other person; however, in many small corporations it is advisable to put restrictions on transfer of shares especially if the persons owning and working in the business must be able to work closely together. This is generally done in the form of a stockholders' agreement.

4. Since the corporation is an independent legal entity it has a life of its own or continuous existence. It does not cease just because one of the owners dies or wishes to retire.

5. There is centralized management which usually rests in the board of directors and is exercised by the officers.

6. As a legal entity it can enter into contracts and sue and be sued and the consent and signature of the owners is not necessary.

7. Corporations have a built-in impetus to increase the capital by reinvesting it, since salaries are normally set at the beginning of the year. In addition, surplus earnings can be set aside for a future date, although there are Federal tax penalties if these surpluses exceed certain amounts.

8. Many companies offer discounts to corporations, an indication that they favor corporate accounts.

9. Retirement funds such as Keogh, defined-contribution plans, money-purchase plans, and other profit-sharing, pension and stock option plans offer greater benefits to corporations.

The disadvantages of a corporation include:

1. It is subject to more governmental regulations than partnerships and sole proprietorships.

2. It may be a more expensive and complex form of business to organize.

3. Record keeping requirements can be very extensive.

4. Operating across state lines can be complicated because of the need of corporations to "qualify to do business" in states where they are not incorporated. This is explained in greater detail later.

5. Ending the corporate existence, and in many cases even changing some of the structure if it requires an amendment to the certificate of incorporation, can be more complicated and costly than for partnerships and proprietorships.

There is one more drawback to a regular corporation (commonly referred to as a C Corporation): The corporation is a person for tax purposes. This means that if it has a profit it must pay a tax on the profits whether the profits were retained by the corporation or distributed to stockholders as dividends. However, if the corporation had a loss, the loss does not work to the benefit of the shareholders. At most the loss can be saved and applied against corporate profits in future years. Yet if the corporation has a profit distributed to shareholders as dividends, they are taxed a second time as dividends to the shareholders who receive the dividends.

That, of course, is the one traditional drawback of a corporation—the double taxation on profits and dividends. And it is for that reason that so many businesspeople have selected proprietorships or partnerships despite their serious disadvantages of unlimited liability.

But with the passage of the Tax Reform Act of 1986 and lowered corporate tax rates, many more people are discovering the very best form of organization is the S Corporation because only this form of organization offers the many advantages of a corporation with the favorable tax treatment afforded the proprietorship or partnership.

WHY AN S CORPORATION?

2

OVERVIEW

The S Corporation combines what is generally considered the best of all possible worlds: it provides the limitations on liability associated with incorporation and the "pass through" taxation of a partnership or proprietorship, i.e. single, not double taxation.

An S Corporation is a corporation that, for most tax purposes, is treated as if it is a partnership or proprietorship. That means it is not a tax-paying entity. Instead, the S Corporation is viewed only as a financial conduit. its income, deductions, credits and losses are passed through to its shareholders who pay whatever tax is due. If, at the end of the year, your S Corporation earns a profit, it does not pay any taxes on that profit. Instead, the profit is recognized as your income and you pay the tax.

On the other hand, if you formed a regular corporation, the profits of that business would be taxed *twice*. First, the corporation would pay a corporate tax on the profit, then when that after-tax profit is distributed to you as a shareholder, you would pay a hefty income tax on it as dividend income. That's what we mean when we refer to the *double taxation* imposed on corporate profits.

For years, most sophisticated businessmen recognized the tax benefits available through an S incorporation. Those benefits have become significantly more important because of the Tax Reform Act of 1986 which adds a vital new incentive for considering S incorporation. In the past, the maximum tax rates for individuals was 4 percent higher for individuals (50 percent) than for corporations (46 percent).

Under the 1986 Tax Reform Act, however, a reverse situation exists. The maximum tax rates for individuals is *6 percent lower* for individuals (28 percent) than for corporations (34 percent). That means that if you form a regular corporation and it has a profit, the profit will be taxed at a maximum rate of 34 percent; whatever is left can be distributed to you as a dividend and can be taxed again at the maximum individual rate of 28 percent. Had you formed an S Corporation, that profit would have been taxed only once, and then at the lower, individual rates.

With this overview of the major benefits of an S Corporation, we can summarize them as:

1. No double taxation.
2 Personal deductions of corporate losses.
3. Lower tax rates.
4. Tax savings on sale of corporate assets.

SINGLE TAXATION AND LOWER TAX RATES

To see how much an S Corporation can actually save in taxes let's use some actual numbers.

Assume your business operates as a regular corporation and earns an annual profit of $100,000. Based on the new 1986 tax rates your corporate and personal taxes on the $100,000 would be $44,323. We calculate that by first deducting $22,250 for corporate taxes. This leaves the corporation with $77,750 to distribute to you as dividend income. If you and your wife are married and file jointly, your tax on the $77,750 is $22,073. This means that between you and the corporation you spent approximately 45 cents on every dollar for taxes!

Now let's assume you formed an S Corporation. That $100,000 in corporate profits would be taxed only once—to you. We do not have to deduct a corporate tax because as an S Corporation there is no corporate tax (federal). Therefore you would pay a personal tax of $28,293 on the $100,000 leaving you approximately $16,000 more after all tax payments. Of course, the actual tax savings will vary based on the amount of profits earned by your corporation and your personal tax situation, however, the combination of one tax instead of two coupled with lower personal tax rate insures lower taxes if you choose an S Corporation form of organization.

Tax Note:
Remember: With an S Corporation you are taxed on corporate earnings whether you take the earnings as dividends or retain the earnings in the corporation. With a regular C Corporation you do

not personally pay taxes on corporate earnings unless first paid to you as dividends. Therefore, the actual tax savings in a given year will depend on the portion of earnings distributed as dividends.

PERSONAL DEDUCTIONS OF CORPORATE LOSSES

Losses accrued by a regular corporation are worthless to the stockholders as a tax-saving device.

However, if your S Corporation has a loss you can apply those losses against other income. For example, if your S Corporation lost $25,000 last year (and you had at least $25,000 invested in the business) you can use the $25,000 as a deduction on your personal return. If you had other income and you are in the 28 percent tax bracket the corporation's $25,000 loss would mean a personal tax savings of approximately $7,000 to you.

Of course, if the corporation has several stockholders, each can take a percentage of the loss allocated to their percentile ownership.

TAX SAVINGS ON THE SALE OF CORPORATE ASSETS

Just as a regular corporation creates a double tax on earned income, so too does it create a double tax situation when the business sells assets that have appreciated.

For example, assume you've been operating a regular corporation for several years and that you've decided to sell the business. If the corporation has assets that have appreciated, under the 1986 Tax Reform Act the appreciated gain on that asset is fully taxable to the corporation. After the corporation pays that tax and remits the remaining balance to you as a stockholder, you'll pay a second tax on any gain you've received. The concept is almost the same as the double taxation on profits discussed above.

If, however, you formed an S Corporation, only one tax would be paid—the tax at the shareholder's level. If the corporation you are about to form will have assets that will appreciate in value, then you have an important added reason for forming an S Corporation.

Tax Tip:
If you have a regular corporation, obviously you should consider converting to an S Corporation. If you do and the corporation has appreciable assets, then the 1986 Tax Reform Act provides that any appreciation that occurred before the switch may be subject to double taxation; appreciation that occurs after the switch will be

taxed only once. Therefore, you should obtain an independent appraisal of the asset at the time you elect S Corporation status.

CAN YOU BENEFIT FROM AN S CORPORATION?

Virtually every type of business operation can benefit by being operated by an S Corporation. Perhaps the only situations where an S Corporation may not be advisable involve businesses that expect to retain rather than distribute profits. Because it is treated as if it is a partnership, an S Corporation must report that its shareholders have earned profits even if it does not distribute those profits. For example, if your S Corporation earns $50,000 in profits and you decide to invest that money in new equipment, your personal return must show the $50,000 of profits as income to you. But even in this situation, the fact that individual tax rates are lower than corporate rates may justify a decision in favor of the S Corporation.

Situations that clearly can benefit from the S Corporation option include:

1. Service industries with modest equipment or capital asset requirements.
2. Fully developed businesses that will not require additional capital investments.
3. Enterprises that will invest in real estate, equipment, or other property that will rapidly appreciate in value.
4. Start-up ventures that are expected to operate at a loss for the first year or two.

Tax Warning:
Most deductions and expenses allowed as deductions for regular corporations are also available to S Corporations, however, there is one exception: deductions based on medical reimbursement or health insurance plans are not available to S Corporations (see chapter on fringe benefits). Still, the other benefits available when the S Corporation option is selected will, usually, far outweigh this drawback.

WHEN TO BE TAXED AS A REGULAR CORPORATION

S Corporation status is one tax strategy of many available to small business owners. Like other tax-saving techniques it is not recommended in all cases. You should elect to be taxed as a regular corporation when:

1. Your enterprise becomes profitable, and you want to build up earnings to expand your business.

    If you choose to be taxed as a regular corporation, your earnings will be subject only to corporate rates which are taxed at lower rates than individual income tax when income is below $75,000. The first $50,000 of corporate profits, for example, is taxed at a 15 percent rate; the next $25,000 is taxed at a 25 percent rate. On the other hand, joint filers are taxed at 15 percent for the first $29,750 of income (and lower for other taxpayers) and at a rate of 28 percent for all income above that level. Not until a corporation's profits go over $75,000 does its rate jump to 34 percent. Therefore, it may be wise to remain a C Corporation until net income exceeds $75,000 when the shift to an S Corporatin will likely be more beneficial.

2. You've owned a profitable service business for several years, and rather than drain earnings from the company, you now want to accumulate them in the corporation and diversify. As above, regular corporate rates may leave more cash for reinvestment. Of course, it may be possible to pull sufficient income out of a C Corporation as salary to avoid double taxation.

3. You formed your S Corporation several years ago as a tax shelter. The shelter's earnings have risen while annual depreciation deductions have diminished. The "shelter" is now poised to become very profitable, throwing profits into your high-bracket personal tax return. The solution: give up S Corporation status and let the profits be taxed at corporate rates. Again, this only is advisable if the corporation will return profits and the annual profits do not exceed $75,000.

4. If there is considerable passive losses, such as through real estate investment, these passive loss generators should be taken out of the S Corporation and owned by a C Corporation or held personally or through some other entity.

A FINAL WORD

How and when you can use an S Corporation will depend upon several factors:

1. The type of business you own.
2. Its profitability.
3. Your personal tax bracket.
4. The types of assets used by your business.
5. Growth prospects.

6. State law and its recognition of the S Corporation status.
7. Other factors.

If you *can* use it, an S Corporation may save you a substantial amount of tax each year... and *help you build more wealth!*

However, consult your tax advisor before you act. He or she may point out other factors which apply in your particular case, or perhaps a tax trap you're nearing.

But don't delay. With the tax savings an S Corporation offers, you may be able to move much more quickly into the financial future you deserve.

INCORPORATING YOUR BUSINESS

3

OVERVIEW

Once you have decided that an S corporation is the form of organization you wish to utilize for a business, you must first organize a valid corporation under state law. These vary from state to state and vary in complexity. However, with planning most people can easily create a corporation without a lawyer saving hundreds of dollars in legal fees.

WHERE TO INCORPORATE

The first question is to decide the state within which to organize the corporation. There are 50 states and the District of Columbia to choose from. You may have heard of the great advantages of incorporating in the State of Delaware, and it is true that a great percentage of the publicly held corporations in this country are incorporated there. There are reasons for this, many of which are no longer valid for public corporations, and most of which never made much sense for a small corporation. As a matter of fact, many of these large Delaware corporations started out in other states and only when they grew in size to become large national corporations, moved their "corporate entity" to Delaware. The State of Delaware's Division of Incorporations sends out a list of these advantages to incorporating in that state to anyone who requests them:

1. The fees payable to the State of Delaware are based upon the number of shares of authorized capital stock, with the no par shares fee one-half the par shares fee.

2. The franchise tax compares favorably with that of any other state.

3. Shares of stock owned by persons outside of the State are not subject to taxation.

4. Shares of stock which are part of the estate of a non-resident decedent are exempt from the State Inheritance Tax Law.

5. The policy of Delaware courts has always been to construe the Corporation Law liberally, to interpret any ambiguities or uncertainties in the wording of the Statutes so as to reach a reasonable and fair construction. This causes the careful investor to have confidence in the security of the investment.

6. The corporation service companies throughout the nation consider the Delaware Corporation Law among the most attractive for organization purposes and the State of Delaware a valuable jurisdiction in which to organize new companies.

7. Directors have greater statutory protection from liability.

Although the above advantages are important, it does not follow that Delaware should be the location of your corporation. There are many reasons for incorporating elsewhere. First, of course, is that most corporations will be established to operate a business which is located somewhere else in the country and which will not likely ever open a branch in Delaware. If your business is, for example, going to be a retail store in New York City, it would be more advisable to set up a New York corporation. If you were to set up a Delaware corporation, and operate a store in New York City, you would still have to qualify "to do business" in the State of New York which would then require filing an application to do business as a foreign corporation, paying of franchise taxes as a foreign corporation in New York, and annual reporting and paying of taxes in New York as well as Delaware. The advantages of Delaware incorporation would have to be very great indeed to overcome the burden for most small businesses of being subject to regulation by two states. Needless to say, incorporating in the state where you are located usually makes the greatest sense. Of course, if the corporation is sufficiently large to benefit from Delaware incorporation it will likely require the services of an attorney whose advice on the state of incorporation should always be carefully considered.

Make your decision on what state to incorporate in on the important factors: First, as we have already mentioned, where your actual physical facilities are can be the most important factor. Second, the costs of incorporating in that state, and if you incorporate in a state other than the one in which you are going to be located, what it will cost to become authorized to do business in the state where you are located. These costs include fees to check and reserve the name you want to use for your corporation, the cost of filing incorporation papers, and whether there is a one time organizational fee or franchise tax (this is often based upon the number of shares you will have authorized for the corporation to issue). If you need to be authorized to do business in another state the filing fees, name reservation fees, and initial franchise fees should be determined and considered. In addition to the initial costs, you must determine what the annual fees are. For example, is there an annual report to file with the Secretary of State and what is the filing fee? Is there an annual franchise tax? Is there a state or local income tax and how is it determined? While these cost factors may be considered, the issues of convenience and taxes are probably more critical factors in selecting the state of incorporation.

Further considerations include whether the laws covering corporations in your state of choice are beneficial to the corporation. For example, some states require three incorporators and three directors. If you plan to have a corporation that only one person is going to own or control it might be that your state might require you to have more board members than you want. The discussion in this book about what goes in the certificate of incorporation will cover many of these items which vary from state to state. Before you make the final decision on the location of your corporation, you should obtain a copy of the corporation statutes and read them for obstacles. These statutes can be found in public libraries and in law libraries and in many instances, the Secretary of State's office will make them available for free or for a small charge. A publication entitled *Martindale-Hubbell Law Directory* which can also be found in public and law libraries contains summaries of all the laws of all 50 states.

Once you have decided what state to incorporate in, a great deal of information about how to set up that corporation free or for minimal fees can be obtained from the appropriate Secretary of State. A listing of the addresses and telephone numbers of persons to contact in the various states is contained at the end of this chapter.

SELECTION OF THE CORPORATION'S NAME

The first step in organizing your corporation is to select a corporate name and then check to see if the state in which you are going to incorporate will allow you to use the name.

Other than your own originality, the only obstacle will be the state statutes which prohibit certain words. Not all states have the same prohibitions, so you should check your particular state. Many prohibited names are used in the name of organizations or corporations, but by and large they are in fields in which special licensing or regulation is required. Often corporations in these fields must be organized pursuant to statutes regulating that particular field, and it is not advisable to attempt to set up such a corporation without the assistance of a lawyer.

In considering the name, you should also check what must be included. All states require that a corporate name include an indication that there is limited liability so that people dealing with the organization know that if it fails, they cannot collect their debts from the owners personally.

The next question will be whether the name you want is already being used by someone else. Even similar names can cause problems because most states will not allow a name which is the same or "deceptively similar" to a name already on record in the state. Therefore, XYZ Corp. may be a problem, for example, even if you are going to be a restaurant and the already existing XYZ, Inc. is a bakery. However, even changing one word in the name may solve the problem. Therefore, XYZ Bakery, Inc. or XYZ Foods, Inc. may be allowed if XYZ, Inc. is refused.

THE REGISTERED AGENT

States generally require that a corporation incorporated there must maintain a registered agent in the state in order to receive communications and to be available to receive summons in law suits and other service. Generally, this agent may be the office of the corporation itself, so if you are physically in the state of incorporation, the corporation itself, or an officer thereof, may be the registered agent. If you incorporate in a state where you do not actually have an office, you need to have an agent there, and there are many organizations in the business of representing corporations for an annual fee, which are easily located in law directories.

FORMING THE CORPORATION

You are now at the stage of readiness to prepare and file a certificate of incorporation (in many states it is titled "Articles of Incorporation"). Many states will supply you with a blank form or with a model form which must be re-typed. There are even complete corporate kits and books available to set up a corporation. *How To Form Your Own Corporation Without A Lawyer* (Enterprise Publishing, 725 Market Street, Wilmington, Delaware 19807) and *The J.K. Lasser Corporation Form-File* (Simon & Schuster, 1230 Avenue of the Americas, New York, New York 10020) are two recommended.

Among the items of information which may be required in a certificate of incorporation are the following:

1. Name of the corporation.
2. Fiscal year.
3. Purposes of the corporation.
4. Aggregate number of shares authorized for issuance, the par value of shares, and the classes of shares if more than one class.
5. Preferences, limitations, and relative rights of shares.
6. Amount of beginning capital.
7. Any provisions regarding shareholders preemptive rights.
8. Any lawful provisions limiting statutory corporate powers.
9. Address of initial registered office and name of person as registered agent at that address.
10. Number of directors constituting initial board of directors.
11. Name and address of each of the initial directors.
12. Name and address of each incorporator.

Of course, not all of these items may be required in the certificate in any particular state, and many of them will not apply or be appropriate in your case. The only way to be sure what is required is to check the state statute, including any updates or recent changes in the state incorporation law.

Once your certificate of incorporation has been drafted and signed it should be mailed or delivered to the Secretary of State's office or other state office as is proper along with the required fees. Generally you will be notified by return mail that the certificate has been accepted and filed. Your evidence of filing is generally a receipt from the state. You may also request from the state a copy of the certificate of incorporation with their certificate of filing and the official date the corporate life began. The fee for this is usually based on the number of pages in the certificate and will be only a few dollars. You may also request a certified copy attesting to the corporate existence as it may come in handy for future transactions.

Help is available in setting up a new corporation. Of course, you can use an attorney to prepare your corporate documents, however, it may be less expensive to use any one of a number of commercial services who incorporate businesses. A partial list of companies that provide incorporation services include:

The Company Corporation
725 Market Street
Wilmington, Delaware 19807

Capital Trust Company
4305 Lancaster Pike
Wilmington, Delaware 19805

Delaware Charter Co.
1105 No. Market Street
Wilmington, Delaware 19899

It should be noted that although their services are located in Delaware, they do set up corporations in other states. You may, however, want to check for similar services in your area.

DISSOLVING YOUR CORPORATION

At some point in time you may want to dissolve your corporation. This will certainly be true when you sell the business assets.

A corporation may be dissolved by:

1. Expiration of the period specified in the corporate charter (Certificate of Incorporation) if any expiration date is stated.

2. A surrender of the charter. When the shareholders of a corporation, by requisite vote, surrender the corporate charter to the state, and is formally accepted by the state.

3. By filing of a Certificate of Dissolution with the Secretary of State of the state of incorporation.

4. Consolidation. When a corporation "A", unites with another corporation "B", to form a third but entirely separate corporation "C", corporations A and B cease to exist and are said to have been dissolved "by consolidation". The new corporation C, assumes all the assets and property rights, privileges as well as the liabilities of former corporations A and B.

5. Merger. When a corporation "A", merges into another corporation "B", only one of the two (corporation "A") is dissolved "by merger". But corporation "B" survives. The surviving corporation (corporation B in this example) absorbs all the assets and property rights, privileges, and often the liabilities of the absorbed corporation, but continues its own separate corporate existence thereafter.

6. A corporation may be dissolved when a condition clearly specified in the corporate charter occurs—such as the death of a principal. This provision is rare, however, as corporations have a perpetual life independent of its principals.

7. Action by the Attorney General. The state (and only the state) can sue to terminate the existence of a corporation. And if satisfied that the state has proven its case (e.g. when the court finds a corporation has not filed required taxes or documents or that it has abused or neglected to use its powers), the court may revoke the corporate charter.

8. Directors' or Shareholders' Petition. The board of directors (or a majority thereof) may be empowered by statute to petition for the dissolution of a corporation upon the occurrence of certain events—e.g. when the assets of the corporation are not sufficient to discharge its liabilities. The stockholders of a majority of all outstanding shares entitled to vote on the issue, may also be empowered by statute to make such petition to the court on similar grounds.

9. Shareholders' Petition Under Deadlock Statutes. A typical so-called "dead-lock statute" commonly provides: "Unless otherwise provided in the certificate of incorporation, the holders of one-half of all outstanding shares of a corporation entitled to vote in an election of directors may present a petition for dissolution on one or more of the following grounds:

    (a) That the directors are so divided respecting the management of the corporation's affairs that the votes required for action by the board cannot be obtained.

    (b) That the shareholders are so divided that the votes required for the election of directors cannot be obtained.

    (c) That there is internal dissension and two or more factions of shareholders are so divided that dissolution would be beneficial to the shareholders."

The dissolution of a corporation carries with it important tax and liability questions and therefore dissolution should be undertaken only after consultation with an attorney and accountant.

Also bear in mind that a dissolution of the corporation is not the same as revocation of S Corporation status. As you will see in Chapter 4, your corporation remains in existence under a switch from S to C status. On the other hand, dissolution of the corporation creates the status of proprietorship or partnership if there are two or more owners.

CHECKLIST

Steps in the Incorporation Process

1. Decide whether to incorporate.

2. Decide where to incorporate.

3. Select a corporate name.

4. Select a registered agent, if necessary.

5. Draft certificate of incorporation.

6. Sign certificate of incorporation and file with Secretary of State with appropriate filing fees.

7. Hold Incorporator's initial meeting to elect directors and transact first business.

8. Hold Organizational meeting of initial Board of Directors.

9. Select corporate seal, stock certificates, issue shares, elect officers and open bank accounts.

10. Apply for Employer Identification Number.

11. Choose a fiscal year.

12. File a "doing business as" certificate, if necessary.

13. Apply for authorization to do business in other states, if necessary.

14. Obtain necessary state and local licenses and/or permits.

15. Elect S Corporation status, if desired.

DEPARTMENT OF CORPORATION
(BY STATE)

ALABAMA

Secretary of State
State Capitol
Montgomery, Alabama 36130
(205/832-3570)

ALASKA

State of Alaska
Department of Commerce and Economic Developoment
Corporations
Juneau, Alaska 99811
(907/465-2530)

ARIZONA

Arizona Corporation Commission
Incorporating Division
2222 West Encanto Boulevard
Phoenix, Arizona 85009
(602/271-4900)

ARKANSAS

Secretary of State
State Capitol
Little Rock, Arkansas 72201
(501/371-1010)

CALIFORNIA

Secretary of State
1230 J Street
Sacramento, California 95814
(916/445-0620)

COLORADO

Secretary of State
1575 Sherman Street, 2nd Floor
Denver, Colorado 80203
(303/839-2361)

CONNECTICUT

Office of the Secretary of State
State of Connecticut
P.O. Box 846, 30 Trinity Street
Hartford, Connecticut 06115
(203/566-4346)

DELAWARE

State of Delaware
Department of State
Division of Incorporations
Townsend Building
P.O. Box 898
Dover, Delaware 19901
(302/678-4111)

DISTRICT OF COLUMBIA

Recorder of Deeds
Washington, D.C. 20001
(202/727-5374)

FLORIDA

Secretary of State
The Capitol
Tallahassee, Florida 32304
(904/488-3680)

GEORGIA

Secretary of State
Corporations Department
Suite 600, Peachtree Center South
225 Peachtree Street, N.E.
Atlanta, Georgia 30303
(404/656-2185)

HAWAII

Director of the Department of Regulatory Agencies
State Capitol
Honolulu, Hawaii 96813
(808/548-6521)

IDAHO

Secretary of State
State of Idaho
Boise, Idaho 83720
(208/334-2300)

ILLINOIS

Secretary of State
Springfield, Illinois 62756
(217/782-7880)

INDIANA

Secretary of State
201 State House
Indianapolis, Indiana 46204
(371/633-6576)

IOWA

Secretary of State
State Capitol
Des Moines, Iowa 50319
(515/281-5864)

KANSAS

State of Kansas
Secretary of State
The State House, 2nd Floor
Topeka, Kansas 66612
(913/296-2236)

KENTUCKY

Secretary of State
Frankfort, Kentucky 40601
(502/564-7330)

LOUISIANA

Secretary of State
P.O. Box 44125
Baton Rouge, Louisiana 70804
(504/925-4704)

MAINE

Secretary of State
State of Maine
Department of State
Augusta, Maine 04333
(207/289-3501)

MARYLAND

State Department of Assessments and Taxation
301 West Preston Street
Baltimore, Maryland 21201
(301/383-2526)

MASSACHUSETTS

Secretary of State
Corporations Division
1 Ashburton Place, 17th Floor
Boston, Massachusetts 02108
(617/727-2850)

MICHIGAN

State of Michigan
Department of Commerce
Corporation Division
P.O. Box 30054
Lansing, Michigan 48909
(517/374-9417)

MINNESOTA

Secretary of State
180 State Office Building
St. Paul, Minnesota 55155
(612/296-6131)

MISSISSIPPI

Secretary of State
Jackson, Mississippi 39205
(601/354-6541)

MISSOURI

Secretary of State
Jefferson City, Missouri 65101
(314/751-2330)

MONTANA

Secretary of State
Capitol
Helena, Montana 59601
(406/449-2034)

NEBRASKA

Secretary of State
Lincoln, Nebraska 68509
(402/471-2556)

NEVADA

Secretary of State
Carson City, Nevada 89710
(702/885-5203)

NEW HAMPSHIRE

Department of Revenue Administration
Returns Processing Division
P.O. Box 637
Concord, New Hampshire 03301
(603/271-3244)

NEW JERSEY

State of New Jersey
Department of State
P.O. Box 1330
Trenton, New Jersey 08625
(609/292-3754)

NEW MEXICO

State Corporation Commission
Franchise Tax Department
P.O. Drawer 1269
Santa Fe, New Mexico 87501
(505/827-2852)

NEW YORK

State of New York
Department of State
Albany, New York 12231
(518/474-4757)

NORTH CAROLINA

Secretary of State
Raleigh, North Carolina 27603
(919/733-4201)

NORTH DAKOTA

Secretary of State
Bismark, North Dakota 58505
(701/224-2900)

OHIO

Secretary of State
30 East Broad Street, 14th Floor
Columbus, Ohio 43215
(614/466-4980

OKLAHOMA

Secretary of State
Oklahoma City, Oklahoma 73105
(405/521-3911)

OREGON

Department of Commerce
Corporation Division
Commerce Building
Salem, Oregon 97310
(503/378-4166)

PENNSYLVANIA

Commonwealth of Pennsylvania
Department of State
Harrisburg, Pennsylvania 17120
(717/787-3006)

RHODE ISLAND

Secretary of State
State House
Providence, Rhode Island 02903
(401/277-2357)

SOUTH CAROLINA

Secretary of State
P.O. Box 11350
Columbia, South Carolina 29211
(803/758-2744)

SOUTH DAKOTA

Secretary of State
Pierre, South Dakota 57501
(605/773-3537)

TENNESSEE

Secretary of State
Corporations Division C1-101
Central Services Building
Nashville, Tennessee 37219
(615/741-2286)

TEXAS

Secretary of State
Austin, Texas 78711
(512/475-2015)

UTAH

Secretary of State
203 State Capitol Building
Salt Lake City, Utah 84114
(801/533-4504)

VERMONT

Secretary of State
Montpelier, Vermont 05602
(802/828-2386)

VIRGINIA

Commonwealth of Virginia
State Corporation Commission
Richmond, Virginia 23209
(804/786-8967)

WASHINGTON

Secretary of State
Olympia, Washington 98504
(206/753-7120)

WEST VIRGINIA

Secretary of State
Charleston, West Virginia 25305
(304/348-2112)

WISCONSIN

Secretary of State
Madison, Wisconsin 53702
(608/266-3590)

WYOMING

Secretary of State
State Capitol
Cheyenne, Wyoming 82002
(305/777-7378)

QUALIFYING YOUR S CORPORATION

OVERVIEW

Any corporation that satisfies the eligibility rules of an S Corporation or "Small Business Corporation" can benefit from its advantageous tax benefits.

The basic requirements are:

- There must be a corporation.
- The corporation must have no more than 35 shareholders.
- Each shareholder must be a natural person or an estate.
- The corporation may have only one class of stock, although there are limited exceptions to this requirement.
- The corporation must be a "Small Business Corporation".

CORPORATE EXISTENCE

In order to qualify as an S Corporation, the business seeking to qualify must be a corporation. If your existing or proposed business operates or will operate as a sole proprietorship or partnership, it must first be converted to a corporation. Only domestic corporations chartered within one of the states, or United States possessions will qualify.

Frequently, a new business will incorporate and immediately thereafter file for S Corporation election.

35 OR FEWER SHAREHOLDERS

The IRS limits to 35 the number of shareholders an S Corporation may have. In calculating whether a corporation has more than 35 shareholders, follow the following guidelines.

- Husbands and wives are considered as one person, even if they own their stock in their separate names. For example, if Mr. Jones owns twenty shares of S Corporation in his name only and Mrs. Jones owns 30 shares in her name only, they will be viewed as one shareholder for S Corporation purposes. Similarly, jointly held stock, e.g. shares owned by John Jones and Mary Jones as joint tenants or tenants in common, is viewed as being owned by one shareholder.

- Shares held in a qualified trust by a trustee or custodian for beneficiaries are usually considered as being owned by the beneficiary not the custodian or trustee. For example, if a parent holds shares as trustee or custodian for each of the parent's three children, there are three shareholders for S Corporation purposes, not one. Therefore, it is important to verify the number of beneficiaries in a trust acquiring shares.

In the event shares of an S Corporation become owned by 36 or more shareholders, the business will lose its S Corporation status. It will be thereafter treated as a regular C Corporation and will be subject to double taxation.

SHAREHOLDER QUALIFICATIONS

Any individual who is either a citizen or resident of the United States as well as estates and certain trusts may be a shareholder in an S Corporation.

Shareholders who do not fit into one of those categories are not qualified to be S Corporation shareholders, and if they obtain shares, the business will lose its S Corporation status.

Since an individual must be a natural person, both partnerships and corporations are disqualified from owning shares in an S Corporation. Therefore, an S Corporation cannot be a subsidiary of another corporation. Further, the individual must be either a citizen or resident of the United States. An alien visiting this country does not qualify as a shareholder. Further, if shares are jointly held, by spouses, for example, and one spouse is a non-resident alien, the corporation has a disqualified shareholder and S Corporation status will be denied. Only residence in the United States qualifies an alien for shareholder status in an S Corporation. Residence in a territory or a possession is not sufficient.

As to estates, a business will not lose its S Corporation status if a qualified shareholder dies and his shares pass to the decedent's estate. However, time limits can be imposed and an estate may become disqualified if the estate remains open an inordinate amount of time. This should be reviewed with counsel for the estate and counsel for the corporation.

Similarly, the estate of a bankrupt may also be a shareholder in an S Corporation. If an individual shareholder files for bankruptcy, his assets, including his shares in the corporation, are placed in the bankrupt's estate and is qualified to be a shareholder in an S Corporation. However, under both a decedent's estate and bankrupt estate, the shares must not be passed on to individuals or parties otherwise unqualified to be a stockholder in an S Corporation.

The matter is more complex when it comes to trusts. Although certain trusts may qualify to become shareholders in an S Corporation, the applicable rules are complex and highly detailed. In the event that a shareholder in an S Corporation intends to establish a trust that includes the corporation shares, qualified legal counsel should be obtained.

Because a corporation can easily lose its S Corporation status if a shareholder transfers shares to an unqualified recipient, all shareholders should enter into an agreement to protect the corporation (and other shareholders) from an involuntary termination. Such an agreement is at the end of Chapter 12. Further, trusts and estates expected to become transferees of S Corporation shares should be first approved by counsel for the corporation.

ONE CLASS OF STOCK

An S Corporation may have only one class of stock issued and outstanding.

Even if the corporation is authorized to issue more than one share of stock (i.e. common and preferred shares), it continues to qualify for S status as long as only one class is issued.

The fact that shares may have different voting rights (i.e. voting and non-voting common stock) do not constitute different classes provided they are treated equally in all other respects with regard to dividends and liquidation.

To determine whether a corporation has more than one class of stock, ask whether every shareholder is entitled to receive the same (1) dividend at the same time as every other shareholder and (2) amount for each share he or she holds and at the same time as every other shareholder in the event of liquidation. If all economic rights are the same, then the shares will be considered the same class.

Tax Warning:
Loans to the corporation may, under certain circumstances, be viewed as creating a second class of stock which then disqualifies the S Corporation status.

The test is whether the loan has the characteristics of an "arms-length" loan bearing conventional lending terms. More lenient terms may be viewed as an equity investment creating the interpretation of a second class of stock.

In order to be considered a loan a shareholder loan must:

1. Be in writing.

2. Require the corporation to pay interest at fixed times—e.g. monthly, quarterly, annually—and set a rate of interest that does not depend on the corporation profits, the corporation discretion, or similar factors.

3. Oblige the corporation to repay the entire principal amount of the loan by a certain date.

4. Not allow the loan to be convertible to stock at either the borrower's or lender's option.

5. The corporation must actually make payments in accordance with the terms of the note.

As suggested above, the safe harbor rules do not present any real problem for a shareholder who seeks to lend money to an S Corporation. The loan terms required by the rule are only those that any creditor would demand before lending money.

SMALL BUSINESS CORPORATION

The term "Small Business Corporation" has never been clearly defined. In fact, we define a Small Business Corporation by defining the type businesses that do not qualify.

Contrary to common belief, the phrase "Small Business Corporation" does not place any ceiling on the sales volume or asset value of the business. And for the most part a Small Business Corporation (S Corporation) is not restricted to the type business in which it may engage.

The only forms of business that may not take advantage of S incorporation are:

1. Financial institutions such as banks, insurance companies, building and loan associations, or mutual savings and loan associations;

2. Foreign corporations, (S Corporation must be incorporated under the laws of any state, possession, or territory of the United States);

3. Corporations that operate in possessions of the United States and use the possessions tax credit against their United States income tax;

4. Domestic International Sales Corporations (DISC's) or former DISC's, and Foreign Service Corporations (FSC's).

A fifth category of ineligible corporations includes affiliated corporations. An S Corporation may not be a subsidiary of a parent corporation. This follows from the fact that shareholders of an S Corporation must be natural persons, estates or certain trusts.

Moreover, a corporation that owns 80 percent or more of all of the stock of another corporation is an ineligible affiliated corporation. If, however, the second corporation has two classes of stock, e.g. voting and non-voting common stock, the S Corporation must own 80 percent or more of each class of stock in order to be disqualified as an affiliated corporation.

ADDITIONAL REQUIREMENTS FOR EXISTING CORPORATIONS

If an existing C Corporation elects to become an S Corporation it must—in addition to the above requirements—satisfy two additional requirements as well.

THE FIVE YEAR RULE

If the regular C Corporation has previously been an S Corporation and revoked or lost its S status within the past five years, it will not be qualified to become an S Corporation. This provision exists to deter shareholders from electing S status in only those years during which their business loses money.

Therefore, the Internal Revenue Service will not approve of an election to be taxed as an S Corporation if the shareholders of the corporation revoked or lost their S Corporation election during the past five years. A possible exception to this rule exists if the corporation shares (or at least a controlling interest) are held by different shareholders than those who revoked or lost the election to be treated as an S Corporation.

Planning Tip:
There is no penalty if shareholders choose to be treated as an S Corporation during the enterprise's first year (when it is likely to lose money because of start-up costs) and then switch to regular C status the following year. At most, the shareholders will be barred from making an S Corporation election for another five years.

PASSIVE INVESTMENT INCOME

If a C Corporation elects to become an S Corporation and has no accumulated earnings and profits (prior profits not distributed as dividends to shareholders), it can qualify for S status regardless of the type or sources of income the corporation has had.

However, if the regular C Corporation does have accumulated earnings and profits when it makes its election for S status, its election may not be recognized. Under this rule, if an S Corporation has (i) accumulated earnings and profits from its C Corporation operations at the end of the S Corporation tax year and (ii) more than 25 percent of its gross income comes from passive investment income sources (dividends, interest, annuities, rents, royalties, and gain from the sale of securities), the election will be lost.

For the passive income rule to apply, the corporation must fall within both sides of the test for three years. In other words, during each of the first three years starting with the election year, the corporation must have accumulated C Corporation earnings and profits and must have passive investment income that is more than 25 percent of its gross income. Should that occur, the S Corporation election is lost in the fourth year but is in effect for the prior three years. For the fourth year the corporation will be taxed as a C Corporation and will remain unable to elect S Corporation status for another five years.

FILING FOR S CORPORATION STATUS

5

OVERVIEW

It is relatively simple to qualify and elect to have your corporation become an S Corporation.

The IRS requires you to do very little work other than to timely file an easily completed Form 2553 ("Election By a Small Business Corporation"), and satisfy the other eligibility requirements.

These requirements, however, should be taken seriously because if the corporation fails to file on time, or improperly completes its forms, the corporation's election will be delayed and this may be costly in terms of taxes.

This chapter will explain the proper procedures for filing and will provide all the needed forms to help you create your own S Corporation.

This chapter, however, only discusses federal requirements. Each state may have its own requirements for recognition as an S Corporation at the state level, and several states do not recognize S Corporation status at all. In these states an S Corporation will be subject to state taxes in the same manner as a C Corporation, although the S Corporation will still enjoy the benefits of S Corporation status as to federal taxes.

DOCUMENTS THAT MUST BE FILED

To satisfy federal requirements, only one document is essential to convert an existing C Corporation to a S Corporation—Form 2553.

A Form 2553 (Election By a Small Business Corporation) is available at any IRS office, however, a current Form 2553 is also included at the end of this chapter and may be used for filing purposes.

Instructions for completing Form 2553 require you to provide the following information.

- The corporation's name and address. If the address is the same as someone else's enter the name of that individual.

- Employer identification number. If you have a new business and applied for an employer identification number (EIN) but have not received it, enter "applied for". If the corporation does not have an EIN, apply for one using Form SS-4 found at the end of this chapter, (mail duplicate copies).

- The principal business activity and principal product or service is entered by code and the code is contained in instructions for Form 1120S (or at end of chapter). Your principal business activity is the one that accounts for the largest percentage of total receipts.

- If the filing is made for the corporation's first year of existence, the earliest of the dates the corporation (1) had shareholders, (2) had assets, or (3) began doing business.

- The total number of shares held by shareholders and have not been re-acquired by the corporation.

- The date of incorporation and state of incorporation.

- The corporation's tax year. A new corporation may automatically elect a tax year ending December 31. If you prefer a tax year other than a calendar year, then parts 2-4 of Form 2553 must be completed. Non-calendar tax years are generally not permitted for S Corporations and will be allowed only in limited circumstances.

- Each shareholder must consent to the election and complete the corresponding information relative to the stock owned, social security number and individual tax year.

Finally, Form 2553 must be signed by an authorized corporate officer and mailed to the IRS office where the corporation files its tax returns.

It is recommended that Form 2553 be sent by certified mail, return receipt requested, so you have proof of filing should a question arise.

OBTAINING SHAREHOLDER CONSENT

All shareholders must consent to an S Corporation election (although only a majority of the outstanding shares are needed to revoke the election. Furthermore, all necessary consents must be filed within the time limit for filing Form 2553.

The following rules apply in determining who must sign and file consents:

- Every person who owned shares during the taxable year must file a consent—even if the person sold his or her shares before the election was filed.

- If shares are held for the benefit of another person, the beneficiary should file a consent. A beneficial owner of stock is ordinarily held by the courts to be the person who is entitled to the financial benefits (dividends or other distributions) of the shares. However, you may want consents from both the beneficiary and the person who holds the stock for the beneficiary.

- Owners of non-voting common stock must also file consents with owners of voting stock.

- If stock is held jointly by husbands and wives, or others, each joint owner or tenant in common should file a consent. In community property states, even if shares of stock are listed in the name of only one spouse, both husband and wife should file consents.

- If shares have passed to an estate, it is generally safe to cover all possibilities by obtaining consents from both the executor of the estate as well as the beneficiaries or legatees of the stock.

If certain shareholders are not available for the filing of the Form 2553 itself, then file extensions for the filing of shareholder consents. In no event should you defer filing the 2553 beyond the required date. An acceptable form for obtaining an extension to filing a shareholder consent is found at the end of this chapter.

It is also possible to obtain shareholders consent using a consent form other than Form 2553. If for example, a shareholder resides in a distant location it may be more convenient to obtain his or her consent using the "shareholders consent" contained at the end of this chapter.

WHEN TO FILE

There are strict rules that govern the filing of Form 2553 for the election of S Corporation status.

- If the election is to be effective for the corporation's present tax year, then Form 2553 must be filed no later than the fifteenth day of the third month of the corporation's taxable year.

- An existing corporation that wants to elect S Corporation status for 1988 can file anytime during 1987, but no later than March 15, 1988.

Caution:
Be certain you allow enough time to meet the two month and fifteen day filing date from the beginning of the tax year. The IRS will not grant an extension for filing the election under any circumstances. Remember, time is of the essence.

FORMS IN THIS SECTION

1. *Form 2553* (with instructions) is the basic application to elect S Corporation status. Be particularly careful to complete all information *and* to file it on time. Note that the 2553 form is to be signed by all the stockholders of the corporation (see Column D of instructions).

2. Shareholder consent may also be submitted on the form—*Shareholder's Consent to S Corporation Election*—when the shareholder cannot conveniently sign Form 2553.

3. Use the *Request For Extension to File Shareholder Consent* if for any reason you cannot obtain the signature of a shareholder within the time required to file 2553. Complete and file the Request For Extension together with the Form 2553 and as soon as possible obtain the shareholder's signature on the Shareholder's Consent and file with the IRS.

4. This section also contains Form SS-4, an *Application For Employee Identification Number*. If the corporation does not have an EID when it files its 2553 application it should mark "applied for" in the appropriate box.

Department of the Treasury
Internal Revenue Service

Instructions for Form 2553
(Revised February 1986)

Election by a Small Business Corporation

(Section references are to the Internal Revenue Code, unless otherwise specified.)

Paperwork Reduction Act Notice.—We ask for this information to carry out the Internal Revenue laws of the United States. We need it to insure that you are complying with these laws and to allow us to figure and collect the right amount of tax. You are required to give us this information.

A. Purpose.—To elect to be treated as an "S Corporation," a corporation must file Form 2553. The election permits the income of the S corporation to be taxed to the shareholders of the corporation except as provided in Subchapter S and section 58(d). (See section 1363.)

B. Who May Elect.—Your corporation may make the election only if it meets the following tests:

1. It is a domestic corporation.

2. It has no more than 35 shareholders. A husband and wife (and their estates) are treated as one shareholder for this requirement. All other persons are treated as separate shareholders.

3. It has only individuals, estates, or certain trusts as shareholders.

4. It has no nonresident alien shareholders.

5. It has only one class of stock. See sections 1361(c)(4) and (5) for additional details.

6. It is not an ineligible corporation as defined in section 1361(b)(2). See section 6(c) of Public Law 97-354 for additional details.

7. It has a calendar tax year or other permitted tax year as explained in instruction G.

8. Each shareholder consents as explained in the instructions for Column D.

See sections 1361, 1362 and 1378 for additional information on the above tests.

C. Where to File.—File this election with the Internal Revenue Service Center where the corporation will file **Form 1120S**, U.S. Income Tax Return for an S Corporation. See the Instructions for Form 1120S for Service Center addresses.

You should keep a copy of Form 2553 for the corporation's files.

D. When to Make the Election.— Complete Form 2553 and file it either: (1) at any time during that portion of the first tax year the election is to take effect which occurs before the 16th day of the third month of that tax year (or at any time during that year, if that year does not extend beyond the period described above) or (2) in the tax year before the first tax year it is to take effect. An election made by a small business corporation after the 15th day of the third month but before the end of the tax year is treated as made for the next year. For example, if a calendar tax year corporation makes the election in April 1985, it is effective for the corporation's 1986 calendar tax year.

For purposes of this election, a newly formed corporation's tax year starts when it has shareholders, acquires assets, or begins doing business, whichever happens first.

E. Acceptance or Non-acceptance of Election.—IRS will notify you if your election is accepted and when it will take effect. You should generally receive determination on your election within 60 days after you have filed Form 2553. Do not file Form 1120S until you are notified that your election is accepted. If you are now required to file **Form 1120**, U.S. Corporation Income Tax Return, or any other applicable tax return, continue filing it until your election takes effect.

You will also be notified if your election is not accepted.

Care should be exercised to ensure the election is received by Internal Revenue Service. If you are not notified of acceptance or non-acceptance of your election within 3 months of date of filing (date mailed), you should take follow-up action by corresponding with the service center where the election was filed. If filing of Form 2553 is questioned, an acceptable proof of filing is: (1) Certified receipt (timely filed); (2) Form 2553 with accepted stamp; (3) Form 2553 with stamped IRS received date; or (4) IRS letter stating that Form 2553 had been accepted.

F. End of Election.—Once the election is made, it stays in effect for all years until it is terminated. During the 5 years after the election has been terminated, the corporation can make another election on Form 2553 only if the Commissioner consents. See section 1362(g). However, the 5-year waiting period does not apply to terminations made under Subchapter S rules in effect for tax years beginning before January 1, 1983. See sections 1362(d), (e), and (f) for rules regarding termination of election.

G. Permitted Tax Year.—Section 1378 provides that no corporation may make an election to be an S corporation for any tax year unless the tax year is a permitted tax year. A permitted tax year is a tax year ending December 31 or any other tax year for which the corporation establishes a business purpose to the satisfaction of IRS. See section 1378(c) if a 50 percent shift in ownership occurs in an existing S corporation after its election is made.

H. Investment Credit Property.— Although the corporation has elected to be an S corporation under section 1362, the tax imposed by section 47 in the case of early disposition of investment credit property will be imposed on the corporation for credits allowed for tax years for which the corporation was not an S corporation. The election will not be treated as a disposition of the property by the corporation. See section 1371(d).

Specific Instructions

Part I.—Part I must be completed by all corporations.

Name and Address of Corporation.—If the corporation's mailing address is the same as someone else's such as a shareholder's, please enter this person's name below the corporation's name.

Employer Identification Number.—If you have applied for an employer identification number (EIN) but have not received it, enter "applied for." If the corporation does not have an EIN, you should apply for one on **Form SS-4**, Application for Employer Identification Number, available from most IRS or Social Security Administration offices. Send Form SS-4 to the IRS Service Center where Form 1120S will be filed.

Principal Business Activity and Principal Product or Service.—Use the Codes for Principal Business Activity contained in the Instructions for Form 1120S. Your principal business activity is the one that accounts for the largest percentage of total receipts. Total receipts are gross receipts plus all other income.

Also state the principal product or service. For example, if the principal business activity is "grain mill products," the principal product or service may be "cereal preparation."

Number of Shares Issued and Outstanding.—Enter only one figure. This figure will be the number of shares of stock that have been issued to shareholders and have not been reacquired by the corporation. This is the number of shares all shareholders own, as reported in column E, Part I.

Item B.—The selected tax year must be a permitted tax year as defined in instruction G.

A newly formed corporation may automatically adopt a tax year ending December 31.

Generally, an existing corporation may automatically change to a tax year ending December 31, if all of its principal shareholders have tax years ending December 31, or if all of its principal shareholders are concurrently changing to such tax year. If a corporation is automatically changing to a tax year ending December 31, it is not necessary for the corporation to file **Form 1128**, Application for Change in Accounting Period. A shareholder may not change his or her tax year without securing prior approval from IRS. For purposes of the automatic change, a principal shareholder is a shareholder who owns 5% or more of the issued and outstanding stock of the corporation. See temporary regulations section 18.1378-1 for additional details.

If a corporation wants to change to a tax year ending December 31, but does not qualify for an automatic change as explained above, it may want to complete Part IV and indicate in an attached statement that it wants to change to a tax year ending December 31.

If a corporation selects a tax year ending other than December 31, it must complete Part II or IV in addition to Part I.

Column D.—Shareholders' Consent Statement.—Each person who is a shareholder at the time the election is made must consent to the election. If the election is made during the corporation's first tax year for which it is effective, any person who held stock at any time during that portion of that year which occurs before the time the election is made must consent to the election although the person may have sold or transferred his or her stock before the election is made. Each shareholder consents by signing in column D or signing a separate consent statement, described below.

The election by a small business corporation is considered made for the following tax year if one or more of the persons who held stock at any time during that portion of that year which occurs before the time the election is made did not consent to the election. See section 1362(b)(2).

If a husband and wife have a community interest in the stock or in the income from it, both must consent. Each tenant in common, joint tenant, and tenant by the entirety also must consent.

A minor's consent is made by the minor or the legal guardian. If no legal guardian has been appointed, the natural guardian makes the consent (even if a custodian holds the minor's stock under a law patterned after the Uniform Gifts to Minors Act).

Continuation Sheet or Separate Consent Statement.—If you need a continuation sheet or use a separate consent statement, attach it to Form 2553. The separate consent statement must contain the name, address, and employer identification number of the corporation and the shareholder information requested in columns C through G of Part I.

If you wish, you may combine all the shareholders' consents in one statement.

Column E.—Enter the number of shares of stock each shareholder owns and the dates the stock was acquired. If the election is made during the corporation's first tax year for which it is effective, do not list the shares of stock for those shareholders who sold or transferred all of their stock before the election was made but who still must consent to the election for it to be effective for the tax year.

Column G.—Enter the month and day that each shareholder's tax year ends. If a shareholder is changing his or her tax year, enter the tax year the shareholder is changing to. If the election is made during the corporation's first tax year for which it is effective, you do not have to enter the tax year of shareholders who sold or transferred all of their stock before the election was made but who still must consent to the election for it to be effective for the tax year.

Signature.—Form 2553 must be signed by the president, treasurer, assistant treasurer, chief accounting officer, or other corporate officer (such as tax officer) authorized to sign.

Part II.—Items H and I of Part II are to be completed by a corporation that selects a tax year ending other than December 31, and that qualifies under section 4.02, 4.03, or 4.04 of Revenue Procedure 83-25, 1983-1 C.B. 689. Items H and I are completed in place of the additional statement asked for in section 7.01 of the procedure. Sections 4.02, 4.03, and 4.04 provide for expeditious approval of certain corporations' requests to adopt, retain, or change to a tax year ending other than December 31. The representation statements in Part II of Form 2553 highlight the three types of requests provided for in the revenue procedure. A corporation adopting, retaining, or changing its accounting period under the procedure must comply with or satisfy all conditions of the procedure.

The revenue procedure applies only to the tax years of corporations which are electing S corporation status by filing Form 2553. A corporation is permitted to adopt, retain, or change its tax year only once under the procedure. It is not necessary for the corporation to file Form 1128 when adopting or changing its tax year under the procedure.

Items H and J of Part II are to be completed by a corporation that is making a request as specified in section 8 of the procedure. Section 8 provides that if a corporation wants to adopt, retain, or change to a tax year not specified under section 4.02, 4.03, or 4.04 of the procedure or certain paragraphs of temporary regulations section 18.1378-1, it should attach a statement to Form 2553 pursuant to the ruling request requirements of Revenue Procedure 85-1, 1985-1 C.B. 404. (Changes to this revenue procedure are usually incorporated annually into a new revenue procedure as the first revenue procedure of the year.) The statement must show the business purpose for the desired tax year.

Approval of tax year selections made under section 4.02, 4.03, or 4.04 of Revenue Procedure 83-25 are generally automatic; however, a request under section 8 is not automatic. If a request is made under section 8, the corporation may want to make the back-up request under Part III. See section 8 of the procedure for details.

Part III.—Check the box in Part III to make the back-up request provided by temporary regulations section 18.1378-1(b)(2)(ii)(A). This section provides that corporations requesting to retain (or adopt) a tax year ending other than December 31, may make a back-up request to adopt or change to a tax year ending December 31, in case the initial request for a fiscal year is denied. In order to make the back-up request, a corporation requesting to retain its tax year ending other than December 31, must qualify for an automatic change of its tax year under temporary regulations section 18.1378-1(b)(1).

Part IV.—Check the box in Part IV to request the IRS to determine your permitted tax year under the provisions of temporary regulations section 18.1378-1(d). If you check the box in Part IV, enter "See Part IV" in the space in item B, Part I, for month and year.

You may attach a schedule to Form 2553 showing any additional information you want the IRS to consider in making the determination. IRS will notify you of the permitted tax year determination. The tax year determination by IRS is final.

★ U.S.G.P.O.: 1986 -491-473/20123

Form **2553**
(Rev. February 1986)

Department of the Treasury
Internal Revenue Service

Election by a Small Business Corporation
(Under section 1362 of the Internal Revenue Code)
▶ For Paperwork Reduction Act Notice, see page 1 of instructions.
▶ See separate instructions.

OMB No. 1545-0146

Expires 1-31-89

Note: *This election, to be treated as an "S corporation," can be approved only if all the tests in Instruction B are met.*

Part I · Election Information

Name of corporation (see instructions) XYZ Corporation	Employer identification number (see instructions) 81-4039261	Principal business activity and principal product or service (see instructions) 6355 Insurance
Number and street 100 Main Street		Election is to be effective for tax year beginning (month, day, year) 1/1/88
City or town, state and ZIP code Anytown, USA 00000		Number of shares issued and outstanding (see instructions) 100

Is the corporation the outgrowth or continuation of any form of predecessor? . . . . ☐ **Yes** ☒ **No**   Date and place of incorporation

If "Yes," state name of predecessor, type of organization, and period of its existence ▶ -   7/15/87 N.Y.

A If this election takes effect for the first tax year the corporation exists, enter the earliest of the following: (1) date the corporation first had shareholders, (2) date the corporation first had assets, or (3) date the corporation began doing business. ▶   7/15/87

B Selected tax year: Annual return will be filed for tax year ending (month and day) ▶ . . . . December 31 . . . .

See instructions before entering your tax year. If the tax year ends any date other than December 31, you must complete Part II or Part IV on back. You may want to complete Part III to make a back-up request.

C Name of each shareholder, person having a community property interest in the corporation's stock, and each tenant in common, joint tenant, and tenant by the entirety. (A husband and wife (and their estates) are counted as one shareholder in determining the number of shareholders without regard to the manner in which the stock is owned.)	D Shareholders' Consent Statement. We, the undersigned shareholders, consent to the corporation's election to be treated as an "S corporation" under section 1362(a). (Shareholders sign and date below.)*	E Stock owned		F Social security number (employer identification number for estates or trust)	G Tax year ends (month and day)
		Number of shares	Dates acquired		
Robert Brown	*Robert Brown*	50	7/15/87	111-11-1111	Dec. 31
Mary Brown	*Mary Brown*	50	7/15/87	111-12-1222	Dec. 31
	SAMPLE				

*For this election to be valid, the consent of each shareholder, person having a community property interest in the corporation's stock, and each tenant in common, joint tenant, and tenant by the entirety must either appear above or be attached to this form. (See instructions for Column D, if continuation sheet or a separate consent statement is needed.)

Under penalties of perjury, I declare that I have examined this election, including accompanying schedules, and statements, and to the best of my knowledge and belief, it is true, correct, and complete.

Signature and Title of Officer ▶ *Robert Brown*   Date ▶ *July 15, 1987*

See Parts II, III, and IV on back.   Form **2553** (Rev. 2-86)

Election by a Small Business Corporation
(Under section 1362 of the Internal Revenue Code)
▶ For Paperwork Reduction Act Notice, see page 1 of instructions.
▶ See separate instructions.

OMB No. 1545-0146

Expires 1-31-89

Note: *This election, to be treated as an "S corporation," can be approved only if all the tests in Instruction B are met.*

Part I Election Information

Name of corporation (see instructions)	Employer identification number (see instructions)	Principal business activity and principal product or service (see instructions)
Number and street		Election is to be effective for tax year beginning (month, day, year)
City or town, state and ZIP code		Number of shares issued and outstanding (see instructions)

Is the corporation the outgrowth or continuation of any form of predecessor? . . . . ☐ **Yes**   ☐ **No** | Date and place of incorporation

If "Yes," state name of predecessor, type of organization, and period of its existence ▶ ----------------------

A If this election takes effect for the first tax year the corporation exists, enter the earliest of the following: (1) date the corporation first had shareholders, (2) date the corporation first had assets, or (3) date the corporation began doing business. ▶

B Selected tax year: Annual return will be filed for tax year ending (month and day) ▶ --

See instructions before entering your tax year. If the tax year ends any date other than December 31, you must complete Part II or Part IV on back. You may want to complete Part III to make a back-up request.

C Name of each shareholder, person having a community property interest in the corporation's stock, and each tenant in common, joint tenant, and tenant by the entirety. (A husband and wife (and their estates) are counted as one shareholder in determining the number of shareholders without regard to the manner in which the stock is owned.)	D Shareholders' Consent Statement. We, the undersigned shareholders, consent to the corporation's election to be treated as an "S corporation" under section 1362(a). (Shareholders sign and date below.)*	E Stock owned		F Social security number (employer identification number for estates or trust)	G Tax year ends (month and day)
		Number of shares	Dates acquired		

*For this election to be valid, the consent of each shareholder, person having a community property interest in the corporation's stock, and each tenant in common, joint tenant, and tenant by the entirety must either appear above or be attached to this form. (See instructions for Column D, if continuation sheet or a separate consent statement is needed.)

Under penalties of perjury, I declare that I have examined this election, including accompanying schedules, and statements, and to the best of my knowledge and belief, it is true, correct, and complete.

**Signature and
Title of Officer ▶**   Date ▶

See Parts II, III, and IV on back.   Form **2553** (Rev. 2-86)

Part II   Selection of Tax Year Under Revenue Procedure 83-25

H   Check the applicable box below to indicate whether the corporation is:

☐ Adopting the tax year entered in item B, Part I.

☐ Retaining the tax year entered in item B, Part I.

☐ Changing to the tax year entered in item B, Part I.

I   Check the applicable box below to indicate the representation statement the corporation is making as required under section 7.01 (item 4) of Revenue Procedure 83-25, 1983-1 C.B. 689.

☐ Under penalties of perjury, I represent that shareholders holding more than half of the shares of the stock (as of the first day of the tax year to which the request relates) of the corporation have the same tax year or are concurrently changing to the tax year that the corporation adopts, retains, or changes to per item B, Part I.

☐ Under penalties of perjury, I represent that shareholders holding more than half of the shares of the stock (as of the first day of the tax year to which the request relates) of the corporation have a tax year or are concurrently changing to a tax year that, although different from the tax year the corporation is adopting, retaining, or changing to per item B, Part I, results in a deferment of income to each of these shareholders of three months or less.

☐ Under penalties of perjury, I represent that the corporation is adopting, retaining, or changing to a tax year that coincides with its natural business year as verified by its satisfaction of the requirements of section 4.042(a), (b), (c), and (d) of Revenue Procedure 83-25.

J   Check here ☐ if the tax year entered in item B, Part I, is requested under the provisions of section 8 of Revenue Procedure 83-25. Attach to Form 2553 a statement and other necessary information pursuant to the ruling request requirements of Revenue Procedure 85-1. The statement must include the business purpose for the desired tax year. See instructions.

Part III   Back-Up Request by Certain Corporations Initially Selecting a Fiscal Year (See Instructions.)

Check here ☐ if the corporation agrees to adopt or to change to a tax year ending December 31 if necessary for IRS to accept this election for S corporation status (temporary regulations section 18.1378-1(b)(2)(ii)(A)). This back-up request does not apply if the fiscal tax year request is approved by IRS or if the election to be an S corporation is not accepted.

Part IV   Request by Corporation for Tax Year Determination by IRS (See Instructions.)

Check here ☐ if the corporation requests the IRS to determine the permitted tax year for the corporation based on information submitted in Part I (and attached schedules). This request is made under provisions of temporary regulations section 18.1378-1(d).

☆ U.S.G.P.O.: 1986-491-473/20122

Codes for Principal Business Activity

These industry titles and definitions are based, in general, on the Standard Industrial Classification System authorized by Regulatory and Statistical Analysis Division, Office of Information and Regulatory Affairs, Office of Management and Budget, to classify enterprises by type of activity in which they are engaged.

Using the list below, enter on page 1, under B, the code number for the specific industry group from which the largest percentage of "total receipts" is derived. "Total receipts" means the total of: gross receipts on line 1a, page 1; all other income on lines 4 through 8, page 1; and income (receipts only) on lines 1b, 1c, and 1d of Schedule K.

On page 2, under H, state the principal business activity and principal product or service that account for the largest percentage of total receipts. For example, if the principal business activity is "Grain mill products," the principal product or service may be "Cereal preparations."

If, as its principal business activity, the corporation (1) purchases raw materials, (2) subcontracts out for labor to make a finished product from the raw materials, and (3) retains title to the goods, the corporation is considered to be a manufacturer and must enter one of the codes (2010-3998) under "Manufacturing."

Agriculture, Forestry, and Fishing
Code
0400	Agricultural production.
0600	Agricultural services (except veterinarians), forestry, fishing, hunting, and trapping.

Mining
Metal mining:
1010	Iron ores.
1070	Copper, lead and zinc, gold and silver ores.
1098	Other metal mining.
1150	Coal mining.

Oil and gas extraction:
1330	Crude petroleum, natural gas, and natural gas liquids.
1380	Oil and gas field services.

Nonmetallic minerals, except fuels:
1430	Dimension, crushed and broken stone; sand and gravel
1498	Other nonmetallic minerals, except fuels.

Construction
General building contractors and operative builders:
1510	General building contractors.
1531	Operative builders.
1600	**Heavy construction contractors.**

Special trade contractors:
1711	Plumbing, heating, and air conditioning.
1731	Electrical work
1798	Other special trade contractors

Manufacturing
Food and kindred products:
2010	Meat products
2020	Dairy products.
2030	Preserved fruits and vegetables
2040	Grain mill products
2050	Bakery products.
2060	Sugar and confectionery products
2081	Malt liquors and malt
2088	Alcoholic beverages, except malt liquors and malt
2089	Bottled soft drinks, and flavorings
2096	Other food and kindred products.
2100	**Tobacco manufacturers.**

Textile mill products:
2228	Weaving mills and textile finishing.
2250	Knitting mills
2298	Other textile mill products

Apparel and other textile products:
2315	Men's and boys' clothing.
2345	Women's and children's clothing.
2388	Other apparel and accessories
2390	Miscellaneous fabricated textile products

Lumber and wood products:
2415	Logging, sawmills, and planing mills
2430	Millwork, plywood, and related products.
2498	Other wood products, including wood buildings and mobile homes
2500	**Furniture and fixtures.**

Paper and allied products.
2625	Pulp, paper, and board mills
2699	Other paper products

Printing and publishing:
2710	Newspapers
2720	Periodicals
2735	Books, greeting cards, and miscellaneous publishing.
2799	Commercial and other printing, and printing trade services

Chemicals and allied products:
2815	Industrial chemicals, plastics materials and synthetics.
2830	Drugs
2840	Soap, cleaners, and toilet goods.
2850	Paints and allied products
2898	Agricultural and other chemical products

Petroleum refining and related industries (including those integrated with extraction):
2910	Petroleum refining (including integrated)
2998	Other petroleum and coal products.

Rubber and misc. plastics products:
3050	Rubber products, plastics footwear, hose, and belting
3070	Misc plastics products.

Leather and leather products:
3140	Footwear, except rubber
3198	Other leather and leather products.

Stone, clay, and glass products:
3225	Glass products.
3240	Cement, hydraulic
3270	Concrete, gypsum, and plaster products.
3298	Other nonmetallic mineral products.

Primary metal industries:
3370	Ferrous metal industries, misc primary metal products.
3380	Nonferrous metal industries.

Fabricated metal products:
3410	Metal cans and shipping containers.
3428	Cutlery, hand tools, and hardware; screw machine products, bolts, and similar products.
3430	Plumbing and heating, except electric and warm air
3440	Fabricated structural metal products.
3460	Metal forgings and stampings.
3470	Coating, engraving, and allied services
3480	Ordnance and accessories, except vehicles and guided missiles.
3490	Misc fabricated metal products.

Machinery, except electrical:
3520	Farm machinery
3530	Construction and related machinery
3540	Metalworking machinery
3550	Special industry machinery
3560	General industrial machinery
3570	Office, computing, and accounting machines.
3598	Other machinery except electrical

Electrical and electronic equipment:
3630	Household appliances
3665	Radio, television, and communication equipment
3670	Electronic components and accessories
3698	Other electrical equipment
3710	**Motor vehicles and equipment**

Transportation equipment, except motor vehicles:
3725	Aircraft, guided missiles and parts.
3730	Ship and boat building and repairing
3798	Other transportation equipment, except motor vehicles

Instruments and related products:
3815	Scientific instruments and measuring devices, watches and clocks
3845	Optical, medical, and ophthalmic goods
3860	Photographic equipment and supplies
3998	**Other manufacturing products.**

Transportation and Public Utilities
Code
Transportation:
4000	Railroad transportation.
4100	Local and interurban passenger transit.
4200	Trucking and warehousing.
4400	Water transportation.
4500	Transportation by air
4600	Pipe lines, except natural gas.
4700	Miscellaneous transportation services.

Communication:
4825	Telephone, telegraph, and other communication services.
4830	Radio and television broadcasting.

Electric, gas, and sanitary services:
4910	Electric services.
4920	Gas production and distribution
4930	Combination utility services.
4990	Water supply and other sanitary services.

Wholesale Trade
Durable:
5008	Machinery, equipment, and supplies.
5010	Motor vehicles and automotive equipment.
5020	Furniture and home furnishings.
5030	Lumber and construction materials.
5040	Sporting, recreational, photographic, and hobby goods, toys and supplies.
5050	Metals and minerals, except petroleum and scrap.
5060	Electrical goods.
5070	Hardware, plumbing and heating equipment and supplies.
5098	Other durable goods

Nondurable:
5110	Paper and paper products
5129	Drugs, drug proprietaries, and druggists' sundries.
5130	Apparel, piece goods, and notions
5140	Groceries and related products.
5150	Farm-product raw materials.
5160	Chemicals and allied products.
5170	Petroleum and petroleum products.
5180	Alcoholic beverages.
5190	Misc nondurable goods.

Retail Trade
Building materials, garden supplies, and mobile home dealers:
5220	Building materials dealers.
5251	Hardware stores.
5265	Garden supplies and mobile home dealers.
5300	**General merchandise stores.**

Food stores:
5410	Grocery stores.
5490	Other food stores

Automotive dealers and service stations:
5515	Motor vehicle dealers.
5541	Gasoline service stations.
5598	Other, automotive dealers.
5600	**Apparel and accessory stores.**
5700	**Furniture and home furnishings stores.**
5800	**Eating and drinking places.**

Misc. retail stores:
5912	Drug stores and proprietary stores
5921	Liquor stores
5995	Other retail stores

Finance, Insurance, and Real Estate
Code
Banking:
6030	Mutual savings banks
6060	Bank holding companies
6090	Banks, except mutual savings banks and bank holding companies

Credit agencies other than banks:
6120	Savings and loan associations.
6140	Personal credit institutions
6150	Business credit institutions
6199	Other credit agencies.

Security, commodity brokers and services:
6210	Security brokers, dealers, and flotation companies
6299	Commodity contracts brokers and dealers; security and commodity exchanges; and allied services.

Insurance:
6355	Life Insurance
6356	Mutual insurance, except life or marine and certain fire or flood insurance companies.
6359	Other insurance companies.
6411	Insurance agents, brokers, and service

Real estate:
6511	Real estate operators and lessors of buildings.
6516	Lessors of mining, oil, and similar property
6518	Lessors of railroad property and other real property
6530	Condominium management and cooperative housing associations
6550	Subdividers and developers
6599	Other real estate

Holding and other investment companies, except bank holding companies:
6742	Regulated investment companies
6743	Real estate investment trusts
6744	Small business investment companies
6749	Other holding and investment companies except bank holding companies

Services
7000	**Hotels and other lodging places.**
7200	**Personal services.**

Business services:
7310	Advertising.
7389	Business services, except advertising

Auto repair; miscellaneous repair services:
7500	Auto repair and services
7600	Misc repair services

Amusement and recreation services:
7812	Motion picture production, distribution, and services
7830	Motion picture theaters
7900	Amusement and recreation services, except motion pictures

Other services:
8015	Offices of physicians, including osteopathic physicians
8021	Offices of dentists
8040	Offices of other health practitioners
8050	Nursing and personal care facilities
8060	Hospitals.
8071	Medical laboratories
8099	Other medical services
8111	Legal services
8200	Educational services
8300	Social services
8600	Membership organizations
8911	Architectural and engineering services.
8930	Accounting, auditing, and bookkeeping.
8980	Miscellaneous services (including veterinarians)

U.S. GOVERNMENT PRINTING OFFICE : 1987 O - 493-200

SHAREHOLDER' CONSENT TO S CORPORATION
ELECTION—SAMPLE

Date: August 1, 1987

Director
Internal Revenue Service Center
10 Oak Street
Anytown, USA 00000

Dear Sir:

By means of this letter, I state my consent to have
the   XYZ Corporation   (name), a
      New York   corporation with offices at
   100 Main Street, Anywhere, New York   treated as
S Corporation under Section 1362 of the Internal Revenue
Code. Pursuant to Form 2553, I offer the following data:

SAMPLE

1. My name is Mary Brown   .

2. I own   50   shares of stock of the   XYZ
    Corporation   .

3. I acquired that stock on   July 15, 1987   .

4. My Social Security number is   111-12-1222   .

5. My tax year ends on   December 31   .

6. The Corporation EID number is   81-4039261   .

Mary Brown
Signature

Mary Brown
Name (Print)

50 Maple Street
Address

Anywhere, USA 00000

555-5555
Tel. No.

SHAREHOLDER' CONSENT TO
S CORPORATION ELECTION—FORM

Date:

Director
Internal Revenue Service Center

Dear Sir:

By means of this letter, I state my consent to have the   (name), a
corporation with offices at   treated as
S Corporation under Section 1362 of the Internal Revenue
Code. Pursuant to Form 2553, I offer the following data:

1. My name is   .

2. I own   shares of stock of the
    .

3. I acquired that stock on   .

4. My Social Security number is   .

5. My tax year ends on   .

6. The Corporation EID number is   .

_____
Signature

_____
Name (Print)

_____
Address

_____

_____
Tel. No.

REQUEST FOR EXTENSION TO FILE
SHAREHOLDERS' CONSENT TO
S CORPORATION ELECTION—SAMPLE

July 15, 1986

Director
Internal Revenue Service
10 Oak Street
Anywhere, USA 00000

Dear Sir:

Be advised XYZ Corporation
("Corporation") requests an extension of the time for
the filing of shareholder consents with respect to the
Corporation's election to be subject to the S incorporation provisions of the Internal Revenue Code. In
support of this request, the following information is
furnished:

1. The Corporation was incorporated under the laws
of the State of New York   , on   July 15   , 1987   .

2. The Corporation first* had assets   on
July 15   , 19 87   .

3. All of the shareholders' consents to the
Corporation election ~~be made under~~ the S incorporation provisions of ~~the Internal Revenue~~ Code have not
and could not be filed on Form 2553, submitted with this
letter, for the following reason:

Mary Brown, holder of 50 shares out of 100 shares issued,
consented to election, however, she is presently out of the
country for one month.

4. Other than   Mary Brown   , all other
shareholders have consented to the election, and each of
those shareholders has consented in writing on Form
2553.

5. The government's interest will not be pre-
judiced by treating the election of the Corporation to
be chaptered under the S incorporation provisions of the
Internal Revenue Code as valid.

By: _____
             Robert Brown
             Title: President

* had assets, or
  had shareholders, or
  did business

REQUEST FOR EXTENSION TO FILE
SHAREHOLDERS' CONSENT TO
S CORPORATION ELECTION—FORM

Director
Internal Revenue Service

Dear Sir:

    Be advised
("Corporation") requests an extension of the time for the filing of shareholder consents with respect to the Corporation's election to be subject to the S incorporation provisions of the Internal Revenue Code. In support of this request, the following information is furnished:

    1. The Corporation was incorporated under the laws of the State of   , on   , 19   .

    2. The Corporation first*   on   , 19   .

    3. All of the shareholders' consents to the Corporation election to be taxed under the S incorporation provisions of the Internal Revenue Code have not and could not be filed on Form 2553, submitted with this letter, for the following reason:

    4. Other than   , all other shareholders have consented to the election, and each of those shareholders has consented in writing on Form 2553.

    5. The government's interest will not be prejudiced by treating the election of the Corporation to be chaptered under the S incorporation provisions of the Internal Revenue Code as valid.

                            By:_____

                                Title:

* had assets, or
  had shareholders, or
  did business

Form **SS-4**
(Rev. November 1985)
Department of the Treasury
Internal Revenue Service

Application for Employer Identification Number

OMB No. 1545-0003

Expires 8-31-88

1 Name (True name. See instructions.)		2 Social security no., if sole proprietor	3 Ending month of accounting year
4 Trade name of business if different from item 1		5 General partner's name, if partnership; principal officer's name, if corporation; or grantor's name, if trust	
6 Address of principal place of business (Number and street)		7 Mailing address, if different	
8 City, state, and ZIP code		9 City, state, and ZIP code	

10 Type of organization ☐ Individual ☐ Trust ☐ Partnership ☐ Plan administrator ☐ Governmental ☐ Nonprofit organization ☐ Corporation ☐ Other (specify)	11 County of principal business location
12 Reason for applying ☐ Started new business ☐ Purchased going business ☐ Other (specify)	13 Acquisition or starting date (Mo., day, year). See instructions.
14 Nature of principal activity (See instructions.)	15 First date wages or annuities were paid or will be paid (Mo., day, year).

16 Peak number of employees expected in the next 12 months (If none, enter "0") ▶	Nonagricultural	Agricultural	Household	17 Does the applicant operate more than one place of business? ☐ Yes ☐ No

18 Most of the products or services are sold to whom? ☐ Business establishments (wholesale) ☐ General public (retail) ☐ Other (specify) ☐ N/A	19 If nature of business is manufacturing, state princ:pal product and raw material used.

20 Has the applicant ever applied for an identification number for this or any other business? ☐ Yes ☐ No

If "Yes," enter name and trade name. Also enter approx. date, city, and state where the application was filed and previous number if known. ▶

Under penalties of perjury, I declare that I have examined this application, and to the best of my knowledge and belief it is true, correct, and complete. | Telephone number (include area code)

Signature and Title ▶   Date ▶

Please leave blank ▶	Geo.	Ind.	Class	Size	Reas. for appl.	**Part I**

- -

Form **SS-4**
(Rev. November 1985)
Department of the Treasury
Internal Revenue Service

Application for Employer Identification Number

OMB No. 1545-0003

Expires 8-31-88

1 Name (True name. See instructions.)		2 Social security no., if sole proprietor	3 Ending month of accounting year
4 Trade name of business if different from item 1		5 General partner's name, if partnership; principal officer's name, if corporation; or grantor's name, if trust	
6 Address of principal place of business (Number and street)		7 Mailing address, if different	
8 City, state, and ZIP code		9 City, state, and ZIP code	

10 Type of organization ☐ Individual ☐ Trust ☐ Partnership ☐ Plan administrator ☐ Governmental ☐ Nonprofit organization ☐ Corporation ☐ Other (specify)	11 County of principal business location
12 Reason for applying ☐ Started new business ☐ Purchased going business ☐ Other (specify)	13 Acquisition or starting date (Mo., day, year). See instructions.
14 Nature of principal activity (See instructions.)	15 First date wages or annuities were paid or will be paid (Mo., day, year).

16 Peak number of employees expected in the next 12 months (If none, enter "0") ▶	Nonagricultural	Agricultural	Household	17 Does the applicant operate more than one place of business? ☐ Yes ☐ No

18 Most of the products or services are sold to whom? ☐ Business establishments (wholesale) ☐ General public (retail) ☐ Other (specify) ☐ N/A	19 If nature of business is manufacturing, state princ:pal product and raw material used.

20 Has the applicant ever applied for an identification number for this or any other business? ☐ Yes ☐ No

If "Yes," enter name and trade name. Also enter approx. date, city, and state where the application was filed and previous number if known. ▶

Under penalties of perjury, I declare that I have examined this application, and to the best of my knowledge and belief it is true, correct, and complete. | Telephone number (include area code)

Signature and Title ▶   Date ▶

Please leave blank ▶	Geo.	Ind.	Class	Size	Reas. for appl.	**Part II**

OPERATING YOUR S CORPORATION

6

OVERVIEW

Operating an S Corporation is no more difficult than operating a C Corporation. There are, however, certain rules that must be followed if the business is to properly fulfill its responsibilities as an S Corporation and maintain its status.

IMMEDIATE STEPS

1. *Transfer Personal Assets To The Corporation*

If you have been operating a business or service prior to S incorporation (as many people do), you can transfer the assets, financial instruments, accounts and debts of the old business to the new corporation, at an agreed sum or consideration and receive shares of stock in exchange. You cannot, however, burden the corporation with more debts than assets. Further, you cannot, sell your personal property to the corporation at inflated prices, or exchange its stock for personal property that is overvalued. Be certain to obtain an appraisal so you can establish a "basis" for your shares and to determine the appreciation of the assets after it becomes part of the S Corporation.

You should also check to determine whether the state will impose a sales tax or transfer tax on the sale of assets.

It will also be necessary to obtain approval from the shareholders and directors of the S Corporation, authorizing the acquisition of assets, assumption of debts and issuance of shares in consideration of the transfer.

2. *Notify All Existing Business Affiliates and Customers or Clients of the New Change to a Corporate Status*

This can be done by personal communication (telephone or letter), or by a small newspaper notice. Generally, all subsequent company records and transactions should be changed to reflect the new "corporate" status of the organization, including the printing of new letterheads, business cards, stationery and sign.

As a seller of assets to the corporation, you should also comply with the Bulk Sales Act in your state which generally provides that creditors of the seller be notified of the intended transfer at least 10 days in advance. As a practical matter, however, this need not be complied with if the existing liabilities are to be fully paid in the ordinary course of business. Similarly, if any assets to be transferred are encumbered or subject to lien or security interest, then authorization to transfer the encumbered asset must be obtained from the lienholder.

3. *Determine State And Local Requirements*

Not only should the parties starting a new business look into the formalities for incorporation, but other possible regulation and clearances must also be considered. Permits and licenses are required for such businesses as real estate brokers, barbers, hairdressers, private investigators, cosmetologists, billiard rooms, pharmacies, nursing homes, notaries, peddlers, newsstands, employment agencies, businesses serving or selling alcoholic beverages, health concerns and hospitals, and educational institutions. Many businesses are regulated by Federal agencies, such as brokerage and securities businesses, air transportation, banking and drug manufacturing companies. Before commencing any new business, you should consider what regulations are applicable so that your business will not be conducted in violation of these rules and regulations. Bear in mind that an S Corporation cannot engage in certain business activities, i.e. banking.

4. *Determine Withholding Taxes*

Any business that hires employees must consider whether it is subject to rules relating to withholding of taxes for local, state and the Federal government, whether it must pay social security tax, unemployment insurance or workmen's compensation, and whether any unions have jurisdiction and what pension or other payments must be made to them. Minimum wage requirements and their applicability should be considered together with the permissibility of hiring minors, and any occupational safety and health regulations. There are, however, no special withholding tax requirements for an S Corporation as compared to a C Corporation.

5. *Keep Separate Financial Records*

Remember that your corporation is viewed in the eyes of the law as a different "legal entity" separate and apart from the owner(s).

Hence, to avoid potential IRS problems, you must maintain separate sets of records, one for your personal affairs, and one for the affairs of the corporation. As a rule, however, it is not necessary to maintain an elaborate bookkeeping system. A separate banking account, and a bookkeeping system that clearly shows what you and the corporation separately earn and pay out, is usually sufficient. A local bookkeeper or accountant can easily set up a convenient accounting and tax system for your business. An S Corporation requires no special bookkeeping procedure.

6. *Set Up Your Corporate Bank Accounts*

To open a corporate bank account, you would need an Employer Identification Number for your corporation. To obtain this, simply file a simple application form, Form SS-4, with the Internal Revenue Service. Another item you'll most probably be required to have by the bank, is a "corporate resolution" duly signed and impressed with the "corporate seal" as an official corporate indication of authorization to open such an account(s). Most banks will provide you with the appropriate corporate resolutions and a corporate seal can be ordered as part of the corporate kit.

7. *Qualify In Other States*

If your new S Corporation is only a local business, it is unlikely that you will have any question as to whether you need to be authorized or qualified to do business in another state. You clearly are doing business in only one place. But what happens if you start advertising in magazines and you get orders from out-of-state? Are you now doing business in more than one state? Or what if you are in the sales business, have a store or sales office only in one place, but have sales representatives who drive to other states and call on potential customers? Does this mean you are now doing business elsewhere? If you start expanding and open up new stores, then you would clearly be doing business in these other locations.

Before we go further into how you decide whether you are "doing business" in another state, let's look at why it matters. If you are doing business in another state, but have not qualified by filing the proper papers and paying the fees, the consequences can be serious. In all states, an unqualified foreign corporation is denied access to the courts of the state, which would mean you could not sue someone in that state in order to enforce a contract or obligation. In addition, in many states fines are imposed by the state when they discover a corporation doing business there without having qualified, and in some cases directors, officers, or agents may be subject to these fines. These consequences could be very serious to your business.

The statutes of many states define what constitutes "doing business" within that state, and these statutes should be consulted.

The model corporation act gives a list of activities, which, in and of themselves alone, do not constitute doing business. Since this act is the basis for the state laws in many states, it is a good guide as to what you can do without having to qualify:

(a) Maintaining or defending any action or suit or any administrative or arbitration proceeding, or effecting settlement thereof or the settlement of claims or disputes.

(b) Holding meetings of its directors or shareholders or carrying on other activities concerning its internal affairs.

(c) Maintaining bank accounts.

(d) Maintaining offices or agencies for the transfer, exchange and registration of its securities, or appointing and maintaining trustees or depositaries with relation to its securities.

(e) Effecting sales through independent contractors.

(f) Soliciting or procuring orders, whether by mail or through employees or agents or otherwise, where such orders require acceptance without this State before becoming binding contracts.

(g) Creating as borrower or lender, or acquiring, indebtedness or mortgages or other security interests in real or personal property.

(h) Securing or collecting debts or enforcing any rights in property securing the same.

(i) Transacting any business in interstate commerce.

(j) Conducting an isolated transaction completed within a period of thirty days and not in the course of a number of repeated transactions of like nature.

If you do have to become authorized to do business as a foreign corporation, the procedure is relatively simple. You obtain from the Secretary of State the application form, complete it and file it with the proper fees.

MAINTAINING CORPORATE RECORDS

Once organized, the S Corporation must maintain a continuous and accurate record of all authorized actions—whether approved by its stockholders or directors.

A complete and detailed record of stockholders and directors meeting—"minutes" as they are called—is important for many reasons:

1. Parties dealing with the corporation may want evidence that the corporate action was approved.
2. Officers and employees within the corporation are entitled to the protection their acts were approved.
3. Accurate minutes is frequently necessary to preserve certain tax benefits or to avoid tax liabilities and penalties.
4. Minutes are oftentimes necessary to prove the corporation is operated as a entity, independent of its principals.

Stockholders' Actions

Stockholders can usually vote on the broadest issues relating to the S Corporation. These typically include change of corporate name, address, purpose, the amount of authorized or type shares and other matters involving the corporate structure. Stockholders' action may also be needed on major legal or financial issues such as to mortgage, encumber, pledge or lease all or substantially all of the corporate assets or to file bankruptcy, merge or consolidate. There are, of course, many other actions that can be taken by stockholders and many of these resolutions can be found within this section. The primary function of the stockholders, however, is to elect the Board of Directors, through whose governance the S Corporation is actually managed.

Stockholders can act officially only as a group. This means that a formal meeting is needed before they can legally bind the corporation. There are some exceptions where the stockholders can consent in writing to a particular action without having to hold a meeting such as in the election to become an S Corporation.

Certain rules and procedures have to be followed for stockholders to properly conduct an official stockholder meeting.

1. Every stockholder has to be properly notified about the time and place of the meeting, who is calling the meeting, and any matters that will be considered at the meeting. It is common in small corporations for the stockholders to do without a formal notice, especially where the by-laws set out the time and place of the regular annual meeting of stockholders. This can be done by having all the stockholders sign a waiver of notice at the meeting. Unscheduled or special meetings of stockholders may require notice, although a signed waiver of notice can also be used at these meetings. For an unscheduled meeting to be legally convened, it is essential that the records show that proper notice was

given, or that the stockholders signed a waiver of notice requirement.

Your articles of incorporation or by-laws will specify where and when a stockholder meeting can legally be held and the book of minutes should show the time and place of each meeting. In this way, you can prove that the meeting complied with the legal requirements.

2. No business can be transacted at stockholders meeting unless a quorum is present. Therefore, it is essential that the book of minutes reflect a quorum of stockholders attended the meeting. The articles of incorporation or the by-laws will usually state the size of the quorum, either in terms of the number of stockholders, or the number of shares that must be represented at the meeting. For example, a by-law that "two-thirds of all stockholders shall constitute a quorum" applies to the number of stockholders, and not to the amount of stock they own. On the other hand, a by-law that "a majority of the outstanding stock shall constitute a quorum" means that a certain number of shares of stock must be represented, regardless of whether the stock is owned by one person or by thousands of people. If there is no rule on a quorum, then whatever number of stockholders shows up for the meeting will constitute a quorum, however, some states require a stated percentage of the outstanding shares be represented at a shareholders' meeting to be valid.

3. Stockholder meetings must have a chairperson to preside over the meeting. It must also have a secretary to record what happened at the meeting. The by-laws will ordinarily designate these officials, such as by specifying that the President serve as chairperson, and the Secretary act as secretary, however, substitutes are usually allowable.

4. The first items of business at every stockholder meeting should be to read and approve the minutes of the previous meeting. Once the minutes are approved, they legally document what occurred at the meeting. They are the most nearly conclusive proof of what the corporation is authorized to do. That is why it is important to show that the minutes have been read and approved as accurate, or that necessary changes have been made.

Directors' Actions

Most of the rules and procedures that apply to stockholders meetings apply equally to meeting of the Board of Directors with several exceptions:

1. Directors will meet far more often than stockholders, and in larger S Corporations may even meet monthly. The Directors can also hold special meetings for interim Board action and in more active S Corporations they will routinely meet more often.

2. The Board—as with stockholders—can only function through a duly called meeting where a quorum of directors (as defined in the by-laws) are present. Directors who may be in conflict with the interests of the S Corporation may, however, not be counted towards the quorum or entitled to vote. An example of this is when the corporation plans to enter into a contract with a company with which the director is affiliated.

3. The Board must be particularly careful to document not only its actions but why the action was taken. Because the board has responsibility to stockholders—and potential liability to other constituencies—it may be called upon to show why its action was prudent—particularly in areas of dividends, loans to officers, major contracts, compensation and policy-making. It is especially critical for the minutes to include or refer to reports, arguments, opinions and other documents to support the reasonableness of the Board's actions.

4. Frequently the Board will be called upon to issue "certified resolutions" or "certificates of vote" which conclusively show to third parties dealing with the corporation that the person acting on behalf of the corporation has the required authority. These forms are contained within this section, and can be easily completed with notary seal and/or corporate seal.

All records, resolutions and minutes should be kept within the corporate minute book and kept for no less than six years—although retaining the records for longer is recommended considering the numerous types of claims that are possible and the varying statute of limitations.

COMPENSATION STRATEGIES

7

OVERVIEW

Another major advantage of an S Corporation is that it allows for greater flexibility in how compensation to officers and key employees can be structured, often reducing personal tax liability or allowing more net income to remain within the family.

COMPENSATION

Because an S Corporation avoids the double taxation of a C Corporation there is little incentive for a shareholder-employee to increase salary simply for purposes of escaping the corporate tax on corporate profits. In an S Corporation the overall tax liability is precisely the same whether the shareholder-employee takes his payment as salary or profits.

For that reason the Internal Revenue Service is not as concerned with the "reasonableness" of compensation with an S Corporation as it is with a C Corporation. On the other hand, the IRS frequently challenges C Corporation shareholder-employees who pay themselves high salaries to avoid the double tax on corporate profits. If the IRS is successful in arguing the compensation level is "unreasonable", the excess salary is recalculated as corporate profits on which it must pay the corporate tax.

There are, however, situations in which the payment of compensation will have an impact and should therefore be structured carefully.

(i) Withholding Taxes: Even though an S Corporation does not pay taxes, it is an entity in the eyes of the law. As an employer, it must withhold a portion of its employees' wages for income tax, social security tax and unemployment insurance tax. Should the S Corporation seek to avoid withholding for these taxes by not paying its owner-employees a salary, it would do so by making a distribution to those employees. Distributions, since they are not wages, would not be subject to withholding taxes.

Both the Internal Revenue Service and the Social Security Administration are alert to this possibility. Both will be quick to take the position that distributions are disguised wages subject to withholding. And both have been successful in making this argument. Shareholders, otherwise entitled to Social Security benefits, have another concern: if they do in fact work for their S Corporation without salary, the Social Security Administration will take the position that distributions they receive are, in fact, wages and that those wages should be applied to reduce the amount of Social Security benefits the shareholder-employee will be entitled to receive. (This problem, it should be noted, exists for both C and S Corporations.)

One way to minimize the impact of the withholding problem is to minimize the amount of wages received by the shareholder-employee. Wages can be reduced to the lowest reasonable amount that can be justified for the services in question. It should be noted, however, that monies taken as salary will reduce passive profits and therefore there will be less earnings to be shielded by passive losses.

(ii) Impact on Basis: We noted that S Corporation losses flow through to the corporation shareholders and may be used as deductions against their other income. We also noted a limitation on that rule: losses can only be used as a deduction if the shareholder has sufficient basis in his stock and debt to cover the amount of the loss. If a shareholder-employee draws all of his income from the S Corporation in the form of wages, his basis in his stock remains unchanged. If, on the other hand, the shareholder draws only a portion of his income as wages, the part he does not draw will become corporate profit at the end of the year. If the money is removed as a distribution of profits, the amount taken in this form will be added to the shareholder's basis in his stock and can therefore be later used against corporate losses.

(iii) Multiple Shareholders: Assume that S Corporation has two shareholders, John and Jane, and that they are unrelated. Both own 100 percent of the shares of S Corporation. Although they agree that both will share profits equally, John, who had put up most of the money to get the business off the ground, does not work for the corporation nor does he draw a salary. Jane works for the corporation full time and is compensated for her services.

Example:
Let's now assume that the IRS determines that Jane's salary was unreasonable and that they conclude it was unreasonable to the extent of $20,000. The result would be that the payment to Jane would be considered a distribution. She would not have to include the $20,000 when reporting her taxable income. However, since the $20,000 payment to Jane is a distribution, the corporation cannot claim it as a deduction for salary. That means the corporation will have an additional $20,000 of income that will flow through to its shareholders. John and Jane will each have to report an extra $10,000 of income —in John's case he will be paying tax on money he never received; Jane, on the other hand, will receive $20,000 and pay tax on $10,000.

Nor do the consequences end there. John's basis in his stock will be increased by $10,000 —his share of the distribution that was treated as a corporate profit. Jane, however, will see her basis reduced by $10,000 (the $20,000 decrease because the distribution is partially offset by a $10,000 increase attributable to her share of the $20,000 distribution treated as a corporate profit).

DETERMINING REASONABLE COMPENSATION

Although there is no one fixed guideline that establishes precisely what constitutes reasonable compensation, there are accepted standards. The most objective test looks to salaries paid to individuals performing comparable services for comparable businesses. Even this test is subject to other considerations. For example, the executive in question may have offered services far greater in effort or scope than would ordinarily be expected. In such cases, a bonus may very well be in order. Straight salary (or bonuses) can be tied to performance standards, e.g. gross sales, an approach that may lead to justifiably high, or low salaries. Other factors that may be considered when determining whether compensation is reasonable include:

1. Business Performance: If the business enjoys a significant increase in sales volume or net profits, higher compensation can be justified.

2. Extensive Experience: An employee with years of experience or special knowledge in a given field generally justifies higher compensation than a less experienced person.

If you anticipate a problem with the salary level, it may be wise to prepare a formal employment contract between yourself and the corporation. This employment contract can then spell out the responsibilities that may help justify the salary level.

While the IRS may look at the level of compensation, as a practical matter the Internal Revenue Service seldom contests salary levels within a small corporation unless there is a clear case of abuse.

INCOME SPLITTING

Starting in 1988, the Tax Reform Act of 1986 provides two basic tax rates for individuals: 15 percent and 28 percent. Given the difference of 13 percent, many taxpayers who form small businesses will be tempted to underpay themselves and maximize the salary they pay to family members, usually children, who are in a lower tax bracket.

To prevent this, the Internal Revenue Code allows the IRS to reallocate income in situations where a family member draws an unreasonably low salary for his efforts. The family member in question does not have to be a shareholder in the S Corporation but may be a spouse, parent, grandparent, child or grandchild of a shareholder. A parent, for example, may be willing to work full time to assist a child and may prefer not to draw a salary to perhaps avoid reducing Social Security benefits.

But there are commonly encountered situations where you can with some degree of safety spread income within the family so it is taxed at the lower 15 percent rate.

For example, if you have two children and want each to receive $100 monthly. If you pay it to them as allowances, you must pay tax on the earnings before you give them the remainder. Assuming you are in the 28 percent bracket, you must earn $280 monthly to give them $200. A better strategy may be to hire your children as employees of the S Corporation. Pay them by the hour to maintain, paint, clean or otherwise perform services for your S Corporation. Their earnings now become a deduction to the business thereby increasing the deductions you add to your personal return.

And don't forget, your children can earn up to $3,000 in 1988 ($2,540 in 1987) without owing any tax. In fact, each can earn $5,000 tax-free if he or she contributes $2,000 to an IRA.

This means that when you pay each child $100 monthly as wages, absolutely no taxes are paid on it. Whatever bracket you're in, you need earn only $200 monthly to give them $200.

Be careful to maintain employment records, showing dates and hours worked. Be sure wages paid are reasonable when compared to work done. If your S Corporation is ever audited, you will need solid backup information to prove your deductions.

In another example, you can also use your S Corporation to split *investment income* with family members, cutting your tax bill and keeping more cash in the family. Assume you earn $10,000 annually from investments and that you are in the 28 percent tax bracket, so the IRS takes $2,800.

If you form an S Corporation instead, and give half the stock to your three children, they can now record their proportionate share of the income on their returns. Each child will report $1,667 of income (one-third of $5,000). Under the 1986 Tax Reform Act each child will be entitled to a $500 standard deduction (assuming the child had no other earnings). Each child will pay tax on $1,167 at a rate of 15 percent. The total tax paid by your children will be $525. Your tax on the $5,000 of income you will report will be $1,400.

Tax Warning:
The examples described above will only work if the children with whom you split your investments are over 14 years of age. Under the Tax Reform Act of 1986, the unearned income of children under the age of 14 will be treated as follows: the first $500 is excluded, the next $500 is taxed at the child's tax rate (assume 15 percent), the remainder is taxed at the parent's rate.

Tax Warning:
If the shareholder-employee's salary appears unreasonably low, the IRS can reallocate income between family members. The criteria for determining whether compensation is too low is the same as determining whether it is too high.

Another income splitting approach is to give your spouse $2,000 to help keep corporate records. If your spouse opens an IRA account and invests the $2,000 in the account each year it will grow to $144,000 in 20 years. And, of course, it will all be tax deferred.

Tax Warning:
This plan will work only if neither you nor your spouse currently participates in a qualified retirement program. The Tax Reform Act of 1986 denies IRA's for individuals who are covered by a retirement plan or who are married to someone who participates in a qualified plan.

FRINGE BENEFITS AND THE S CORPORATION

8

OVERVIEW

The legislative history of S Corporations show several changes in the rules regarding fringe benefits.

Prior to 1982 an S Corporation could provide the same fringe benefits—medical, accident, disability, life insurance plans—that a C Corporation could and do so on the same terms. Premiums paid by the corporation were deductible as a business expense; benefits received by the employee were excluded from taxable income. Therefore, in terms of fringe benefits the S Corporation featured no disadvantage.

However, in 1982 Congress sought to provide the S Corporation with as many partnership tax features as possible. Most of the changes worked to help entrepreneurs who sought the benefits of limited liability associated with incorporation and the single tax on earnings available in the sole proprietorship or partnership.

When S Corporations were taxed on a par with partnerships, Congress applied the rule on partnerships and fringe benefits to S Corporations. This means that the S Corporation cannot deduct as a business expense the cost of fringe benefits provided to most shareholder-employees. As is the case with partnerships, the shareholder-employee who receives a benefit must include that benefit when reporting taxable income.

Such benefits include:

1. Premiums paid by the S Corporation for medical and disability plans.

2. Premiums paid for $50,000 group life insurance policies.

3. Meals and lodging furnished by the S Corporation to the employee but for the convenience of the company.

4. The $5,000 death benefit exclusion available to the estate of an employee whose employer provides this benefit.

WHO IS QUALIFIED TO RECEIVE BENEFITS?

The important point to remember is that fringe benefits may be provided to non-shareholder-employees. As with a regular C Corporation the cost of those benefits are deductible by the S Corporation and non- taxable to the employee. Therefore, an S Corporation features absolutely no disadvantage in recruiting and retaining valuable employees who, of course, will expect a competitive fringe benefit package.

Therefore, only employees who are stockholders of the S Corporation are ineligible to receive tax-free fringe benefits. If the corporation provides fringe benefits to stockholder-employees, the cost of the fringe benefits would not be deductible by the S Corporation and would nevertheless be taxable to the stockholder-employee.

The rule described above applies to all shareholder-employees who own more than 2 percent of the S Corporation stock or, if the corporation has both voting and non-voting stock, more than 2 percent of the corporations total combined voting stock. If either of these ownership requirements is satisfied for just one day of the corporation tax year, the rule applies.

Example:
On January 1, 1988 Mary Smith owned 3 percent of S Corporation stock. On January 2, 1988 she sold her stock interest but continued to remain employed by the corporation for the rest of the year.

Under these circumstances Mary would be ineligible to receive tax-free fringe benefits for all of 1988 (as she owned over 2 percent during a part of 1988), however, she may receive tax-free benefits starting January 1, 1989.

The disqualification of stockholder-employees who own over 2 percent of the shares also extends to an employed relative who owns no shares. The term "relative" includes spouse, parents, grandparents, children, and grandchildren. Furthermore, this disqualification extends to an employed relative who owns no shares but is related to a disqualified shareholder who is not an employee of the corporation.

The obvious legislative intent in disqualifying "relatives" is to prevent a disqualified stockholder from indirectly benefitting from tax-free fringe benefits provided the relative, and, of course, it also avoids a stockholder from using a relative as a "straw" so as to frustrate the intent of the law.

The drawback to a stockholder-employee of not obtaining tax-free fringe benefits is, of course, relatively minor when measured against the many attributes of an S Corporation.

There are, however, two approaches that may even resolve this fringe benefit problem:

1. A common solution to the problem is to divide your business activities into two corporations—a C Corporation and S Corporation. The C Corporation may provide a service, or perhaps sell a product to the S Corporation. The C Corporation—with nominal income—may provide the fringe benefits and operate at a break-even or near break-even basis. Essentially, the C Corporation becomes a conduit for furnishing tax-exempt, tax-deductible fringe benefits.

The fact that the same individual owns both corporations would not be a disqualification for this strategy, provided the corporations were operated as separate and distinct entities.

2. It is always possible to adjust a stockholder-employees compensation levels so that the stockholder-employee can purchase a comparable package of benefits designed for his specific needs. While this compensation would be deductible by the corporation (as salary) it would nevertheless be taxable to the stockholder-employee.

RETIREMENT PLANS

Unlike other fringe benefits, stockholder-employees may participate along with other employees in qualified retirement plans set up by the S Corporation.

In 1982 when the Tax Equity and Fiscal Responsibility Act (TEFRA) was passed, Congress placed S Corporations, C Corporations and partnerships on equal footing respect to qualified retirement plans. In large measure, there are few significant differences in the treatment accorded the three types of business forms.

The benefits provided by a qualified retirement plan are:

1. The corporation is permitted to take a deduction for the full amount of its contribution to the plan;

2. The shareholder-employee does not include as income either the

contribution made on his or her behalf by the corporation or the earnings on the contribution until the time he or she receives a distribution from the qualified plan.

However, there are limits on the amount an employer may contribute on behalf of shareholder-employees. Those limits are very similar to the requirements concerning compensation—only a reasonable salary will be treated as compensation when paid to a shareholder-employee. Similarly, the contribution made on behalf of a shareholder-employee must be reasonable when considered along with other compensation paid to the shareholder-employee.

If the S Corporation has an HR 10 Plan, it may deduct that portion of contributions it uses to purchase life insurance for shareholder-employees. To that extent, the use of a qualified plan may, at least partially solve the problem of fringe benefits for stockholder-employees.

There are, however, two serious considerations in adopting a qualified retirement plan by an S Corporation.

1. Should the stockholder-employees choose to form an Employee Stock Ownership Plan (ESOP), formation of a Trust will be necessary. However, Trusts are not eligible to own shares in an S Corporation and such ownership would cause the S Corporation to lose its status. Many companies are establishing ESOP's with the idea of encouraging the ESOP to take over ownership of the company at a future date. When this becomes the primary objective of an ESOP the corporation should consider switching from S status to C status.

2. Shareholders of an S Corporation may not receive loans from a qualified plan if they hold 5 percent or more of the corporate shares. C Corporations do not have this restriction. In determining the percentages of stock ownership listed above, the employee is considered the owner of shares owned by a spouse, children, parents, grandparents and grand children.

Tax Warning:
There are other rules that govern retirement plans.

One caution is to avoid a "top heavy" plan which imposes complex requirements. A "top heavy" plan exists if 60 percent or more of the plan's benefits are for the benefit of key employees. A key employee who 1) is an officer of the corporation or 2) owns 5 percent or more of the S Corporation stock or 3) is one of ten employees who owns the greatest interest in the corporation or 4) receives more than $150,000 a year in compensation from the corporation.

Another problem may arise with retirement plans when a C Corporation converts to S Corporation status. Loans made by the pension plan while the entity was a C Corporation become dis-

qualified for an S Corporation exposing the plan to potential penalties.

Because retirement plans are so technical, consider seeking professional advice—often provided free of charge from most banks and financial institutions.

AVAILABILITY OF FRINGE BENEFIT

FRINGE BENEFIT	C CORP. EMPLOYEE	2% S CORP SHAREHOLDER	EARNED INCOME PARTNER	PASSIVE PARTNER	SELF-EMPLOYED
Health & Accident	Yes	No	No	No Yes under new law to 25%	No
Group-Term Life	Yes	No	No	No	No
Qualified Group Legal	Yes	Yes	Yes	No	Yes
Education Assist.	Yes	Yes	Yes	No	Yes
Dependent Care Assistance	Yes	Yes	Yes	No	Yes
No-Additional-Cost Services	Yes	Yes	Yes	No	No
Qualified Employee Discounts	Yes	Yes	Yes	No	No
Working Condition Fringes	Yes	Yes	Yes	No	No
Diminimus Fringe Benefits	Yes	Yes	Yes	No	No

TAX BENEFITS FROM CORPORATE LOSSES

9

OVERVIEW

One of the great benefits of the S Corporation is that its stockholders have several ways to personally take advantage of the corporate losses. Of course, stockholders will—at least in most cases—prefer their corporation earn a profit, but the fact they can "write off" at least a portion of the losses can be somewhat consoling

SECTION 1244 STOCK

One tax benefit stockholders of either a C or S Corporation can take advantage of is to use Section 1244 Stock.

Summarily, Section 1244 Stock allows shareholders of a failed corporation to write off up to $50,000 in any one year, against either capital gains or ordinary income ($100,000 if the taxpayers file a joint return).

Under present tax rules, losses suffered by a shareholder when his stock becomes worthless are capital losses and can be used only in a limited manner. If the losses are long-term losses (held for more than six months), they can be applied to offset capital gains, and then if there are excess capital losses, they can be used to offset ordinary income but only up to a maximum of $3,000. This means that if a taxpayer has $2,000 of capital gains and $20,000 of long-term capital losses, $15,000 of capital losses cannot be used in the current tax year but must be carried forward. $2,000 of the losses will offset the $2,000 gain, and another $3,000 can be used to offset ordinary income; that leaves a balance of $15,000 of the total $20,000 loss that is unused in the current tax year, and must be held over to be applied to future years earnings.

However, if the shareholder had the same $20,000 loss on 1244 shares he could have applied the $20,000 against an equivalent amount of income in that year. Assuming this shareholder has $20,000 in earnings he could have eliminated his total tax liability for the year through the accelerated write off.

The advantages of 1244 stock are obvious and there are absolutely no disadvantages, therefore it is important that every corporation that qualifies issue stock pursuant to Section 1244 of the Internal Revenue Code.

The procedure is simple. Reference to the 1244 Stock issue may be contained in the by-laws or minutes of Incorporators of Directors (see appendix), and any attorney can see to it that the paperwork is properly documented.

In order to use Section 1244 Stock, the corporation must satisfy five criteria, none of which conflict with S Corporation requirements. The five criteria are:

1. The corporation must be a United States corporation.
2. The corporation may not be a holding company.
3. The total amount paid by shareholders for their stock must not be more than $1 million.
4. The stock must have been issued for cash or property and may not have been issued for services or in exchange for other shares of stock.
5. During the five tax years that preceded the year in which the stock became worthless, the corporation derived more than half of its income from non-passive sources. (Passive sources include income from royalties, rents, dividends, interest, annuities, and sales or exchanges of stock or other securities.)

It should be noted that although the benefits of capital have been eliminated under the Tax Reform Act, the concept of capital gains as well as limits on capital losses remain. Also, under the new law the differential between short-term losses and long-term losses is no longer in effect.

OPERATING LOSSES

Although S Corporation losses flow through to its shareholders, those losses can be deducted by shareholders on their returns only if they do not exceed the total of shareholders' basis in their stock and any debt owed to them by the corporation. "Basis" is a tax term that generally means the cost of the asset.

However, if an S Corporation's losses exceed a shareholder's basis the shareholder cannot deduct his full loss but must limit it to his basis and any excess must be carried over until such time as he has a sufficient basis to cover the loss.

Therefore, to fully take advantage of the S Corporation tax loss provisions it is important to understand how basis is determined, how basis increases or decreases and how the tax loss carryover provisions work.

DETERMINING BASIS

Basis is determined by combining the cost of the stock together with any debts made to the corporation. We can, however, consider each separately.

The general rule is that a shareholder's basis in S Corporation stock is the price paid for the stock. If, for example, a shareholder paid $500 for 50 shares of stock, her basis per share is $50 and her total or aggregate basis is $500.

However, if the shareholder transfers property to the S Corporation in exchange for shares, the shareholder's basis is determined by whether the transfer is a taxable event. Typically when a new business is formed, the transfer of property for shares is not a taxable event. In those cases, basis equals: (1) the basis of the property in the shareholder's hands when he or she transferred it to the corporation, (2) less the amount of any cash paid to the shareholder for the property, and (3) plus any gain the shareholder recognizes on the transfer.

If the stock was simply exchanged for property and the transfer was a taxable event, the basis of the stock would be the fair market value of the property at the time of transfer. It should be noted, however, that a transfer property to the corporation generally results in a non-taxable event.

Tax Tip:
When transferring property to your own corporation always obtain a professional appraisal to establish value.

Of course, if the stock is inherited by a stockholder the basis to the stockholder is the fair market value of the shares at the time of the decedent's death. Similarly, if the shares were gifted, the transferee accepts the shares at the transferors basis at the time of the gift.

Loans made to a corporation constitute part of the basis.

If a shareholder lends money to an S Corporation, his basis is the amount of the loan. If a shareholder renders services or property in exchange for a note, the shareholder's basis is the amount of the note.

Of course, a shareholder has a basis only in money actually loaned to the corporation, not money loaned to the corporation by a third-party.

The mere fact that a shareholder guarantees a corporate note is not sufficient for that debt to become part of the shareholder's basis. The shareholder must be more than "at risk". The shareholder actually has to expend the funds in payment of the debt before it becomes part of his basis. Therefore, if a corporation defaults on a note and the shareholder as quarantor is required to pay the note, he will have obtained a basis in corporate debt by the amount actually paid on the guarantee.

CHANGES IN BASIS

An S Corporation's shareholder will experience a change in his stock basis annually to reflect the corporation's profit or loss for the year. For example, if a shareholder has a stock basis of $20,000 and the corporation earns a profit of $5,000 for the year, the new basis will be $25,000. Conversely, if the corporation lost $5,000 the basis would have been reduced to $15,000 at the end of the year.

Therefore, to determine annual adjustments in basis, each S Corporation shareholder should increase or decrease his basis by the proportionate share of any profit or loss. However, if the S Corporation makes a non-taxable distribution (dividend payment) to shareholders, their basis is reduced by the amount of the distribution.

If a shareholder has basis in both stock and debt, there is a formula for determining which of the two basis changes when the corporation operates at a profit of loss. The general rule is that both accounts are determined separately unless operating losses exceed the shareholder's basis in his stock. In that case, the shareholder may deduct the loss only if he has sufficient basis in debt owed to him by the corporation to cover the loss. If the corporation operates at a profit the next year, the increase in basis would be applied to the debt basis first and the excess, if any, to stock.

A simple formula is as follows:

1. Decreases in basis caused by operating losses are applied first to the basis in stock and then to the basis in debt.

2. If operating losses have been used to decrease the basis in debt and there is a profit in a succeeding year, the debt basis must be

increased until it is completely replaced; then remaining profits can increase the basis of stock.

3. A shareholder can deduct losses only if the losses do not exceed the total amount of the shareholder's basis in stock and debt. If losses do exceed the combined basis, the shareholder may carry them forward indefinitely and until such time as (i) the shareholder has increased his basis through additional investments in stock or loans to the corporation or (ii) operating profits supply sufficient basis to cover the losses.

Tax Tip:
If you are an S Corporation's sole stockholder, and anticipate losses for the year, you may want to loan or invest further funds into the corporation so as to increase your basis to match the losses and thereby take the entire loss in the current year.

As a shareholder of an S Corporation you cannot, however, repay loans to yourself without it being a taxable event. Because loans made to an S Corporation will be treated unlike loans made to a C Corporation, you should review the tax consequences with an advisor before loaning money to the S Corporation. In many cases the taxable consequences associated with debt repayment are sufficiently significant to determine whether an S Corporation or some other form of organization will be used.

TAX PROBLEMS TO AVOID

OVERVIEW

The one distinguishing feature of the S Corporation is that its profits are not subject to taxation at the corporate level. However, there are exceptions to this general rule; an S Corporation may be taxed under several circumstances discussed in this chapter.

However, it should be first pointed out the the tax possibilities discussed in this section of the chapter apply only to corporations that previously operated as C Corporations and later switched to S Corporation status.

Corporations that start out as S Corporations can most likely bypass this chapter.

The three tax-creating situations we will cover in this chapter include:

1. Excess passive investment income.
2. Capital gains.
3. Taxes arising from a sale or disposition of property in a liquidation.

EXCESS PASSIVE INVESTMENT INCOME

An S Corporation is obligated to pay a tax on excess passive investment income earned during a tax year when it also operated as a regular C Corporation and had earnings or profits, from other sources or business activities.

Obviously, this tax can only apply to corporations that began as a C Corporation and later switched to S Corporation status.

Passive investment income, for purposes of an S Corporation tax include:

- rents
- dividends
- interest
- annuities
- royalties
- proceeds from the sale or exchange of stock or other securities

Although this problem most commonly occurs when shareholders of a C Corporation elect to switch to S Corporation in a year during which the C Corporation had earnings, it may also occur when there is a merger between a C and S Corporation.

Tax Tip:
The way to avoid the tax on passive investment is to have the corporation distribute its accumulated earnings and profits to its shareholders before the end of the tax year. Although the shareholders will be required to declare the distribution as taxable dividend income, the corporation will escape tax liability if the distribution is made before the end of the tax year.

CAPITAL GAINS

A capital gain occurs when a "capital asset" is sold for more than its basis. (Cost plus improvements less depreciation.) Typically, a capital asset usually is a fixed asset (real estate, equipment, etc.) used to produce income.

The Tax Reform Act of 1986 provides that capital gains are to be taxed as if they constitute ordinary income. However, the Tax Reform Act left undisturbed the procedures for determining capital gains as part of a taxpayers income. This was probably done so the concept of capital gains can be reintroduced in future tax changes, if warranted.

Because capital gains enjoyed favorable treatment, Congress was concerned that S Corporations would be organized solely to take advantage of a one-time capital gain benefit. To avoid this the new tax law prescribes an S Corporation will have to pay a tax on capital gains if four criteria exist:

1. The net capital gain must be in excess of $25,000.
2. The corporation has taxable income in excess of $25,000.

3. The net capital gain must constitute more than 50 percent of the corporations taxable income for the year.

4. The corporation a) was not an S Corporation for each of the three years prior to the tax year in question or b) has been in business for less than four years and has not been an S Corporation throughout the period.

All four criteria must be present before the S Corporation has a liability for capital gain tax. The tax applies only to the capital gain in excess of $25,000. Further, the tax rate is the lower of a) 28 percent or b) the tax if the corporation had not been an S Corporation.

Tax Tip:
To avoid the capital gains tax consider one of several options:
a) Wait at least three years before selling capital assets at a gain.
b) Sell capital assets with values of less than $25,000 in any one taxable year.

LIQUIDATION OF ASSETS

Prior to the Tax Reform Act of 1986, if a corporation sold appreciated property for a gain as part of a complete liquidation, the corporation would not be taxed on the gain. Alternatively, the gain would pass through to the shareholders and be taxable to them if the gain received was greater than their investment in their shares. This is no longer the situation.

Since passage of the new Tax Act, if a regular C Corporation disposes of an appreciated asset, it must pay a tax on the gain, and the shareholders will pay a tax at their level if the distribution received represents a gain to them.

Unfortunately, switching to an S Corporation does not totally solve the problem. The 1986 tax law requires the S Corporation to pay a tax on any appreciation of its property that occurred before the switch to S status, but only if the sale or distribution that is part of the liquidation occurs within ten years of the day the S Corporation becomes effective. Therefore, the tax that can be assessed against the S Corporation is limited to the appreciation that took place before the conversion. Appreciation that occurs after the conversion to S status is gain that flows through to the shareholders of the S Corporation. It should be noted, however, that C Corporations converting to S corporation status by December 31, 1986 avoid this problem.

Tax Tip:
If a C Corporation is to convert to S status, it should obtain an appraisal on its capital assets so the appreciation occurring after

conversion can be distinguished from the appreciation prior to conversion.

Note:
The 1986 Tax Reform Act has provided limited relief from this provision for C Corporations whose assets do not exceed $10 million if more than 50 percent of their stock is owned by fewer than 11 individuals. If the corporation's assets total $5 million or less, the new provisions do not affect it at all. The exemption for these $5 and $10 million dollar corporations, however, applies only to liquidating sales that are completed before January 1, 1989.

RECAPTURE OF INVESTMENT TAX CREDITS

Another problem area is that of Investment Tax Credits (ITC's).

The new tax laws effectively eliminated ITC's, however, it still applies in a more limited way.

If an S Corporation has an ITC, the unused credit is automatically passed through to the shareholders. However, if the S Corporation sells property on which it took an ITC as a C Corporation, the S Corporation becomes liable for the recapture of the ITC. Of course, this only applies to corporations that switch from C status to S Status.

SELLING S CORPORATION SHARES

11

OVERVIEW

A shareholder may sell or transfer his shares to a third-party, or as is often the case with an S Corporation, the shareholder may elect to transfer part or all of his shares back to the corporation.

There are oftentimes important tax ramifications based on how the sale is structured, and this is certainly true in the case of an S Corporation where the rules are particularly complex.

REDEMPTIONS

A "redemption" occurs when a shareholder transfers all or part of his shares back to the corporation. The corporation then owns the shares, however, as is typically the case the corporation retires the shares as non-voting treasury stock.

A shareholder may redeem or transfer his shares to the corporation for a wide variety of reasons:

1. The shareholder's basis in his stock has been reduced, and he wants to take a long-term capital loss by selling a portion of his shares in a year when he will realize long-term gains on other holdings.

2. An existing shareholder, because of the desire to retire from active business, wishes to sell all of his shareholdings back to the corporation, so the corporation can issue new shares to the buyer of the business.

3. Planning reduced participation in the business, a majority share-

holder is willing to sell a portion of his shares back to the corporation in order to equalize his holdings with those of the minority shareholder.

4. The selling shareholder wishing to obtain a tax-free distribution from the S Corporation, and sells a portion of his shareholdings back to the business for the distribution.

The transfer of shares back to the corporation may be treated either as a distribution or a sale (or exchange).

How the transaction is characterized is critical to the selling shareholder because of the difference in tax treatments of a distribution versus a sale or exchange.

If the transfer of stock is treated as a distribution, the shareholder may receive a tax-free payment of money from the corporation. If a transfer is found to be a sale or exchange, the shareholder will end up with either a capital gain or loss, depending upon the basis he had in the stock before the transfer. A shareholder receiving a distribution may have to recognize the distribution as ordinary income if the distribution exceeds his basis.

In large measure we can define a distribution as all transactions that do not meet the criteria of a sale or exchange.

The key criteria for a sale or exchange (and hence taxable) is if upon completion of the transfer there will be a meaningful or significant change at the corporate or shareholder level. That determination, in turn, rests on five points:

1. The shareholder transfers all of his stock;
2. There is a substantially disproportionate redemption of stock;
3. The redemption takes place as part of a partial liquidation of the S Corporation; or
4. The transfer is viewed as a redemption that is not equivalent to a dividend;
5. The shareholder's stock in the S Corporation exceeds 35 percent of his estate and the shares are sold back to the corporation in order to provide the estate with money to pay death taxes.

(i) Sale of All Shares: If a shareholder sells all of his shares back to the corporation, there has been a meaningful change at both the shareholder and corporate levels. Such a transfer will constitute a sale or exchange only if the selling shareholder completely severs his relationship with the S Corporation. In order to satisfy this requirement, the selling shareholder may not continue on as an officer, employee, or director of the S Corporation. The selling shareholder may, however, serve the corporation as an independent contractor.

It is cautioned, however, that the Internal Revenue Service carefully scrutinizes independent contractor arrangement and it is wise to have counsel prepare appropriate independent contractor agreements to document the nature of the relationship.

The selling shareholder will not be considered as having completely terminated his interest if the shareholder's spouse, children, grandchildren or parents will continue to own stock in the corporation. In that case, the sale to the corporation will be viewed as a distribution. The same result is obtained if the selling shareholder retains an option to purchase shares in the S Corporation.

(ii) Transfer Is Not a Dividend: This test is satisfied if the shareholder can show that as a result of the transfer there has been a meaningful reduction in the shareholder's pro rata interest in the S Corporation. This test, therefore, only applies to situations where the corporation has more than one shareholder and the comparative ownership of the shareholders can be evaluated.

In determining whether there has been a meaningful reduction in the shareholder's proportionate interest, the IRS looks at voting power. For example, if a shareholder who owns 95 percent of the corporation stock sells 44 percent back to the corporation, the IRS will probably view the transfer as a distribution rather than a sale because the transferring shareholder will end up with 51 percent of the stock and will retain voting control.

If, instead, that shareholder had sold sufficient outstanding stock so that he retained exactly half the voting stock, the transfer would be considered as a sale or exchange since the selling shareholder would no longer have voting control.

The IRS claims most other partial share redemptions, even those involving a minority shareholder, may qualify as sales or exchanges. Of course, if there is a pro rata transfer by all shareholders, there will not be a meaningful change, and the transfers will be treated as distributions.

(iii) Disproportionate Reductions: A transfer of shares back to the S Corporation will be treated as a sale or exchange if the selling shareholder can show:

1. The selling shareholder will then own less than 50 percent of the total voting power of the corporation after the transfer.

2. After the transfer the selling shareholder will not own more than 79 percent of the percentage of voting stock the shareholder had before the transfer.

3. If the S Corporation has non-voting common stock, the selling shareholder may not be left with more than 79 percent of the total

amount of stock he held before the transfer. In this test, the percentages are based on the fair market value of the shares.

TAX TREATMENT

Based on the factors described above, the primary difference between a distribution and a sale or exchange occurs when a shareholder transfers fewer than all of his shares to the corporation. In such a case the shareholder will receive an immediate benefit (tax-free money) if the transfer is viewed as a distribution; the cost, however, will be a reduced basis in stock. This means the shareholder's use of operating losses of the S Corporation in subsequent years will be limited. Should the shareholder be viewed as having sold or exchanged his shares, he may have a capital gain or loss on the shares he transfers; the shareholder's basis in his remaining shares will be unchanged and he will be in a position to use subsequent losses, if they occur, to the extent of that basis.

If a transfer is considered a sale or exchange the following tax implications will occur.

1. If the selling shareholder transfers all of his shares back to the corporation, he will lose the benefit of all unused carryover losses, (i.e. losses the shareholder was unable to use in previous years because he had an insufficient basis in his stock). Should there be unused losses, the selling shareholder might instead sell fewer than all his shares and hold the remainder until such time that his basis can permit him to make use of the losses.

2. If the shareholder receives more for his stock than his basis in the shares, he will have capital gain. If he receives less than his basis, he will have a capital loss. If the shareholder sells fewer than all of his shares and remains with an ownership interest of more than 50 percent of the corporation value, the capital loss will not be allowed by the IRS.

3. If the S Corporation holds property on which it took an investment tax credit, the selling shareholder may be liable for the recapture of the credit.

If the shareholder is viewed as receiving a distribution when he redeems his shares to the corporation: 1) The amount received from the corporation is tax-free to the extent of the shareholder's basis in his shares. 2) If the distribution exceeds the shareholder's basis in his shares, the excess is treated as a capital gain—the shareholder may not apply the excess against any basis he may have in corporate debt.

SALE TO THIRD PARTIES

Instead of redeeming shares back to the corporation, the selling shareholder may sell to a third-party—either another shareholder or a person with the corporation.

Of course, the new stockholder must be one qualified to be an S Corporation stockholder otherwise the S status election will be subject to revocation.

If there is a sale to a third-party, the tax consequences to the selling shareholder are precisely the same as a sale or exchange to the corporation. The shareholder who purchases the shares will be obligated to pro rate with the selling stockholder his pro rata share of income and loss that flows through to him.

CLOSING THE BOOKS

Whenever there is a sale and exchange (whether to the corporation or a third-party) the selling stockholder and buyer have the option to:

1. Keep the corporate books (financial) open, thereby adjusting the pro rata share of profits and losses.
2. Close the books as of the transfer date. This will essentially create two short tax years and the selling shareholder will report only his share of flow-through profits or losses for that portion of the year during which he owned his shares.

Since there is no way to predict what will happen after a shareholder leaves the corporation, it is impossible to determine which approach will work best in a given situation. If, however, the S Corporation is running in the red when the shareholder sells his back to the business, a prudent approach might be to close the books as of the date of the sale. That way the shareholder gets the benefit of those losses. This approach makes even more sense if the corporation business is seasonal and its high season will follow the sale.

When the selling shareholder and buyer agree to close the books the parties should complete the forms that follow.

INSTRUCTIONS TO CLOSE CORPORATE BOOKS WHEN A SHAREHOLDER SELLS ALL HIS SHARES

The form that appears on the next page must be used if a shareholder sells all of his shares in the S Corporation, and the selling and buyer shareholders agree to create two short tax years.

When completed, the form must be attached to the corporation income tax form (Form 1120S). Every shareholder who owned the S Corporation stock at any time during the course of the tax year, even if only for one day, must consent to the closing of the corporation books upon the transfer of all of the shareholder's shares.

This form may be used when the shareholder sells his or her shares to either the S Corporation or to an individual.

ELECTION TO CLOSE CORPORATE BOOKS—SAMPLE

Date: July 18, 1988

XYZ Corporation
Corporate Name

100 Main Street
Address

Anytown, USA 00000

Employer Identification Number: 81-4039261

    This Election is hereby made as an Attachment to Form 1120S for the above captioned Corporation's Tax Year which ends   December 31 , 19 88 .

    The above Corporation hereby elects to have the provisions of Internal Revenue Code Section 1377(a)(1) enforced as if the Corporation's taxable year consisted of two taxable years, the first of which shall end July 1   , 1988   .

    The reason for this election is that   Robert Brown , a shareholder of the Corporation sold all of his shares in the Corporation, and terminated his interest in the Corporation, on July 1   , 1988   .

    Pursuant to this election, the Corporation's tax year, which runs a calendar year from January 1 through December 31, will consist of the following two parts:
(1) January 1 , 19 88   , through June 30   , 19 88 , and
(2) July 1   , 1988   , through December 30 , 1988   .

XYZ Corporation

By: *Adam Smith*

Adam Smith, President

SHAREHOLDERS' CONSENT

    The undersigned who include every person or party who was a shareholder of the above Corporation at any time during calendar year 1988   all consent to the above election.

Shareholder Name	Shareholder Signature
Robert Brown	*Robert Brown*
Mary Brown	*Mary Brown*
Adam Smith	*Adam Smith*

ELECTION TO CLOSE CORPORATE BOOKS—FORM

Date:

_____

Corporate Name

_____

Address

_____

Employer Identification Number:

This Election is hereby made as an Attachment to Form 1120S for the above captioned Corporation's Tax Year which ends _____, 19__.

The above Corporation hereby elects to have the provisions of Internal Revenue Code Section 1377(a)(1) enforced as if the Corporation's taxable year consisted of two taxable years, the first of which shall end _____, 19__.

The reason for this election is that _____, a shareholder of the Corporation sold all of his shares in the Corporation, and terminated his interest in the Corporation, on _____, 19__.

Pursuant to this election, the Corporation's tax year, which runs a calendar year from January 1 through December 31, will consist of the following two parts:
(1) _____, 19__, through _____, 19__, and
(2) _____, 19__, through _____, 19__.

By:_____

SHAREHOLDERS' CONSENT

The undersigned who include every person or party who was a shareholder of the above Corporation at any time during calendar year 19__ all consent to the above election.

Shareholder Name   Shareholder Signature

_____   _____

_____   _____

_____   _____

TERMINATING THE S CORPORATION ELECTION

12

OVERVIEW

Once having made the decision to elect S Corporation status, the shareholders retain the right to switch back to C Corporation status, just as a C Corporation may elect to become an S Corporation. However, when the decision is made to switch from S Corporation status to C Corporation status, it is termed a revocation of S status.

It is also possible to lose the benefits of S Corporation status if the corporation fails to comply with Internal Revenue Code requirements necessary to maintain S Corporation status. When the Internal Revenue Service ends the S Corporation status for non-compliance the involuntary ending is referred to as a termination of election.

REVOCATION OF S STATUS

Revocation of S status automatically occurs when shareholders who own more than 50 percent of all outstanding shares of corporate stock notify the Internal Revenue Service of their election to discontinue as an S Corporation. For purposes of determining a majority, both voting and non-voting shares are included as one class.

Example:
Ralph owns 100 shares of stock in S Corporation. Henry and Mary each own 40 shares. Ralph controls the decision to revoke the S

status election since he owns more than one-half the outstanding shares (100 out of 180 shares). Of course, a shareholder's agreement may provide that the vote of a higher percentage of shares is necessary to revoke S Corporation status.

A sample and blank "Revocation Notice" is included at the end of this chapter. It should be addressed to the nearest regional office of the Internal Revenue Service and, of course, must be signed by the shareholders electing to revoke S Chapter. The notice must also be signed on behalf of the Corporation by an authorized corporate officer (President or Treasurer) notwithstanding that such officer may also be a shareholder who personally does not elect revocation.

EFFECTIVE DATE OF REVOCATION

When shareholders decide to revoke the S status election, there are three possible dates upon which the revocation will become effective, and the corporation will thereinafter be taxed as a regular C Corporation.

The three possibilities include:

1. *On the date the consent form is filed, or some later date.*

Example:
You file the revocation notice form on April 10, 1987, and ask that S Corporation status end on June 30, 1987. One tax return is filed for the enterprise as an S Corporation (January 1–June 30). Another tax return is filed for it as a regular corporation (July 1–December 31).

2. *The first day of the corporation's taxable year.* The filing deadline is the 15th of the 3rd month of the corporation's taxable year; (March 15 for calendar year corporations).

Example:
Your corporation operates on a December 31 calendar year for tax purposes. In early 1987, you decide to give up S corporation tax status. If you want your business to be taxed as a regular corporation for all of 1987, file the revocation notice on or before March 15, 1987. The corporation will then be taxed as a regular C Corporation beginning January 1, 1988.

3. *On the first day of the next year.*

Example:
You file the revocation notice form on April 10, 1987, and ask that S Corporation status end on December 31, 1987. The 1988 tax return is filed for a regular C Corporation.

INVOLUNTARY TERMINATIONS

In order to remain an S Corporation, the corporation must continue in all respects to qualify as a small business corporation, with the same requirements as when it first obtained S Corporation status.

Should the S Corporation fail to satisfy one or more requirements needed to qualify it as a small business corporation, its S status ends as of the day the disqualifying event occurs.

Therefore it's worthwhile to review the qualifications for S election if you are to avoid an involuntary termination by the Internal Revenue Service.

1. *Do not permit more than 35 shareholders in your S Corporation.* Once a corporation has the maximum number of shareholders (35), you should keep track of what your other shareholders do with their stock. For example, should a married couple divorce and each take half the shares they jointly held, they will count as two shareholders, not one. Similarly, if a parent gives shares to his or her children, each child adds to the total of shareholders. Therefore, each shareholder must understand these restrictions to avoid the corporation inadvertently ending up with more than 35 shareholders.

2. *Do not issue shares to ineligible shareholders.* S Corporation status is terminated when organizations have ineligible shareholders. Therefore, do not issue shares to:

- A corporation
- Any person who is a non-resident alien of the United States
- A trust (certain trusts are eligible to be shareholders in an S Corporation, but you should check with your tax advisor before issuing shares to a trust)
- A partnership

Similarly, a shareholder cannot transfer his shares to any of the above ineligible parties.

The best way to avoid these problems is to enter into a buy-sell agreement that requires a shareholder to offer his or her shares to the corporation before transferring them to any other buyer. If such an agreement is used, you should take care to place a legend on each share certificate indicating the shares are subject to a restriction on their transferability; a similar statement should be placed in the corporation articles of incorporation and in its by-laws. An appropriate legend is found on the sample stock certificate found in the back section of this book.

A buy-sell agreement of the type described above will insure that no shareholder transfers shares to an ineligible purchaser such as a corporation or a partnership. A sample buy-sell agreement ("Shareholders' Agreement") is included at the end of this chapter. Shareholders should also be reminded to review their S Corporation ownership with their estate planner to avoid transfers to nonqualifying trusts.

3. *Avoid disqualifying loans.* If a corporation's shareholders lend too much money to the corporation (rather than putting their investment in at risk in exchange for common stock), the IRS may treat the loan as an investment in stock—and hold that stock to be of a different class than the one originally issued. The result is that the corporation will be viewed as having more than one class of stock and will be ineligible for S Corporation treatment. The rules for permissible lending limits are the same for S Corporations as they are for regular C Corporations. Further, loans must carry legitimate loan terms—a fair interest rate, an unconditional promise to repay, a definite repayment date, and is not subordinated to other debts. If your loan carries normal lending terms, the likelihood is that it will not be treated as a second class of stock. If you intend lending money to your corporation in amounts greater than your investment in its stock, you should consider clearing the amount and terms of the loan with your tax advisor before completing the arrangement.

Of course, issuance of a second class of stock is a disqualifying event. An S Corporation is permitted to have only one class of stock. The exception to this rule allows an S Corporation to create a second class of common stock that differs from the first class only with respect to voting rights.

4. *Comply with tax year requirements.* Although not a violation of the requirements concerning a small business corporation, an S Corporation may lose its status if it does not use a proper tax year. In most instances, S Corporations are required to use a calendar year since they are obliged to use the year as their owner's tax year.

5. *Avoid intracorporate relationships.* Another way to lose S Corporation status is to permit the S Corporation to enter into a parent-subsidiary with another corporation. And you should not allow it to enter into an affiliation with another corporation (i.e. owning 80 percent of the stock of another corporation). And remember: S Corporation status is available only to domestic (U.S.) corporations.

6. *Watch passive income limits.* If you are switching from a regular corporation to an S Corporation and the regular corporation was profitable, not more than 25 percent of its gross receipts can be "passive income". Although that term has been redefined under the Tax Reform Act of 1986, for our purposes it includes all non-operating income, e.g. interest, dividends, or rent. If your passive income begins to approach 25 percent of total corporate revenues, then confer with your accountant for ways to redistribute passive

earnings so the corporation can continue to qualify. The test for excessive passive income applies to an S Corporation that has (i) accumulated earnings and profits from its C Corporation operations and those earnings and profits remain in the S Corporation for three consecutive S Corporation tax years and (ii) passive income for three consecutive tax years, and the passive income exceeds 25 percent of the S Corporation gross receipts for each of those years.

7. *Avoid disqualifying business activities.* For example, an S Corporation cannot become a banking or financial institution or become an insurance company. If there is a question whether a new business activity would disqualify the S status, the corporation should obtain a ruling from the Internal Revenue Service.

WHEN YOU LOSE YOUR S STATUS

When a terminating or disqualifying event occurs, the corporation has the responsibility to report it to the IRS. The statement must include the date the disqualifying event occurred and the nature of the event (i.e. sold shares to an ineligible purchaser, exceeded passive income limits, etc.).

However, if you can show the IRS that you inadvertently violated one of the above rules, the Service may allow you to correct the problem, and keep your business an S Corporation.

> *Example:*
> *One of your 35 stockholders (a married couple) divorces and divides their stock, so there are now 36 stockholders. But other stockholders quickly move to purchase the stock held by the ex-husband or ex-wife.*

> *Result:*
> *The number of stockholders returns to 35. Since no tax is avoided, the IRS will most likely allow S Corporation status to continue.*

It is important to show your willingness to spot and correct any violation of S Corporation rules.

EFFECT OF TERMINATION

If a corporation's election to be taxed as an S Corporation is revoked or terminated, it then becomes a C Corporation. As a general rule, it cannot elect to return to S status until the fifth year after the year in which the revocation or termination occurred. For example, if an S Corporation revoked its S election on April 15, 1983, and it was a calendar year corporation, it cannot become an S Corporation again until January 1, 1988.

Although the IRS can waive the five-year rule, it seldom does so where there was a revocation or an intentional termination unless there has been a change of ownership amongst a majority of the corporation's shareholders.

THE FORMS IN THIS SECTION

1. The *Revocation Notice* is used to terminate the S Corporation election. It must be signed by the shareholders who own fifty percent or more of the outstanding shares, and mailed to the IRS.

2. The *Shareholders' Agreement* should be signed by all shareholders when they first elect to adopt S Corporation status. This agreement essentially prevents a shareholder from transferring his shares to a stockholder who would disqualify the S Corporation status. The shares of stock should carry a legend making reference to the restriction on transfer.

REVOCATION NOTICE—SAMPLE

Date: December 31, 1988

Director
Internal Revenue Service Center
10 Oak Street
Anytown, USA 00000

Re: <u>XYZ Corporation</u>
          Corporation
   <u>100 Main St., Anywhere,</u> USA 00000
          Address
   <u>81-4039261</u>
          EID Number

SAMPLE

Dear Sir:

Please be advised that the above XYZ Corporation , (Corporation) hereby revokes its election to be taxed as an S Corporation under the provisions of Section 1362 of the Internal Revenue Code. The Corporation has a total of 100 shares of stock issued and outstanding as of this date. This revocation shall be effective as of December 31 , 1988 . The consent by a requisite number of stockholders is contained below.

Sincerely,
XYZ Corporation

By: *Adam Smith*
Authorized Officer

SHAREHOLDERS' CONSENT

The undersigned, record owners of more than fifty percent of the outstanding stock of XYZ Corporation (Corporation) as of the date of this notice, have consented to the revocation of the Corporation's election to be treated as an S Corporation under Section 1362 of the Internal Revenue Code.

Name	Signature	Number of Shares Owned
Robert Brown	*Robert Brown*	50
Adam Smith	*Adam Smith*	50

REVOCATION NOTICE—FORM

Date:

Director
Internal Revenue Service Center

Re:_____
                           Corporation

_____
                             Address

_____
                           EID Number

Dear Sir:

Please be advised that the above
_____, (Corporation) hereby revokes
its election to be taxed as an S Corporation under the
provisions of Section 1362 of the Internal Revenue Code.
The Corporation has a total of   shares of stock
issued and outstanding as of this date. This revocation
shall be effective as of   , 19   . The
consent by a requisite number of stockholders is contained below.

Sincerely,

By:_____
                      Authorized Officer

SHAREHOLDERS' CONSENT

The undersigned, record owners of more than fifty
percent of the outstanding stock of
(Corporation) as of the date of this notice, have
consented to the revocation of the Corporation's
election to be treated as an S Corporation under Section
1362 of the Internal Revenue Code.

Name   Signature   Number of Shares Owned

_____   _____   _____

_____   _____   _____

_____   _____   _____

SHAREHOLDERS' AGREEMENT—SAMPLE

This agreement is made on the 15th day of
July   , 19 87 , by and between
XYZ Corporation   , a   New York   corporation,
and   Robert Brown and Mary Brown   , who are all
shareholders (Shareholders) of   XYZ Corporation.   .

Whereas, the Corporation has elected to be taxed as
an S Corporation as permitted by the Internal Revenue
Code of the United States, and that each Shareholder has
consented to that election; and

Whereas, the Shareholders believe it is in their
mutual interests for the Corporation to continue as an S
Corporation as long as the holders of   percent of
the outstanding shares of stock agree the Corporation
shall be an S Corporation, it is hereby mutually agreed
that:

1.   Unless the approval of all of the Shareholders
is first obtained, no Shareholder shall gift, hypo-
thecate, encumber, sell, donate, or in any way transfer
shares of stock in the Corporation without first obtaining (a) the written opinion of the legal counsel to the
corporation that the transfer will not cause the corporation to lose its status as an S Corporation and (b) the
transferee's written consent that he or she will be
bound by all the terms of this Agreement. Any actual or
attempted transfer of shares of stock in violation of
paragraph 1 above will be null, void and without legal
effect.

2.   No Shareholder shall refuse to provide any
consent or execute other document that may now or hereinafter be required by the Internal Revenue Code, any
regulations promulgated under the Internal Revenue Code
or the Internal Revenue Service that may be as a condition for maintaining the Corporation election to be
taxed as an S Corporation.

3.   In the event any Shareholder violates or
refuses to perform in accord-ance with the provisions of
paragraphs 1 and/or 2 above, the other Shareholders
shall, in addition to monetary damages, enforce this
Agreement by requesting any form of legal or equitable
relief or remedy that requires specific performance from
the Shareholder in accordance with this Agreement.

4. In the event that the Corporation loses its S Corporation status and such loss is attributable in whole or in any part to the failure of one or more Shareholders to act in accordance with the provisions of paragraphs 1 and/or 2 above, then each Shareholder who failed to comply with the provisions of paragraphs 1 and/or 2 above shall be jointly and severally liable for all losses incurred by the Corporation and the other Shareholders as a result or consequence of said violation.

5. Each Shareholder, upon the signing of this Agreement, shall return to the Secretary of the Corporation, all stock certificates he or she may now own and shall receive in substitution therefor a share certificate for the same number of shares. The new certificate shall contain a printed legend stating that the shares represented by the certificate are subject to the restrictions on transfer set out in this Agreement.

6. In the event that the Internal Revenue Code provisions governing S Corporation status are amended or changed in any way, this Agreement will be modified by such modification or modifications are necessary in order for the Shareholders to continue to receive the benefit of S incorporation status.

7. This Agreement shall terminate upon the occurrence of any one of the following events:

    a. The written agreement of the holders of 51 percent of the outstanding shares of the Corporation or

    b. The repeal of the Internal Revenue Code provisions allowing for the election of S Corporation status and the failure of the Internal Revenue Code, or any future law replacing the Internal Revenue Code, to provide a substitute for the single taxation approach to corporate profits and dividends currently provided by the existing S Corporation provisions of the Internal Revenue Code.

8. This Agreement will be binding upon and exists for the benefit of the parties to this Agreement, and, subject to the restrictions set out in this Agreement, upon their heirs, assigns, personal representatives and successors.

9. This Agreement is governed by the laws of New York   .

IN WITNESS WHEREOF, the parties have executed this Agreement on the date first above written.

XYZ Corporation

By: *Robert Brown, Pres.*

ATTEST:

SAMPLE

By: *Henry Jones*

WITNESS: SHAREHOLDERS:

Henry Jones   *Robert Brown*
Henry Jones   Robert Brown
                                   Mary Brown
                                   Mary Brown

SHAREHOLDERS' AGREEMENT—FORM

This agreement is made on the   day of
          , 19   , by and between
                              , a   corporation,
and   , who are all
shareholders (Shareholders) of   .

Whereas, the Corporation has elected to be taxed as
an S Corporation as permitted by the Internal Revenue
Code of the United States, and that each Shareholder has
consented to that election; and

Whereas, the Shareholders believe it is in their
mutual interests for the Corporation to continue as an S
Corporation as long as the holders of   percent of
the outstanding shares of stock agree the Corporation
shall be an S Corporation, it is hereby mutually agreed
that:

1. Unless the approval of all of the Shareholders
is first obtained, no Shareholder shall gift, hypo-
thecate, encumber, sell, donate, or in any way transfer
shares of stock in the Corporation without first obtaining (a) the written opinion of the legal counsel to the
corporation that the transfer will not cause the corporation to lose its status as an S Corporation and (b) the
transferee's written consent that he or she will be
bound by all the terms of this Agreement. Any actual or
attempted transfer of shares of stock in violation of
paragraph 1 above will be null, void and without legal
effect.

2. No Shareholder shall refuse to provide any
consent or execute other document that may now or hereinafter be required by the Internal Revenue Code, any
regulations promulgated under the Internal Revenue Code
or the Internal Revenue Service that may be as a condition for maintaining the Corporation election to be
taxed as an S Corporation.

3. In the event any Shareholder violates or
refuses to perform in accord-ance with the provisions of
paragraphs 1 and/or 2 above, the other Shareholders
shall, in addition to monetary damages, enforce this
Agreement by requesting any form of legal or equitable
relief or remedy that requires specific performance from
the Shareholder in accordance with this Agreement.

4. In the event that the Corporation loses its S
Corporation status and such loss is attributable in
whole or in any part to the failure of one or more
Shareholders to act in accordance with the provisions of
paragraphs 1 and/or 2 above, then each Shareholder who
failed to comply with the provisions of paragraphs 1
and/or 2 above shall be jointly and severally liable for
all losses incurred by the Corporation and the other
Shareholders as a result or consequence of said
violation.

5. Each Shareholder, upon the signing of this
Agreement, shall return to the Secretary of the Corporation, all stock certificates he or she may now own and
shall receive in substitution therefor a share
certificate for the same number of shares. The new
certificate shall contain a printed legend stating that
the shares represented by the certificate are subject to
the restrictions on transfer set out in this Agreement.

6. In the event that the Internal Revenue Code
provisions governing S Corporation status are amended or
changed in any way, this Agreement will be modified by
such modification or modifications are necessary in
order for the Shareholders to continue to receive the
benefit of S incorporation status.

7. This Agreement shall terminate upon the
occurrence of any one of the following events:

> a. The written agreement of the holders of
> percent of the outstanding shares of the
Corporation or

> b. The repeal of the Internal Revenue Code
provisions allowing for the election of S Corporation status and the failure of the Internal
Revenue Code, or any future law replacing the
Internal Revenue Code, to provide a substitute for
the single taxation approach to corporate profits
and dividends currently provided by the existing S
Corporation provisions of the Internal Revenue Code.

8. This Agreement will be binding upon and exists
for the benefit of the parties to this Agreement, and,
subject to the restrictions set out in this Agreement,
upon their heirs, assigns, personal representatives and
successors.

9. This Agreement is governed by the laws of

IN WITNESS WHEREOF, the parties have executed this Agreement on the date first above written.

By:_____

ATTEST:

By:_____

WITNESS: SHAREHOLDERS:

_____   _____

_____   _____

_____   _____

_____   _____

_____   _____

_____   _____

APPENDIX

THE FORMS IN THIS SECTION

This section contains numerous forms designed to simplify the procedures for maintaining proper corporate records:

1. Notice of Organization Meeting
2. Waiver of Notice of Organization Meeting
3. Minutes of Organization Meeting of Directors
4. Waiver of Notice—Shareholders Meeting
5. Minutes, First Shareholders Meeting
6. Minutes, Special Shareholders Meeting
7. Stockholder Resolution for S Corporation
8. By-Laws
9. Stock Transfer Ledgers
10. Stock Certificates with Restrictions

NOTICE OF ORGANIZATION MEETING
OF INCORPORATORS AND DIRECTORS

TO: _____

_____

_____

PLEASE BE ADVISED THAT:

We, the undersigned, do hereby constitute a
majority of the directors named in the Articles of
Incorporation of_____,
a   corporation;

Pursuant to state law, we are hereby calling an
organization meeting of the Board of Directors and
incorporators named in the Articles of Incorporation of
the above named corporation; for the purpose of adopting
by-laws, electing officers, and transacting such other
business as may come before the meeting; and

Said organization meeting shall be held at _____

_____

on   , 19   , at   o'clock   .m.

_____   _____

_____   _____

RECEIPT OF NOTICE

_____   _____
Addressee-Director   Date Received

WAIVER OF NOTICE OF ORGANIZATION
MEETING OF INCORPORATORS AND DIRECTORS
OF_____

      We do hereby constitute the incorporators and
directors of the above named corporation and do hereby
waive notice of the organization meeting of directors
and incorporators of the aforesaid corporation.

      Furthermore, we hereby agree that said meeting
shall be held at   o'clock   .m. on
        , 19   at the following place:

_____.

      We do hereby affix our names to show our waiver of
notice of said meeting.

_____   _____

_____   _____

Dated:

MINUTES OF ORGANIZATION MEETING
OF BOARD OF DIRECTORS OF

_____

The organizational meeting of the Board of
Directors of   , was held
at   on
                  , 19   , at   :00   .m.
Present was   ,
              ,   , being
the persons designated as the Directors in the Articles
of Incorporation.

acted as temporary Chairman of
the meeting and   acted as
temporary Secretary.

The Chairman announced that the meeting had been
duly called by the Incorporators of the Corporation.

The Chairman reported that the Articles of Incor-
poration of the Corporation had been duly filed with the
State of   on   , 19   .
The Certificate of Incorporation and a copy of said
Articles of Incorporation were ordered to be inserted in
the Minutes as a part of the records of the meeting.

A proposed form of By-laws for the regulation and
the management of the affairs of the Corporation was
then presented at the meeting. The By-laws were read
and considered and, upon motion duly made and seconded,
it was:

RESOLVED, that the form of By-laws of the Corporation, as presented to this meeting, a copy of which is directed to be inserted in the Minute Book of the Corporation be, and the same are hereby approved and adopted as the By-laws of the Corporation.

The following persons were nominated officers of the Corporation to serve until their respective successors are chosen and qualify:

PRESIDENT:

VICE PRESIDENT:

SECRETARY:

TREASURER:

The Chairman announced that the aforenamed persons had been elected to the office set opposite their respective names.

The President thereupon took the chair and the Secretary immediately assumed the discharge of the duties of that office.

The President then stated that there were a number of organizational matters to be considered at the meeting and a number of resolutions to be adopted by the Board of Directors.

The form of stock certificates was then exhibited at the meeting. Thereupon, a motion duly made and seconded, it was:

RESOLVED, that the form of stock certificates presented at this meeting be, and the same is hereby adopted and approved as the stock certificate of the Corporation, a specimen copy of the stock certificate to be inserted with these Mintues.

FURTHER RESOLVED, that the officers are hereby authorized to pay or reimburse the payment of all fees and expenses incident to and necessary for the organization of this Corporation.

The Board of Directors then considered the opening of a corporate bank account to serve as a depository for the funds of the Corporation. Following discussion, on motion duly made and seconded, it was:

RESOLVED, that the Treasurer be authorized, empowered and directed to open an account with

and to deposit all funds of the Corporation, all drafts, checks and notes of the Corporation, payable on said account to be made in the corporate name signed by

FURTHER RESOLVED, that officers are hereby authorized to execute such resolutions (including formal Bank Resolutions), documents and other instruments as may be necessary or advisable in opening or continuing said bank account. A copy of the applicable printed form of Bank Resolution hereby adopted to supplement these Minutes is ordered appended to the Minutes of this meeting.

It is announced that the following persons have offered to transfer the property listed below in exchange for the following shares of the stock of the Corporation:

Name	Payment Consideration, or Property	Number of Shares

Upon motion duly made and seconded, it was:

RESOLVED, that acceptance of the offer of the above-named person is in the best interest of the Corporation and necessary for carrying out the corporate business, and in the judgement of the Board of Directors, the assets proposed to be transferred to the Corporation are reasonably worth the amount of consideration deemed therefor, and the same hereby is accepted, and that upon receipt

of the consideration indicated above, the President
and the Secretary are authorized to issue certificates of fully-paid, nonassessable capital stock of
this Corporation in the amounts indicated to the
above-named persons.

In order to provide for the payment of expenses of
incorporation and organization fo the Corporation, on
motion duly made, seconded and unanimously carried, the
following resolution was adopted:

RESOLVED, that the President and the Secretary
and/or Treasurer of this Corporation be and they
are hereby authorized and directed to pay the
expenses of this Corporation, including attorney's
fees for incorporation, and to reimburse the persons who have made disbursements thereof.

After consideration of the pertinent issues with
regard to the tax year and accounting basis, on motion
duly made, and seconded and unanimously carried, the
following resolution was adopted:

RESOLVED, that the first fiscal year of the
Corporation shall commence on
and end on

FURTHER RESOLVED, that the President be and is hereby authorized and directed to enter into employment contracts with certain employees, such contract shall be for the term and the rate stated in the attached Employment Agreements.

FURTHER RESOLVED, that it shall be the policy of the Corporation to reimburse each employee or to pay directly on his behalf all expenses incidental to his attendance at conventions and seminars as may be approved by the President. Reimbursement shall include full reimbursement for commercial and private transportation expenses, plus other necessary and ordinary out-of-pocket expenses incidental to the said travel, including meals and lodging.

A general discussion was then held concerning the immediate commencement of business operations as a Corporation and it was determined that business operations of the Corporation would commence as of

It was agreed that no fixed date would be set for holding meetings of the Board of Directors except the regular meetings to be held immediately after the annual meetings of shareholders as provided in the By-laws of the Corproation but that meetings of the Directors would be periodically called by the President and Secretary or others as provided by the By-laws.

Upon motion duly made, seconded and unanimously carried, it was:

RESOLVED, that the officers of the Corporation are hereby authorized to do any and all things necessary to conduct the business of the Corporation as set forth in the Articles of Incorporation and By-laws of the Corporation.

Upon motion duly made, seconded, and unanimously carried the following resolution was adopted:

RESOLVED, that, if required, that
be, and hereby is, appointed
Resident Agent in the State of   .
The office of the Resident Agent will be located
at   .

The Chairman then presented to the meeting the question of electing the provisions of Section 1244 of the Internal Revenue Code. He noted that this Section permits ordinary loss treatment when either the holder of Section 1244 stock sells or exchanges such stock at a loss or when such stock becomes worthless. After a discussion, the following preamble was stated and the following resolution was unanimously:

RESOLVED, THAT:

WHEREAS, this Corporation qualifies as a small business corporation as defined in Section 1244, but

WHEREAS, the Board of Directors are concerned over future tax law changes modifying Section 1244 as presently enacted (subsequent to the Revenue Act of 1978) and thus desire to safeguard this Corporation's 1244 election by complying with prior law as well as present law, and

WHEREAS, pursuant to the requirements of Section 1244 and the Regulations issued thereunder, the following plan has been submitted to the Corporation by the Board of Directors of the Corporation:

(a) The plan as hereafter set forth shall, upon its adoption by the Board of Directors of the Corporation immediately become effective.

(b) No more than   shares of common stock are authorized to be issued under this plan, such stock to have a par value of $ per share.

(c) Stock authorized under this plan shall be issued only in exchange for money, or property susceptible to monetary valuation other than capital stock, securities or services rendered or to be rendered. The aggregate dollar amount to be received for such stock shall not exceed $1,000,000, and the sum of each aggregate dollar amount and the equity capital of the Corporation (determined on the date of adoption of the plan) shall not exceed $1,000,000.

(d) Any stock options granted during the life of this plan which apply to the stock issuable hereunder shall apply solely to such stock and to no other and must be exercised within the period in which the plan is effective.

(e) Such other action as may be necessary shall be taken by the Corporation to qualify the stock to be offered and issued under this plan as "Section 1244 Stock", as such term is defined in the Internal Revenue Code and the regulations issued thereunder.

NOW, THEREFORE, the foregoing plan to issue Section 1244 Stock is adopted by the Corporation and the appropriate officers of the Corporation are authorized and directed to take all actions deemed by them necessary to carry out the intent and purpose of the recited plan.

There being no further business requiring Board action or consideration;

On motion duly made, seconded and carried, the meeting was adjourned.

Dated:

_____
Secretary of the Meeting

WAIVER OF NOTICE,
FIRST MEETING OF SHAREHOLDERS

     We the undersigned, being the shareholders of
the_____,
agree that the first meeting of shareholders be held on
the date and at the time and place stated below in order
to elect officers and transact such other business as
may lawfully come before the meeting. We hereby waive
all notice of such meeting and of any adjournment
thereof.

Place of Meeting_____

Date of Meeting_____

Time of Meeting_____

                        _____

                        _____

                        _____

                        _____

                        _____

Dated:_____ _____
                                                             Shareholders

MINUTES, FIRST MEETING
OF SHAREHOLDERS

The first meeting of the shareholders of _____
_____ was held at _____
_____ on the _____
day of _____, 19_____, at _____
o'clock _____.m.

The meeting was duly called to order by the President. He stated the purpose of the meeting.

Next, the Secretary read the list of shareholders as they appear in the record book of the Corporation. He reported the presence of a quorum of shareholders.

Next, the Secretary read a waiver of notice of the meeting, signed by all shareholders. On a motion duly made, seconded and carried, the waiver was ordered appended to the minutes of this meeting.

Next, the President asked the Secretary to read:

(1) the minutes of the organization meeting of the Corporation; and (2) the minutes of the first meeting of the Board of Directors.

A motion was duly made, seconded and carried unanimously that the following resolution be adopted:

WHEREAS, the minutes of the organization meeting of the Corporation and the minutes of the first meeting of the Board of Directors have been read to this meeting, and

WHEREAS, by-laws were adopted and directors and officers were elected at the organization meeting, it is hereby

RESOLVED that this meeting approves and ratifies the election of the said directors and officers of this Corporation for the term of _____ years, and approves, ratifies and adopts said by-laws as the by-laws of the corporation. It is further

RESOLVED that all acts taken and decisions made at the organization meeting and the first meeting of the Board are approved and ratified. It is further

RESOLVED that signing of these minutes constitutes full ratification by the signatories and waiver of notice of the meeting.

There being no further business, the meeting was adjourned, Dated the _____day of_____, 19_____.

_____
Secretary

_____

_____

_____

Directors

Appended hereto:

   Waiver of notice of meeting.

MINUTES OF SPECIAL MEETING OF STOCKHOLDERS

A special meeting of the stockholders of the
Corporation was held at
in the City of   , in the State of
                        , on   , 19   ,
at   .m.

The meeting was called to order by   ,
the President of the Corporation, and   ,
the Secretary of the Corporation , kept the records of
the meeting.

The Secretary reported that a quorum of stockholders were present in person or were represented by
proxy, the aggregate amount representing more than
of the outstanding stock entitled to vote on the resolutions proposed at the meeting.

The Secretary reported that the following
stockholders were present in person:

Names   Number of Shares

_____   _____

_____   _____

_____   _____

_____   _____

and that the following stockholders were represented by
proxy:

Names	Names of Proxies	Number of Shares
_____	_____	_____
_____	_____	_____
_____	_____	_____
_____	_____	_____

The Secretary presented and read a waiver of notice of the meeting signed by each stockholder entitled to notice of the meeting, which waiver of notice was ordered to be filed with the minutes of the meeting.

On motion duly made and seconded, and after due deliberation, the following resolution(s) was/were unanimously voted upon:

That the Corporation elect to be subject to and taxed pursuant to Section 1362 of the Internal Revenue Code.

The Secretary reported that all shares of common stock had been voted in favor of the foregoing resolution(s) and no shares of common stock had been voted against the resolutions, said vote therefore representing 100 percent of the outstanding shares entitled to vote thereon.

The President thereupon declared that the resolution(s) had been duly adopted.

There being no further business, upon motion, the meeting adjourned.

A True Record

Attest

_____
Secretary

RESOLUTION OF STOCKHOLDERS OF

_____

BE IT KNOWN, that at a special meeting of the Stockholders of the Corporation wherein all the Stockholders were present, in person or by proxy, and voting throughout, it was upon motion duly made and seconded that it be <u>unanimously</u>

<u>Voted</u>: That the Corporation elect to be subject to the provisions of Section 1362 of the Internal Revenue Code and be deemed and taxed as an S Corporation.

<u>Voted</u>: That the President of the Corporation execute and file all documents and undertake such further acts which in his discretion is deemed necessary or advisable to carry out the tenor and performance of the foregoing vote.

IN WITNESS WHEREOF, I have affixed my name as Secretary and have caused the corporate seal of said Corporation to be hereunto affixed, this   day of   , 19   .

A True Record
Attest

_____
Secretary

BY-LAWS
OF

_____

ARTICLE I
OFFICES

   Thr principal office of the Corporation in the
State of   shall be located in
                    , County of   .
The Corporation may have such other offices, either
within or without the State of   , as
the Board of Directors may designate or as the business
of the Corporation may require from time to time.

ARTICLE II
SHAREHOLDERS

   SECTION 1. <u>Annual Meeting</u>. The annual meeting of
the shareholders shall be held on the   day in the
month of   in each year, beginning with
the year 19   , at the hour of   o'clock   .m.,
for the purpose of electing Directors and for the
transaction of such other business as may come before
the meeting. If the day fixed for the annual meeting
shall be a legal holiday in the State of   ,
such meeting shall be held on the next succeeding
business day. If the election of Directors shall not be
held on the day designated herein for any annual meeting
of the shareholders, or at any adjournment thereof, the
Board of Directors shall cause the election to be held
at a special meeting of the shareholders as soon
thereafter as conveniently may be.

   SECTION 2. <u>Special Meetings</u>. Special meetings of
the shareholders, for any purpose or purposes, unless
otherwise prescribed by statute, may be called by the
President or by the Board of Directors, and shall be
called by the President at the request of the holders of
not less than   percent (%) of all the
outstanding shares of the Corporation entitled to vote
at the meeting.

   SECTION 3. <u>Place of Meeting</u>. The Board of Directors
may designate any place, either within or without the
State of   , unless otherwise prescribed
by statute, as the place of meeting for any annual
meeting or for any special meeting. A waiver of notice
signed by all shareholders entitled to vote at a meeting
may designate any place, either within or without the
State of   , unless otherwise prescribed

by statute, as the place for the holding of such meeting. If no designation is made, the place of meeting shall be the principal office of the Corporation.

SECTION 4. _Notice of Meeting_. Written notice stating the place, day and hour of the meeting and, in case of a special meeting, the purpose or purposes for which the meeting is called, shall unless otherwise prescribed by statute, be delivered not less than (   ) nor more than (   ) days before the date of the meeting, to each shareholder of record entitled to vote at such meeting. If mailed, such notice shall be deemed to be delivered when deposited in the United States Mail, addressed to the shareholder at his address as it appears on the stock transfer books of the Corporation, with postage thereon prepaid.

SECTION 5. _Closing of Transfer Books or Fixing of Record_. For the purpose of determining shareholders entitled to notice of or to vote at any meeting of shareholders or any adjournment thereof, or shareholders entitled to receive payment of any dividend, or in order to make a determination of shareholders for any other proper purpose, the Board of Directors of the Corporation may provide that the stock transfer books shall be closed for a stated period, but not to exceed in any case fifty (50) days. If the stock transfer books shall be closed for the purpose of determining shareholders entitled to notice of or to vote at a meeting of shareholders, such books shall be closed for at least (   ) days immediately preceding such meeting. In lieu of closing the stock transfer books, the Board of Directors may fix in advance a date as the record date for any such determination of shareholders, such date in any case to be not more than (   ) days and, in case of a meeting of shareholders, not less than (   ) days, prior to the date on which the particular action requiring such determination of shareholders is to be taken. If the stock transfer books are not closed and no record date is fixed for the determination of shareholders entitled to notice of or to vote at a meeting of shareholders, or shareholders entitled to receive payment of a dividend, the date on which notice of the meeting is mailed or the date on which the resolution of the Board of Directors declaring such dividend is adopted, as the case may be, shall be the record date for such determination of shareholders. When a determination of shareholders entitled to vote at any meeting of shareholders has been made as provided in this section, such determination shall apply to any adjournment thereof.

SECTION 6. Voting Lists. The officer or agent having charge of the stock transfer books for shares of the corporation shall make a complete list of the shareholders entitled to vote at each meeting of shareholders or any adjournment thereof, arranged in alphabetical order, with the address of and the number of shares held by each. Such list shall be produced and kept open at the time and place of the meeting and shall be subject to the inspection of any shareholder during the whole time of the meeting for the purposes thereof.

SECTION 7. Quorum. A majority of the outstanding shares of the Corporation entitled to vote, represented in person or by proxy, shall constitute a quorum at a meeting of shareholders. If less than a majority of the outstanding shares are represented at a meeting, a majority of the shares so represented may adjourn the meeting from time to time without further notice. At such adjourned meeting at which a quorum shall be present or represented, any business may be transacted which might have been transacted at the meeting as originally noticed. The shareholders present at a duly organized meeting may continue to transact business until adjournment, notwithstanding the withdrawal of enough shareholders to leave less than a quorum.

SECTION 8. Proxies. At all meetings of shareholders, a shareholder may vote in person or by proxy executed in writing by the shareholder or by his duly authorized attorney-in-fact. Such proxy shall be filed with the secretary of the Corporation before or at the time of the meeting. A meeting of the Board of Directors may be had by means of a telephone conference or similar communications equipment by which all persons participating in the meeting can hear each other, and participation in a meeting under such circumstances shall constitute presence at the meeting.

SECTION 9. Voting of Shares. Each outstanding share entitled to vote shall be entitled to one vote upon each matter submitted to a vote at a meeting of shareholders.

SECTION 10. Voting of Shares by Certain Holders. Shares standing in the name of another corporation may be voted by such officer, agent or proxy as the By-Laws of such corporation may prescribe or, in the absence of such provision, as the Board of Directors of such corporation may determine.

Shares held by an administrator, executor, guardian or conservator may be voted by him, either in person or by proxy, without a transfer of such shares into his name. Shares standing in the name of a trustee may be voted by him, either in person or by proxy, but no trustee shall be entitled to vote shares held by him without a transfer of such shares into his name.

Shares standing in the name of a receiver may be voted by such receiver, and shares held by or under the control of a receiver may be voted by such receiver without the transfer thereof into his name, if authority so to do be contained in an appropriate order of the court by which such receiver was appointed.

A shareholder whose shares are pledged shall be entitled to vote such shares until the shares have been transferred into the name of the pledgee, and thereafter the pledgee shall be entitled to vote the shares so transferred.

Shares of its own stock belonging to the Corporation shall not be voted, directly or indirectly, at any meeting, and shall not be counted in determining the total number of outstanding shares at any given time.

SECTION 11. Informal Action by Shareholders. Unless otherwise provided by law, any action required to be taken at a meeting of the shareholders, or any other action which may be taken at a meeting of the shareholders, may be taken without a meeting if a consent in writing, setting forth the action so taken, shall be signed by all of the shareholders entitled to vote with respect to the subject matter thereof.

ARTICLE III
BOARD OF DIRECTORS

SECTION 1. General Powers. The business and affairs of the Corporation shall be managed by its Board of Directors.

SECTION 2. Number, Tenure and Qualifications. The number of directors of the Corporation shall be fixed by the Board of Directors, but in no event shall be less than (   ). Each director shall hold office until the next annual meeting of shareholders and until his successor shall have been elected and qualified.

SECTION 3. Regular Meetings. A regular meeting of the Board of Directors shall ble held without other notice than this By-Law immediately after, and at the same place as, the annual meeting of shareholders. The Board of Directors may provide, by resolution, the time and place for the holding of additional regular meetings without notice other than such resolution.

SECTION 4. _Special Meetings_. Special meetings of the Board of Directors may be called by or at the request of the President or any two directors. The person or persons authorized to call special meetings of the Board of Directors may fix the place for holding any special meeting of the Board of Directors called by them.

SECTION 5. _Notice_. Notice of any special meeting shall be given at least one (1) day previous thereto by written notice delivered personally or mailed to each director at his business address, or by telegram. If mailed, such notice shall be deemed to be delivered when deposited in the United States Mail so addressed, with postage thereon prepaid. If notice be given by telegram, such notice shall be deemed to be delivered when the telegram is delivered to the telegraph company. Any directors may waive notice of any meeting. The attendance of a director at a meeting shall constitute a waiver of notice of such meeting, except where a director attends a meeting for the express purpose of objecting to the transaction of any business because the meeting is not lawfully called or convened.

SECTION 6. _Quorum_. A majority of the number of directors fixed by Section 2 of this Article III shall constitute a quorum for the transaction of business at any meeting of the Board of Directors, but if less than such majority is present at a meeting, a majority of the directors present may adjourn the meeting from time to time without further notice.

SECTION 7. _Manner of Acting_. The act of the majority of the directors present at a meeting at which a quorum is present shall ble the act of the Board of Directors.

SECTION 8. _Action Without a Meeting_. Any action that may be taken by the Board of Directors at a meeting may be taken without a meeting if a consent in writing, setting forth the action so to be taken, shall be signed before such action by all of the directors.

SECTION 9. _Vacancies_. Any vacancy occurring in the Board of Directors may be filled by the affirmative vote of a majority of the remaining directors though less than a quorum of the Board of Directors, unless otherwise provided by law. A director elected to fill a vacancy shall be elected for the unexpired term of his predecessor in office. Any directorship to be filled by reason of an increase in the number of directors may be filled by election by the Board of Directors for a term of office continuing only until the next election of directors by the shareholders.

SECTION 10. Compensation. By resolution of the
Board of Directors, each director may be paid his
expenses, if any, of attendance at each meeting of the
Board of Directors, and may be paid a stated salary as
director or a fixed sum for attendance at each meeting
of the Board of Directors or both. No such payment
shall preclude any director from serving the Corporation
in any other capacity and receiving compensation
therefor.

SECTION 11. Presumption of Assent. A director of
the Corporation who is present at a meeting of the Board
of Directors at which action on any corporate matter is
taken shall be presumed to have assented to the action
taken unless his dissent shall be entered in the minutes
of the meeting or unless he shall file his written
dissent to such action with the person acting as the
Secretary of the meeting before the adjournment thereof,
or shall forward such dissent by registered mail to the
Secretary of the Corporation immediately after the
adjournment of the meeting. Such right to dissent shall
not apply to a director who voted in favor of such
action.

ARTICLE IV
OFFICERS

SECTION 1. Number. The officers of the Corporation
shall be a President, one or more Vice Presidents, a
Secretary and a Treasurer, each of whom shall be elected
by the Board of Directors. Such other officers and
assistant officers as may be deemed necessary may be
elected or appointed by the Board of Directors, including a Chairman of the Board. In its discretion, the
Board of Directors may leave unfilled for any such
period as it may determine any office except those of
President and Secretary. Any two or more offices may be
held by the same person, except for the offices of
President and Secretary which may not be held by the
same person. Officers may be directors or shareholders
of the Corporation.

SECTION 2. Election and Term of Office. The
officers of the Corporation to be elected by the Board
of Directors shall be elected annually by the Board of
Directors at the first meeting of the Board of Directors
held after each annual meeting of the shareholders. If
the election of officers shall not be held at such
meeting, such election shall be held as soon thereafter
as conveniently may be. Each officer shall hold office
until his successor shall have been duly elected and
shall have qualified, or until his death, or until he

shall resign or shall have been removed in the manner hereinafter provided.

SECTION 3. Removal. Any officer or agent may be removed by the Board of Directors whenever, in its judgement, the best interests of the Corporation will be served thereby, but such removal shall be without prejudice to the contract rights, if any, of the person so removed. Election or appointment of an officer or agent shall not of itself create contract rights, and such appointment shall be terminable at will.

SECTION 4. Vacancies. A vacancy in any office because of death, resignation, removal, disqualification or otherwise, may be filled by the Board of Directors for the unexpired portion of the term.

SECTION 5. President. The President shall be the principal executive officer of the Corporation and, subject to the control of the Board of Directors, shall in general supervise and control all of the business and affairs of the Corporation. He shall, when present, preside at all meetings of the shareholders and of the Board of Directors, unless there is a Chairman of the Board, in which case the Chairman shall preside. He may sign, with the Secretary or any other proper officer of the Corporation thereunto authorized by the Board of Directors, certificates for shares of the Corporation, any deeds, mortgages, bonds, contracts, or other instruments which the Board of Directors has authorized to be executed, except in cases where the signing and execution thereof shall be expressly delegated by the Board of Directors or by these By-Laws to some other officer or agent of the Corporation, or shall be required by law to be otherwise signed or executed; and in general shall perform all duties incident to the office of President and such other duties as may be prescribed by the Board of Directors from time to time.

SECTION 6. Vice President. In the absence of the President or in event of his death, inability or refusal to act, the Vice President shall perform the duties of the President, and when so acting, shall have all the powers of and be subject to all the restrictions upon the President. The Vice President shall perform such other duties as from time to time may be assigned to him by the President or by the Board of Directors. If there is more than one Vice President, each Vice President shall succeed to the duties of the President in order of rank as determined by the Board of Directors. If no such rank has been determined, then each Vice President shall succeed to the duties of the President in order of date of election, the earliest date having the first rank.

SECTION 7. Secretary. The Secretary shall: (a) keep the minutes of the proceedings of the shareholders and of the Board of Directors in one or more minute books provided for that purpose; (b) see that all notices are duly given in accordance with the provisions of these By-Laws or as required by law; (c) be custodian of the corporate records and of the seal of the Corporation and see that the seal of the Corporation is affixed to all documents, the execution of which on behalf of the Corporation under its seal is duly authorized; (d) keep a register of the post office address of each shareholder which shall be furnished to the Secretary by such shareholder; (e) sign with the President certificates for shares of the Corporation, the issuance of which shall have been authorized by resolution of the Board of Directors; (f) have general charge of the stock transfer books of the Corporation; and (g) in general perform all duties incident to the office of the Secretary and such other duties as from time to time may be assigned to him by the President or by the Board of Directors.

SECTION 8. Treasurer. The Treasurer shall: (a) have charge and custody of and be responsible for all funds and securities of the Corporation; (b) receive and give receipts for moneys due and payable to the Corporation from any source what-soever, and deposit all such moneys in the name of the Corporation in such banks, trust companies or other depositaries as shall be selected in accordance with the provisions of Article VI of these By-Laws; and (c) in general perform all of the duties incident to the office of Treasurer and such other duties as from time to time may be assigned to him by the President or by the Board of Directors. If required by the Board of Directors, the Treasurer shall give a bond for the faithful discharge of his duties in such sum and with such sureties as the Board of Directors shall determine.

SECTION 9. Salaries. The salaries of the officers shall be fixed from time to time by athe Board of Directors, and no officer shall be prevented from receiving such salary by reason of the fact that he is also a director of the Corporation.

ARTICLE V
INDEMNITY

The Corporation shall indemnify its directors, officers and employees as follows:

(a) Every director, officer, or employee of the Corporation shall be indemnified by the Corporation against all expenses and liabilities, including counsel fees, reasonably incurred by or imposed upon him in connection with any proceeding to which he may be made a party, or in which he may become involved, by reason of his being or having been a director, officer, employee or agent of the Corporation or is or was serving at the request of the Corporation as a director, officer, employee or agent of the corporation, partnership, joint venture, trust or enterprise, or any settlement thereof, whether or not he is a director, officer, employee or agent at the time such expenses are incurred, except in such cases wherein the director, officer, or employee is adjudged guilty of willful misfeasance or malfeasance in the performance of his duties; provided that in the event of a settlement the indemnification herein shall apply only when the Board of Directors approves such settlement and reimbursement as being for the best interests of the Corporation.

(b)   The Corporation shall provide to any person who is or was a director, officer, employee, or agent of the Corporation or is or was serving at the request of the Corporation as a director, officer, employee or agent of the corporation, partnership, joint venture, trust or enterprise, the indemnity against expenses of suit, litigation or other proceedings which is specifically permissible under applicable law.

(c)   The Board of Directors may, in its discretion, direct the purchase of liability insurance by way of implementing the provisions of this Article V.

ARTICLE VI
CONTRACTS, LOANS, CHECKS AND DEPOSITS

SECTION 1. Contracts. The Board of Directors may authorize any officer or officers, agent or agents, to enter into any contract or execute and deliver any instrument in the name of and on behalf of the Corporation, and such authority may be general or confined to specific instances.

SECTION 2. Loans. No loans shall be constracted on behalf of the Corporation and no evidences of indebtedness shall be issued in its name unless authorized by a resolution of the Board of Directors. Such authority may be general or confined to specific instances.

SECTION 3. Checks, Drafts, etc. All checks, drafts or other orders for the payment of money, notes or other evidences of indebtedness issued in the name of the Corporation, shall be signed by such officer or officers, agent or agents of the Corporation and in such manner as shall from time to time be determined by resolution of the Board of Directors.

SECTION 4. Deposits. All funds of the Corporation not otherwise employed shall be deposited from time to time to the credit of the Corporation in such banks, trust companies or other depositaries as the Board of Directors may select.

ARTICLE VII
CERTIFICATES FOR SHARES AND THEIR TRANSFER

SECTION 1. Certificates for Shares. Certificates representing shares of the Corporation shall be in such form as shall be determined by the Board of Directors. Such certificates shall be signed by the President and by the Secretary or by such other officers authorized by law and by the Board of Directors so to do, and sealed with the corporate seal. All certificates for shares shall be consecutively numbered or otherwise identified. The name and address of the person to whom the shares represented thereby are issued, with the number of shares and date of issue, shall be entered on the stock transfer books of the Corporation. All certificates surrendered to the Corporation for transfer shall be cancelled and no new certificate shall be issued until the former certificate for a like number of shares shall have been surrendered and cancelled, except that in case of a lost, destroyed or mutilated certificate, a new one may be issued therefor upon such terms and indemnity to the Corporation as the Board of Directors may prescribe.

SECTION 2. Transfer of Shares. Transfer of shares of the Corporation shall be made only on the stock transfer books of the Corporation by the holder of record thereof or by his legal representative, who shall furnish proper evidence of authority to transfer, or by his attorney thereunto authorized by power of attorney duly executed and filed with the Secretary of the Corporation, and on surrender for cancellation of the certificate for such shares. The person in whose name shares stand on the books of the Corporation shall be deemed by the Corporation to be the owner thereof for all purposes. Provided, however, that upon any action undertaken by the shareholders to elect S Corporation status pursuant to Section 1362 of the Internal Revenue Code and upon any shareholders agreement thereto restricting the transfer of said shares so as to dis-qualify said S Corporation status, said restriction on transfer shall be made a part of the by-laws so long as said agreement is in force and effect.

ARTICLE VIII
FISCAL YEAR

The fiscal year of the Corporation shall begin on the   day of   and end on the day of   of each year.

ARTICLE IX
DIVIDENDS

The Board of Directors may from time to time declare, and the Corporation may pay, dividends on its outstanding shares in the manner and upon the terms and conditions provided by law and its Articles of Incorporation.

ARTICLE X
CORPORATE SEAL

The Board of Directors shall provide a corporate seal which shall be circular in form and shall have inscribed thereon the name of the Corporation and the state of incorporation and the words, "Corporate Seal".

ARTICLE XI
WAIVER OF NOTICE

Unless otherwise provided by law, whenever any notice is required to be given to any shareholder or director of the Corporation under the provisions of these By-Laws or under the provisions of the Articles of Incorporation or under the provisions of the applicable Business Corporation Act, a waiver thereof in writing, signed by the person or persons entitled to such notice, whether before or after the time stated therein, shall be deemed equivalent to the giving of such notice.

ARTICLE XII
AMENDMENTS

These By-Laws may be altered, amended or repealed and new By-Laws may be adopted by the Board of Directors at any regular or special meeting of the Board of Directors.

The above By-Laws are certified to have been adopted by the Board of Directors of the Corporation on the   day of   , 19   .

_____
Secretary

STOCK TRANSFER LEDGER

NAME OF STOCKHOLDER	PLACE OF RESIDENCE		CERTIFICATES ISSUED		FROM WHOM SHARES WERE TRANSFERRED	
			CERTIF. NOS.	NO. SHARES	(IF ORIGINAL ISSUE ENTER AS SUCH)	

AMOUNT PAID THEREON	DATE OF TRANSFER OF SHARES	TO WHOM SHARES ARE TRANSFERRED	CERTIFICATES SURRENDERED		NUMBER OF SHARES HELD (BALANCE)	VALUE OF STOCK TRANSFER TAX STAMP AFFIXED
			CERTIF. NOS.	NO. SHARES		

These shares are subject to restrictions on transfer pursuant to a shareholder agreement.

SHARES

NUMBER

This Certifies that

is the owner of

fully paid and non-assessable Shares of the above Corporation transferable only on the books of the Corporation by the holder hereof in person or by duly authorized Attorney upon surrender of this Certificate properly endorsed.

In Witness Whereof, the said Corporation has caused this Certificate to be signed by its duly authorized officers and to be sealed with the Seal of the Corporation.

Dated

APPENDIX

2

THE FORMS IN THIS SECTION

1. *Form 1120S: U.S. Income Tax Return for S Corporation*

    This form contains complete instructions for preparing and filing the corporation's income tax return at the end of its fiscal year, together with a sample tax return.

2. *Form 4562: Depreciation and Amortization*

    This form contains both instructions and depreciation and amortization attachment to the year end Form 1120S tax return.

3. *Schedule K-1: Shareholder Income*

    This form is used by shareholders of the S Corporation to report their share of income, credits, deductions and other "pass-through" items.

1986

Department of the Treasury
Internal Revenue Service

Instructions for Form 1120S

U.S. Income Tax Return for an S Corporation

(Section references are to the Internal Revenue Code, unless otherwise noted.)

Paperwork Reduction Act Notice

We ask for this information to carry out the Internal Revenue laws of the United States. We need it to ensure that taxpayers are complying with these laws and to allow us to figure and collect the right amount of tax. You are required to give us this information.

Voluntary Contributions To Reduce the Public Debt

Quite often, inquiries are received about how voluntary contributions to reduce the public debt may be made. A corporation may contribute by enclosing a separate check, payable to "Bureau of the Public Debt," with the tax return. Please keep the contribution to reduce the public debt separate from any amount payable with the tax return. Tax remittances should be made payable to "Internal Revenue Service."

Changes You Should Note
Tax Reform Act of 1986 (Act)

The Act made many changes to the Internal Revenue Code that affect the S corporation and shareholders of the S corporation. See pages 14 and 15 of these instructions for Changes Made by the Act that affect the S corporation and its shareholders for the 1986 calendar year, 1986–87 fiscal year (FY), and 1987 tax year.

Reminders

● **Preaddressed Label.**—Use the pre-addressed label and envelope that comes with the tax package to help speed up the processing of your return.

● **Optional Writeoff of Certain Tax Preferences.**—Do not take a deduction for any qualified expenditures to which an election under section 58(i) (new section 59(e) after 1986) applies. Instead, pass the expenditures and information needed to compute this deduction through to your shareholders on the schedule attached for line 19 of Schedule K-1. Each shareholder will take the deductible amount, if any, on his or her own return. See the instructions for line 16 of Schedule K and line 19 of Schedule K-1 for more information.

● **Depletion.**—Do not deduct depletion on oil and gas wells on the S corporation return. Instead, pass the information needed to compute this deduction through to the shareholders on Schedule K-1 or on an attached schedule for line 19 of Schedule K-1. The shareholders will determine the deductible amount on their own returns. See the instructions for line 16

of Schedule K and line 19 of Schedule K-1 for more information.

Registration of Tax Shelter

If an S corporation is a tax shelter, or if the corporation is involved in a tax shelter, or if the corporation is considered to be the organizer of a tax shelter, or if the corporation is a pass-through entity of the shelter benefits, there are reporting requirements under section 6111 for both the corporation and its shareholders.

See **Form 8264,** Application for Registration of a Tax Shelter, and **Form 8271,** Investor Reporting of Tax Shelter Registration Number, and their related instructions for information the corporation must provide to IRS and to the shareholders to enable them to comply with these requirements.

The corporation must enter its tax shelter registration number in item C of Schedule K-1 if applicable. Also, complete item O on page 2 of Form 1120S.

General Instructions
Purpose of Form

Form 1120S is used if a domestic corporation has filed **Form 2553,** Election by a Small Business Corporation, to be an S corporation and its election is in effect. Do not file your first Form 1120S until you have been notified by the IRS that your election is accepted and the tax year it will take effect.

If you need more information, get **Publication 589,** Tax Information on S Corporations.

Filing Form 1120S
Who Must File

You must file Form 1120S if: (a) you elected by filing Form 2553 to be taxed as an S corporation, (b) IRS accepted your election, and (c) the election remains in effect.

End of Election

Once the election is made, it stays in effect for all years until it is terminated. During the 5 years after the tax year the election has been terminated, the corporation can make another election on Form 2553 only if the Commissioner consents. See section 1362(g), and related regulations.

The election ends **automatically** in any of the following cases:

a. The corporation is no longer a small business corporation as defined in section 1361(b). The ending of an election in this manner is effective as of the day on which the corporation ceases to be a small business corporation. See sections 1362(d)(2) and 1362(e) for more information.

b. If, for each of three consecutive tax years, the corporation has both subchapter C earnings and profits, and gross receipts more than 25% of which are derived from passive investment income as defined in section 1362(d)(3)(D), the election shall terminate on the first day of the first tax year beginning after the third consecutive tax year. The corporation must pay a tax for each year it has excess net passive income. See specific instructions for line 25a for details on how to figure the tax

c. When an existing S corporation (section 1378(c)(1)) has a more than 50% change in ownership and has not adopted a permitted tax year as defined in section 1378(b) for any tax year following the year it has more than 50% change in ownership. See section 1378(c) for details. For tax years beginning after 1986, section 1378(c) is repealed. See Changes Made by the Act that affect 1987 tax years for more information.

The election may be revoked if shareholders who collectively own a majority of the stock in the corporation consent to a revocation. So long as the specified date is on or after the date of consent to the revocation, the revocation is effective as of the specified date. If no date is specified, the revocation is effective as of the beginning of a tax year if it is made on or before the 15th day of the 3rd month of such tax year. If no date is specified and the revocation is made after the 15th day of the 3rd month, it is not effective until the beginning of the following tax year. See section 1362(d)(1) for more information.

When To File

In general, file Form 1120S by the 15th **day** of the 3rd month after the end of the tax year. Use **Form 7004,** Application for Automatic Extension of Time To File Corporation Income Tax Return, to request an automatic 6-month extension of time to file Form 1120S.

Period To Be Covered by 1986 Return

File the 1986 return for calendar year 1986 and fiscal years beginning in 1986 and ending in 1987. If the return is for a fiscal year, fill in the tax year spaces on the form.

Note: *The 1986 Form 1120S may also be used if: (1) the corporation has a tax year of less than 12 months that begins and ends in 1987; and (2) the 1987 Form 1120S is not available by the time the corporation is required to file its return. However, the corporation must show its 1987 tax year on the 1986 Form 1120S and incorporate any tax law changes that are effective for tax years beginning after December 31, 1986. See Changes Made by the Act that affect 1987 tax years at the end of these instructions.*

Final Return

If the corporation ceases to exist, check the box for Final Return in item F at the top of the form.

Change in Address

If there has been a change in address from the previous year, check the box for Change in Address in item F at the top of Form 1120S.

Amended Return

To correct an error in a Form 1120S already filed, file an amended Form 1120S and check the box for Amended Return in item F at the top of the form. If the amended return results in a change to income, or a change in the distribution of any income or other information provided to shareholders, an amended Schedule K-1 (Form 1120S) must also be filed with the amended Form 1120S and given to each shareholder. Write "AMENDED" across the top of the corrected Schedule K-1 you give each shareholder.

Designation of Tax Matters Person (TMP)

An S corporation may designate an individual shareholder as the TMP for a specific corporate tax year by attaching a statement to the return that:

1. Identifies by name, address, and taxpayer identification number the corporation and the individual shareholder designated as the TMP,

2. Declares that the attached statement is a designation of a TMP for the tax year to which the return relates (an S corporation may not designate a TMP for any tax year other than the tax year for which the return is being filed), and

3. Is signed by a corporate officer authorized to sign the corporation's return.

Where To File

If the corporation's principal business, office, or agency is located in ▼	Use the following Internal Revenue Service Center address ▼
New Jersey, New York (New York City and counties of Nassau, Rockland, Suffolk, and Westchester)	Holtsville, NY 00501
New York (all other counties), Connecticut, Maine, Massachusetts, Minnesota, New Hampshire, Rhode Island, Vermont	Andover, MA 05501
Alabama, Florida, Georgia, Mississippi, South Carolina	Atlanta, GA 31101
Kentucky, Michigan, Ohio, West Virginia	Cincinnati, OH 45999
Kansas, Louisiana, New Mexico, Oklahoma, Texas	Austin, TX 73301
Alaska, Arizona, California (counties of Alpine, Amador, Butte, Calaveras, Colusa, Contra Costa, Del Norte, El Dorado, Glenn, Humboldt, Lake, Lassen, Marin, Mendocino, Modoc, Napa, Nevada, Placer, Plumas, Sacramento, San Joaquin, Shasta, Sierra, Siskiyou, Solano, Sonoma, Sutter, Tehama, Trinity, Yolo, and Yuba), Colorado, Idaho, Montana, Nebraska, Nevada, North Dakota, Oregon, South Dakota, Utah, Washington, Wyoming	Ogden, UT 84201
California (all other counties), Hawaii	Fresno, CA 93888
Illinois, Iowa, Missouri, Wisconsin	Kansas City, MO 64999
Arkansas, Indiana, North Carolina, Tennessee, Virginia	Memphis, TN 37501
Delaware, District of Columbia, Maryland, Pennsylvania	Philadelphia, PA 19255

Accounting Methods

Figure ordinary income using the method of accounting regularly used in keeping the corporation's books and records. Such method may include the cash receipts and disbursements method, an accrual method or any other method permitted by the Internal Revenue Code. In all cases, the method adopted must clearly reflect income. (See section 446.) Several changes were made to tax law regarding accounting methods. See Changes Made by the Act at the end of these instructions for details.

Unless the law specifically states otherwise, a corporation may change the method of accounting used to report income in earlier years (for income as a whole or for any material item) only by first getting consent on **Form 3115**, Application for Change in Accounting Method. Also see **Publication 538**, Accounting Periods and Methods.

Rounding Off to Whole-Dollar Amounts

You may show the money items on the return and accompanying schedules as whole-dollar amounts. To do so, drop any amount less than 50 cents, and increase any amount from 50 cents through 99 cents to the next higher dollar.

Change in Accounting Period

To change an accounting period, see regulations section 1.442-1 and **Form 1128**, Application for Change in Accounting Period. Also see Publication 538. For tax years beginning after 1986, certain fiscal year corporations will have to change to calendar year. See Changes Made by the Act that affect 1987 tax years at the end of these instructions for more information.

Paying the Tax

The corporation must pay the tax due (line 27, page 1) in full within 2½ months after the end of the tax year.

Deposit corporation income tax payments with a Federal Tax Deposit Coupon (**Form 8109**). Make these tax deposits with either a financial institution qualified as a depositary for Federal taxes or the Federal Reserve bank or branch servicing the geographic area where the corporation is located. Do not submit deposits directly to an IRS office; otherwise, the corporation may be subject to a penalty. Records of deposits will be sent to IRS for crediting to the corporation's account. See the instructions contained in the coupon book (Form 8109) for more information.

To get more deposit forms, use the reorder form (Form 8109A) provided in the coupon book.

For additional information concerning deposits, see **Publication 583**, Information for Business Taxpayers.

Penalties

a. Form 1120S is required to be filed by sections 6037 and 6012. A corporation that does not file its tax return by the due date, including any extensions, may have to pay a penalty of 5% a month, or fraction of a month, up to a maximum of 25%, for each month the return is not filed. (The penalty is imposed on the net amount due. See section 6651(a)(1).) The minimum penalty for not filing a tax

return within 60 days of the due date for filing (including extensions) is the lesser of the underpayment of tax or $100.

b. A corporation that does not pay the tax when due generally may have to pay a penalty of ½% a month or fraction of a month, up to a maximum of 25%, for each month the tax is not paid. (The penalty is imposed on the net amount due. See section 6651(a)(2).)

These penalties will not be imposed if the corporation can show that not filing or not paying was due to reasonable cause and not willful neglect.

The penalties are in addition to the interest charge imposed on unpaid tax at a rate under section 6621.

Stock Ownership in Foreign Corporations

If the corporation owned at least 5% in value of the outstanding stock of a foreign personal holding company, attach the statement required by section 551(c).

A taxpayer who controls a foreign corporation, or who is a 10% or more shareholder of a controlled foreign corporation, may have to file **Form 5471**, Information Return With Respect to a Foreign Corporation.

Net Operating Loss and Other Deductions

An S corporation may not take the deduction for net operating losses provided by section 172 and the special deductions in sections 241 through 250 (except section 248).

The corporation's net operating loss is allowed as a deduction from the shareholders' gross income. (Section 1366.)

Attachments

Attach **Form 4136**, Computation of Credit for Federal Tax on Gasoline and Special Fuels, after page 4, Form 1120S. Attach schedules in alphabetical order and other forms in numerical order.

To assist us in processing the return, we ask that you complete every applicable entry space on Form 1120S and Schedule K-1. Please do not attach statements and write "See attached" in lieu of completing the entry spaces on Form 1120S and Schedule K-1.

If you need more space on the forms or schedules, attach separate sheets and show the same information in the same order as on the printed forms. But show your totals on the printed forms. Please use sheets that are the same size as the forms and schedules. Attach these separate sheets after all the schedules and forms. Be sure to put the taxpayer's name and employer identification number (EIN) on each sheet.

Unresolved Tax Problems

IRS has a Problem Resolution Program for taxpayers who have been unable to resolve their problems with IRS. If the corporation has a tax problem it has been unable to resolve through normal channels, write to the corporation's local IRS district director or call the corporation's local IRS office and ask for Problem Resolution Assistance. This office will take responsibility for your problem and ensure that it receives proper attention. Although the Problem Resolution Office cannot change the tax law or make technical decisions, it can frequently clear up misunderstandings that may have resulted from previous contacts.

Signature

The return must be signed and dated by the president, vice president, treasurer, assistant treasurer, chief accounting officer, or any other corporate officer (such as tax officer) authorized to sign.

A receiver, trustee, or assignee must sign and date any return he or she is required to file on behalf of a corporation.

If your corporate officer fills in Form 1120S, the Paid Preparer's space under "Signature of Officer" should remain blank. If someone prepares Form 1120S and does not charge the corporation, that person should not sign the return. Certain others who prepare Form 1120S should not sign. For example, a regular, full-time employee of the corporation such as a clerk, secretary, etc., does not have to sign.

In general, anyone paid to prepare Form 1120S must sign the return and fill in the other blanks in the Paid Preparer's Use Only area of the return.

The preparer required to sign the return MUST:

● Complete the required preparer information.

● Sign, by hand, in the space provided for the preparer's signature. (Signature stamps or labels are not acceptable.)

● Give a copy of Form 1120S to the taxpayer in addition to the copy filed with IRS.

Tax return preparers should be familiar with their responsibilities. See **Publication 1045**, Information and Order Blanks for Preparers of Federal Income Tax Returns, for more details.

Transfers to Corporation Controlled by Transferor

If a person acquires stock or securities of a corporation in exchange for property, and no gain or loss is recognized under section 351, the transferor and transferee must attach the information required by regulations section 1.351-3.

Information Returns That May Be Required

Form 966. Corporate Dissolution or Liquidation.

Form 1096. Annual Summary and Transmittal of U.S. Information Returns. (For transmitting Form 1099-R information for 1986, use **Form W-3G**, Transmittal of Certain Information Returns.)

Form 1098. Mortgage Interest Statement. This form is used to report the receipt from any individual of $600 or more of mortgage interest in the course of the corporation's trade or business.

Forms 1099-A, B, DIV, INT, MISC, OID, PATR and R. You may have to file these information returns to report abandonments and acquisitions through foreclosure, proceeds from broker and barter exchange transactions, certain dividends, interest payments, medical and dental health care payments, miscellaneous income, original issue discount, patronage dividends, and total distributions from profit-sharing plans, retirement plans, and individual retirement arrangements. Also use certain of these returns to report amounts that were received as a nominee on behalf of another person.

For more information, see **Publication 916**, Information Returns.

Use Form 1099-DIV to report actual dividends paid by the corporation. Only distributions from accumulated earnings and profits are classified as dividends. These dividends qualify for the dividend exclusion under section 116. Do not issue Form 1099-DIV for dividends received by the corporation that are allocated to shareholders on line 2 of Schedule K-1.

Note: *Every corporation must file information returns if it makes payments of rents, commissions, or other fixed or determinable income (see section 6041) totaling $600 or more to any one person in the course of its trade or business during the calendar year.*

Form 5713. International Boycott Report. Every corporation that had operations in, or related to, a boycotting country, company, or national of a country must file Form 5713. In addition, persons who participate in or cooperate with an international boycott may have to complete Schedule A or Schedule B and Schedule C of Form 5713 to compute their loss of the following items: the foreign tax credit, the deferral of earnings of a controlled foreign corporation, IC-DISC benefits, and FSC benefits.

Form 8281. Information Return for Publicly Offered Original Issue Discount Instruments. This form is used by issuers of publicly offered debt instruments having OID to provide the information required by section 1275(c).

Form 8300. Report of Cash Payments Over $10,000 Received in a Trade or Business. This form is used to report the receipt of more than $10,000 in cash or foreign currency in one transaction (or a series of related transactions).

Windfall Profit Tax. Generally, the S corporation will notify each shareholder of any income tax deduction for windfall profit tax on **Form 6248**, Annual Information Return of Windfall Profit Tax. Include on line 19 of Schedule K-1, or on the statement attached for line 19 of Schedule K-1, the shareholder's share of windfall profit tax. The individual shareholder figures his or her overpaid windfall profit tax on **Form 6249**, Computation of Overpaid Windfall Profit Tax.

Caution: *Some S corporations may elect to be treated as authorized to act on behalf of the shareholders. If the corporation makes this election, the preceding paragraph will not apply. See the instructions for Form 6249 for details on how the corporation claims the overpaid windfall profit tax on Form 1120S.*

Passive Activity Provisions (Fiscal Year (FY) Corporations Only)

New section 469 limits losses and credits from passive activities for tax years beginning after 1986. The limitations apply to shareholders of the S corporation and not the S corporation itself. To assist shareholders with tax years beginning after 1986 in figuring the section 469 limitations, the 1986-87 fiscal year corporation must report income or loss and credits separately on Schedules K and K-1 for each of the following types of passive activities:

● Trade or business passive activity.

● Rental real estate activity.

● Rental activity other than real estate rental.

Trade or Business Passive Activity.— Generally, a passive activity is any activity of the S corporation involving the conduct of any trade or business in which a shareholder does not materially participate. Any working interest in oil or gas property as defined in section 469(c)(3) is excluded. A shareholder is treated as materially participating only if the shareholder is involved in the operation of the trade or business on a regular, continuous, and substantial basis. See section 469(h) and related regulations for more information.

Rental Activity Other Than Real Estate Rental.—This term means an activity the income from which consists of payments principally for the use of tangible property. Certain rental activities that involve the performance of substantial services may be treated as a trade or business and not as a rental activity. See instructions for line 5 of page 1 for details.

Rental Real Estate Activity.—A rental real estate activity is a rental activity which involves the rental or leasing of real estate. See instructions for line 5 of page 1 for details.

Specific Instructions

Employer Identification Number. If the employer identification number (EIN) on the label is wrong or if you did not receive a label, write the correct number at the top of the return.

A corporation that does not have an EIN should apply for one on **Form SS-4**, Application for Employer Identification Number. Obtain this form at most IRS or Social Security Administration offices. Send Form SS-4 to the same Internal Revenue Service Center to which Form 1120S is mailed. If the EIN has not been received by the filing time for Form 1120S, write "Applied for" in the space for the EIN. See Publication 583 for additional information.

Business Code No.—See "Codes for Principal Business Activity" at the end of these instructions.

Total Assets. Enter the total assets, as determined by the accounting method regularly used in maintaining the corporation's books and records, at the end of the corporation's tax year. If there are no assets at the end of the tax year, enter the total assets as of the beginning of the tax year.

Page 1 Changes (FY Corporations Only)

Certain line items on page 1 do not apply when Form 1120S is filed by fiscal year corporations. This is a result of tax law changes which necessitate that S corporations with tax years ending after 1986 figure their income or loss and report income or loss to their shareholders in a manner different than the 1986 calendar year S corporation.

1. Adjustments to Page 1 To Provide for Separate Computation of Income or Loss of Any Trade or Business Passive Activity(ies) on Page 1.—The following items of income and expense (for the entire tax year) are not reported on page 1 so that

Page 3

only income and expense items relating to trade or business passive activity(ies) remain on page 1:

a. Income and expenses attributable to rental real estate activities or other rental activities generally are not reported on page 1 because such rental activity losses are subject to different rules than trade or business passive activity losses under section 469 limitations. See section 469 for details. Rental real estate activity income or loss is reported on line 1b of Schedule K, and other rental activity income or loss is reported on line 1c of Schedule K.

b. Income or loss from a working interest in any oil or gas property; as defined in section 469(c)(3), is not reported on page 1. Report this income or loss on line 6 of Schedule K.

c. Portfolio income and related expenses are not reported on page 1. Portfolio income includes interest, dividends, royalty income, and annuity income not derived in the ordinary course of a trade or business; gain or loss on the disposition of property which normally produces that income; gain or loss on the disposition of property held for investment; and any income, gain, or loss which is attributable to an investment of working capital. Generally, expenses related to portfolio income must be clearly and directly allocable to such income. See section 469(e)(1) for details on portfolio income and related expenses. Report portfolio income (reduced by applicable expenses) on line 1d or 2 of Schedule K.

2. See Changes Made by the Act at the end of these instructions for other changes that affect the reporting of income and expenses by FY corporations.

Gross Income

Note: *Do not include any income that is tax exempt in lines 1 through 8, or any nondeductible expenses in lines 10 through 22. However, these income and expense items are used in figuring the amount for line 23 or 24 of Schedule L. Also, see instructions for line 16 of Schedule K and line 19 of Schedule K-1.*

A corporation that receives any exempt income other than interest, or holds any property or engages in an activity that produces exempt income, must attach to its return an itemized statement showing the amount of each type of exempt income and the expenses allocated to each type.

Line 1
Gross receipts
Enter gross receipts or sales from all business operations except those you report on lines 4 through 8.

Extensive changes were made to tax law provisions regarding long-term contracts and installment sales. See Changes Made by the Act at the end of these instructions before completing line 1.

For reporting advance payments and long-term contracts, see regulations sections 1.451-3 and 1.451-5.

If you use the installment method, enter on line 1c the gross profit on collections from installment sales and carry the same amount to line 3. Attach a schedule showing for the current year and 3 preceding years. (a) gross sales, (b) cost of goods sold, (c) gross profit, (d) percentage

Page 4

of gross profit to gross sales, (e) amount collected, and (f) gross profit on amount collected.

Line 2
Cost of goods sold and/or operations
See the instructions for Schedule A.

Line 4
FY corporations see Page 1 Changes (above) regarding portfolio income (investment income) before completing line 4. Enter the total taxable interest and the total nonqualifying dividends. See **Publication 550,** Investment Income and Expenses, for additional information.

Taxable interest
Include taxable interest from all sources. Do not include interest exempt from tax and interest on tax-free covenant bonds.

Nonqualifying dividends
Nonqualifying dividends are taxable dividends that are included in ordinary income and for which the individual shareholder is not entitled to an exclusion under section 116. These dividends come from the following:

● Foreign corporations, including a controlled foreign corporation.

● Exempt organizations (charitable, fraternal, etc.) and exempt farmers' cooperative organizations.

● Regulated investment companies (including Money Market Funds) and real estate investment trusts, unless the companies have told you how much of the dividends qualify for the exclusion or as capital gain dividends.

Qualifying dividends are taxable dividends received in tax years beginning before 1987 from domestic corporations not listed above. They are passed through to the shareholders on Schedules K and K-1, line 2. See section 116 for more information.

Line 5
Gross rents
(Calendar Year Corporations Only)
Enter the gross amount you received for renting property. Enter expenses attributable to rental income on the proper deduction lines (10–22).

The corporation may be limited in the amount of deductions for renting a vacation home if a shareholder uses the property for personal purposes. (See section 280A.)

Before deducting any interest expense, see the instructions for lines 16a–c, page 1, and lines 13c(1) and (2) of Schedules K and K-1 to determine if the interest on rental property is investment interest.

(FY Corporations Only)
Fiscal year corporations do not report income and expenses from certain rental activities on page 1 of Form 1120S. Income or loss from rental real estate activities or other rental activities, except as explained below, are reported separately on lines 1b, 1c, and 6 of Schedule K.

Rental activities are subject to different rules than other passive activities. Generally, rental real estate activities are not subject to material participation rules. However, where significant services are provided in connection with the rental of real estate (such as in the renting of hotel rooms), the activity is treated as a trade or business activity and not a rental activity

and as such is subject to the material participation rules. Also, in order for the rental of tangible property to be considered a rental activity, the income from the activity must consist of payments principally for the use of the tangible property, rather than for the performance of substantial services. As in the case of a hotel, if significant services are involved, the rental service would be a trade or business and not a rental activity and thus would be subject to the material participation rules. If a rental service is treated as a trade or business, income and expenses from the activity are reported on page 1 of Form 1120S and not on lines 1b and 1c of Schedule K.

Line 8
Other income
Enter any other taxable income not listed above and explain its nature on an attached schedule. Examples of other income are recoveries of bad debts deducted in earlier years under the specific charge-off method; the amount of credit for alcohol used as a fuel that was figured on **Form 6478,** Credit for Alcohol Used as Fuel; the amount of the credit for Federal tax on gasoline and special fuels to the extent that it reduced your income tax (see **Form 4136,** Computation of Credit for Federal Tax on Gasoline and Special Fuels, for details); and refunds of taxes deducted in earlier years. Do not include those items requiring separate computations by shareholders that must be reported on Schedule K. (See the instructions for Schedules K and K-1.) Do not offset current year's taxes with tax refunds.

If "other income" consists of only one item, identify it by showing the account caption in parentheses on line 8. A separate schedule need not be attached to the return in this case.

Do not net any expense item (such as interest) with a similar income item. Report all expenses on lines 10 through 22.

Deductions

Note: *FY corporations see instructions for "Page 1 Changes (FY Corporations Only)" at the beginning of the Specific Instructions for "Gross Income" before completing lines 10 through 22.*

Limitations on deductions
1. Transactions between related taxpayers.— See section 267 for rules on treatment of losses, expenses, and interest on transactions between related taxpayers.

2. Limitation on deductions for tax preference items.—If the S corporation was a C corporation for any of the three immediately preceding years, it may be required to reduce deductions for the following tax preference items by a certain percentage:

a) Section 1250 capital gain (20%);

b) Amortizable basis of pollution control facilities (generally 20% but 15% for property placed in service before January 1, 1985);

c) Intangible drilling and exploration and development costs (see section 291(b)); and

d) Depletion of iron ore and coal (including lignite) (15%).

See sections 1363(b)(4) and 291 for more information.

3. See section 58(i) regarding qualified expenditures under sections 173, 174(a), 263(c), 616(a), and 617. These expenditures are passed through separately to shareholders to allow them the write-off option under section 58(i). See instructions for line 16 of Schedule K and line 19 of Schedule K-1.

4. Business start-up expenses.—Section 195 provides that business start-up expenses be amortized over a period of at least 60 months.

Line 10
Compensation of officers
Enter on line 10 the total compensation of all officers.

Line 11
Salaries and wages
Enter on line 11a the amount of total salaries and wages (other than salaries and wages deducted elsewhere on your return) paid or incurred for the tax year.

Enter on line 11b the applicable jobs credit from **Form 5884, Jobs Credit.** See Instructions for Form 5884 for more information.

If a shareholder or a member of the family of one or more shareholders of the corporation renders services or furnishes capital to the corporation for which reasonable compensation is not paid, the IRS may make adjustments in the items taken into account by such individuals and the value of such services or capital. See section 1366(e).

Line 12
Repairs
Enter the cost of incidental repairs, such as labor and supplies, that do not add to the value of the property or appreciably prolong its life. New buildings, machinery, or permanent improvements that increase the value of the property are not deductible. They are chargeable to capital accounts and may be depreciated or amortized.

Do not include section 179 expense items. See instructions for line 8 of Schedules K and K-1 for details on reporting these items to shareholders.

Line 13
Bad debts
You may treat bad debts in either of two ways: (a) as a deduction for specific debts that become worthless in whole or in part, or (b) as a deduction for a reasonable addition to a reserve for bad debts. (Section 166.)

If the corporation uses the reserve method, attach a schedule for 1986 that separately lists:

1. Trade notes and accounts receivable outstanding at the end of the year;
2. Sales on account;
3. Amount added to reserve—current year's provision;
4. Amount added to reserve—recoveries;
5. Amount charged against reserve; and
6. Reserve for bad debts at end of year.

An S corporation may choose either method on its first return in which it takes a bad debt deduction. It must use that method for following years unless it receives permission to change. Apply on Form 3115 if you want to change the method of figuring bad debts.

For tax years beginning after 1986, the reserve method for figuring bad debts is repealed. See Changes Made by the Act that affect 1987 tax years for more information.

Line 15
Taxes
Enter taxes paid or incurred on business property for carrying on a trade or business, if not reflected in cost of goods sold. Federal import duties and Federal excise and stamp taxes are deductible only if paid or incurred in carrying on the trade or business of the corporation. Taxes incurred in the production or collection of income, or for the management, conservation, or maintenance of property held for the production of income, may be considered to be deductible only under section 212. These are not deductible on line 15; they are reported separately on Schedules K and K-1, line 9.

Do not deduct taxes assessed against local benefits that increase the value of the property assessed (such as for paving, etc.); Federal income taxes; estate, inheritance, legacy, succession, and gift taxes; or taxes reported elsewhere, such as in Schedule A.

Do not deduct section 901 foreign taxes. These taxes are reported separately to shareholders on line 14 of Schedules K and K-1.

See section 189(b) for information on amortizing real property construction period taxes. Section 189 is repealed for costs incurred after 1986 in tax years ending after 1986.

Lines 16a–16c
Interest
Caution: Include on lines 16a and 16b interest expense on indebtedness incurred after December 16, 1969, to purchase or carry property held for investment (including net lease property). Also include interest expense not incurred in the trade or business of the corporation required to be reported on line 9 of Schedules K and K-1. Property held for investment includes all investments held for producing taxable income or gain. It does not generally include property used in a trade or business. See the instructions for Schedules K and K-1, line 13b, for a description of investment income.

Note: FY corporations see Page 1 Changes at the beginning of the Specific Instructions and section 163(d)(4)(D) for changes that may affect the way interest expense is reported.

For more information, see section 163(d) and **Form 4952,** Investment Interest Expense Deduction.

Line 16a
Enter interest on all indebtedness incurred for the operation of the corporation that is deductible by either the corporation or the shareholders (that is not claimed elsewhere on the return).

Generally, both accrual and cash basis corporations must deduct prepaid interest payments over the period of the prepayment instead of when actually paid. (See section 461(g).)

Do **not** include on line 16a:
● Amounts claimed elsewhere on the return such as on Schedule A.
● Amounts paid or accrued during the year for real property construction period interest. See section 189 for more information. Section 189 is repealed for costs incurred after 1986 in tax years ending after 1986.

The interest and carrying charges on straddle positions cannot be deducted. Instead, capitalize these amounts. See section 263(g) for exceptions.

Line 16b
See Caution under Lines 16a–16c above before completing line 16b. The line 16b amount is entered on lines 13a(2) and 13a(3) of Schedule K.

Line 17a
Depreciation
The rules for computation of depreciation for property placed in service after 1986 have been substantially changed. See Form 4562A for more information. (The corporation may elect to use the new provisions for property placed in service after July 31, 1986.)

Enter depreciation expense from Form 4562. Include amortization expense from Form 4562 on line 22.

Do not include any expense deduction for recovery property (section 179) on this line. This amount is not deductible by the corporation. Instead, it is passed through to the shareholders on line 8 of Schedule K-1 (or on a statement attached to Schedule K-1).

Line 18
Depletion
Do not report depletion deductions for oil and gas properties on this line. Each shareholder figures depletion on these properties under section 613A(c)(13). See the Instructions for line 16 of Schedule K and line 19 of Schedule K-1 for information on oil and gas depletion that must be supplied to the shareholders by the corporation.

Line 20
Pension, profit-sharing, etc., plans
Employers who maintain a pension, profit sharing, or other funded deferred compensation plan, whether or not qualified under the Internal Revenue Code and whether or not a deduction is claimed for the current tax year, generally are required to file one of the forms listed below:

Form 5500, Annual Return/Report of Employee Benefit Plan (with 100 or more participants).

Form 5500-C, Return/Report of Employee Benefit Plan (with fewer than 100 participants).

Form 5500-R, Registration Statement of Employee Benefit Plan.—Complete the applicable form for each plan with fewer than 100 participants.

Form 5500EZ.—Complete this form for a one participant plan.

There are penalties for failure to file these forms on time. **Note:** There is a new penalty for overstating the pension plan deduction for returns filed after October 22, 1986. See new section 6659A.

Line 21
Employee benefit programs
Enter the amount of contributions to employee benefit programs (such as insurance and health and welfare programs) that are not an incidental part of a pension, profit-sharing, etc., plan included in line 20.

Section 1372, added by Public Law 97-354 (Subchapter S Revision Act of 1982 (Act)), provides for partnership-type rules for fringe benefits. Generally, section 6(d) of the Act provides that, in the case of existing fringe benefits of a corporation which as of September 28, 1982, was an S corporation, section 1372 (added by the Act) only applies for tax years beginning after December 31, 1987. For this purpose, existing fringe benefits means any employee fringe benefit of a type which the corporation provided to its employees as of September 28, 1982. See Act section 6(d) for exceptions to this rule and other details.

Also include the corporation's contributions to a qualified group legal services plan established for the exclusive benefit of employees (including shareholders) or their spouses or dependents.

Line 22
Other deductions

Enter any other authorized deductions for which there is no line on page 1 of the return. Do not include those items requiring separate computations which must be reported on Schedules K and K-1. Do not deduct losses incurred in transactions which were not connected with the corporation's trade or business. Report these losses separately to shareholders on Schedules K and K-1, line 9.

Do not include qualified expenditures to which an election under section 58(i) applies. See instructions for line 16 of Schedule K and line 19 of Schedule K-1 for details on treatment of these items.

Include in line 22 the deduction taken for amortization. See instructions for Form 4562 and Form 4562A for more information.

In most cases, you may not take a deduction for any part of any item allocable to a class of exempt income. (See section 265 for exceptions.) Items directly attributable to wholly exempt income must be allocated to that income. Items directly attributable to any class of taxable income must be allocated to that taxable income.

If an item is indirectly attributable both to taxable income and to exempt income, allocate a reasonable proportion of the item to each, based on all the facts in each case.

Attach a statement showing (1) the amount of each class of exempt income and (2) the amount of expense items allocated to each such class. Show the amount allocated by apportionment separately.

In the case of a farming syndicate, a deduction for amounts paid for feed, seed, fertilizer, or other similar farm supplies is allowed only in the tax year in which these items are actually used or consumed. For definitions, exceptions to the general rule, and special rules for orchard and vineyard expenses, see section 278. Section 278 is repealed for costs incurred after 1986 in tax years ending after 1986.

For special treatment of certain expenses incurred in the production of films, books, records, or similar property, see section 280. Section 280 is repealed for costs incurred after 1986 in tax years ending after 1986.

Generally, the corporation can deduct all ordinary and necessary travel and entertainment expenses paid or incurred in the corporation's trade or business. However, the corporation cannot deduct an expense paid or incurred for a facility (such as a yacht or hunting lodge) that is used for an activity that is usually considered entertainment, amusement, or recreation. (The corporation may be able to deduct the expenses if the amount is treated as compensation and reported on Form W-2 for an employee or on Form 1099-MISC for an independent contractor.) See Publication 463, Travel, Entertainment, and Gift Expenses, for more details.

For tax years beginning after 1986, extensive changes were made to tax law provisions regarding deductions for meals and entertainment expenses. See Changes Made by the Act that affect 1987 tax years for more information.

Line 24
Ordinary income (loss)

This is nonseparately computed income or loss as defined in section 1366(a)(2). This income or loss is entered on line 1a of Schedule K.

Line 24 income is not used in figuring line 25a or 25b tax. See instructions for line 25a for figuring taxable income for purposes of line 25a or 25b tax.

Line 25a

If the corporation has always been a subchapter S corporation, the line 25a tax does not apply to the corporation. If the corporation has subchapter C earnings and profits at the close of its tax year, has passive investment income that is in excess of 25% of gross receipts, and has taxable income at year end, the corporation must pay a tax on the excess net passive income. Complete lines 1 through 3 and line 9 of the worksheet below to make this determination. If line 2 is greater than line 3 and the corporation has taxable income (see taxable income instruction below), it must pay the tax. Complete a separate schedule using the format of lines 1 through 10 or 11 of the worksheet to figure the tax. Enter the tax on line 25a, page 1, Form 1120S, and attach the computation schedule to Form 1120S.

Reduce each item of passive income passed through to shareholders by its portion of tax on line 25a. See section 1366(f)(3).

Worksheet

1. Enter gross receipts for the tax year (see section 1362(d)(3)(C) for gross receipts from the sale of capital assets)*. . . . . . _____
2. Enter passive investment income as defined in section 1362(d)(3)(D)* . . . . . . _____
3. Enter 25% of line 1 (If line 2 is less than line 3, stop here. You are not liable for this tax.) . . _____
4. Excess passive investment income—Subtract line 3 from line 2 _____
5. Enter expenses directly connected with the production of income on line 2 (see section 1375(b)(2))* . . . . . . _____
6. Net passive income—Subtract line 5 from line 2 . . . . _____
7. Divide amount on line 4 by amount on line 2 . . . . _____ %
8. Excess net passive income—Multiply line 6 by line 7 . . . _____
9. Enter taxable income (see instructions for taxable income below) . . . . . . _____
10. Tax on excess net passive income—All filers enter 46% of

the smaller of line 8 or 9. (Calendar year filers and FY filers whose tax year ends on or before 6-30-87, enter this tax on line 25a, page 1, Form 1120S. Filers with tax years which include 7-1-87, continue computation below.) . . . . . _____ _____

11. Filers with fiscal years which include 7-1-87, compute tax as follows:
    a. Enter 34% of the smaller of line 8 or 9 . . . . . . _____
    b. Line 10 × number of days in tax year before 7/1/87 / number of days in tax year _____
    c. Line 11a × number of days in tax year after 6/30/87 / number of days in tax year _____
    d. Add lines 11b and 11c. Enter here and on line 25a, page 1 Form 1120S. . . . . _____

*Income and expenses on lines 1, 2, and 5 are from total operations for the tax year. This includes applicable income and expenses from page 1, Form 1120S, as well as those that are reported separately on Schedule K. See sections 1362(d)(3)(D)(ii)–(v) for exceptions regarding lines 2 and 5.

Taxable income (line 9 of the worksheet)

Line 9 income is defined in section 1374(d). You figure this income by completing lines 1 through 28 of **Form 1120**, U.S. Corporation Income Tax Return. Include the Form 1120 computation with the worksheet computation you attach to Form 1120S. You do not have to attach the schedules, etc., called for on Form 1120. However, you may want to complete certain Form 1120 schedules, such as Schedule D (Form 1120) if you have capital gains or losses.

Line 25b

If net capital gain, line 10a, Schedule D (Form 1120S), is $25,000 or less, the corporation is not liable for income tax or minimum tax. If the net capital gain is more than $25,000, see Instructions for Part IV, Tax Computation of Schedule D (Form 1120S), to determine if the corporation is liable for income tax or minimum tax.

Line 25c

Section 1371(d) provides that an S corporation is liable for investment credit recapture attributable to credits allowed for tax years for which the corporation was not an S corporation.

Include the corporation's section 47 recapture tax in the total amount to be entered on line 25c. Write to the left of the line 25c total the amount of recapture tax and the words "section 47 tax," and attach **Form 4255**, Recapture of Investment Credit, to Form 1120S.

Schedule A
Cost of Goods Sold and/or Operations

Cost of Operations

If the entry on line 2, page 1 of Form 1120S, is for the cost of operations, complete Schedule A, even if inventories are not used.

Valuation methods

Your inventories can be valued at: (a) cost, (b) cost or market value (whichever is lower), or (c) any other method approved by the Commissioner of Internal Revenue, if that method conforms to the provisions of the applicable regulations cited below.

Taxpayers using erroneous valuation methods must change to a method permitted for Federal income tax purposes. To make this change, file Form 3115. For more information, see regulations section 1.446-1(e)(3) and Rev. Proc. 84-74, 1984-2 C.B. 738.

In line 8a, check the method(s) used for valuing inventories. Under "lower of cost or market," market generally applies to normal market conditions when there is a current bid price prevailing at the date the inventory is valued. When no regular open market exists or when quotations are nominal because of inactive market conditions, use fair market prices from the most reliable sales or purchase transactions that occurred near the date the inventory is valued. For additional requirements, see regulations section 1.471-4.

Inventory may be valued below cost when the merchandise is unsalable at normal prices or unusable in the normal way because the goods are "subnormal" (that is because of damage, imperfections, shop wear, etc.) within the meaning of regulations section 1.471-2(c). Such goods may be valued at a current bona fide selling price less direct cost of disposition (but not less than scrap value) when the taxpayer can establish such a price. See regulations section 1.471-2(c) for additional requirements.

If this is the first year the "Last-in-First-out" (LIFO) inventory method was either adopted or extended to inventory goods not previously valued under the LIFO method, as provided in section 472, attach **Form 970,** Application To Use LIFO Inventory Method, or a statement with Form 1120S and check the LIFO box in line 8b. In line 8c, enter the amount or percent (estimates may be used) of total closing inventories covered under section 472.

If you have changed or extended your inventory method to LIFO and have had to "write up" your opening inventory to cost in the year of election, report the effect of this writeup as income (line 8, page 1) proportionally over a 3-year period that begins in the tax year you made this election. (Section 472(d))

If you are engaged in manufacturing or production, you must use the full absorption method of inventory costing. If you are not using it, you must change to this method. Under it, both direct and certain indirect production costs are included for inventory valuation purposes. Use Form 3115 to change to full absorption. For details, see Rev. Proc. 75-40, 1975-2, C.B. 571, regulations section 1.471-11; and Rev. Rul. 81-272, 1981-2 C.B. 116.

Additional Information

Be sure to answer the questions and provide other information in items G through P. The instructions that follow are keyed to these items.

Question K
Foreign financial accounts

Check the Yes box if either **1.** or **2.** below applies to you. Otherwise, check the No box.

1. At any time during the year, the corporation had an interest in or signature or other authority over a financial account in a foreign country

(such as a bank account, securities account, or other financial account). Exception. Check No if either of the following applies to you:
- The combined value of the accounts was $10,000 or less during the whole year.
- The accounts were with a U.S. military banking facility operated by a U.S. financial institution.

2. The corporation owns more than 50% of the stock in any corporation that would answer the question "Yes" based on Item 1 above.

Get form **TD F 90-22.1,** Report of Foreign Bank and Financial Accounts, to see if the corporation is considered to have an interest in or signature or other authority over a financial account in a foreign country (such as a bank account, securities account, or other financial account).

If question K is checked Yes, file form TD F 90-22.1 by June 30, 1987, with the Department of the Treasury at the address shown on the form. Form TD F 90-22.1 is not a tax return, so do not file it with Form 1120S.

Form TD F 90-22.1 can be obtained from IRS Forms Distribution Centers.

Also, if question K is checked Yes, write the name of the foreign country or countries. Attach a separate sheet if you need more space.

Schedule K and Schedule K-1
Shareholder's Share of Income, Credits, Deductions, etc.

Note: *FY corporations see instructions for "FY Corporations Only" throughout the Specific Instructions for Schedule K and Schedule K-1 before completing the schedules.*

Purpose

Schedule K is a summary schedule of all the shareholders' share of the corporation's income, deductions, credits, etc. Schedule K-1 shows each shareholder's separate share. A copy of each shareholder's K-1 is attached to the Form 1120S filed with the IRS. A copy is kept as a part of the corporation's records, and each shareholder receives his or her own separate copy.

Be sure to give each shareholder a copy of the Shareholder's Instructions for Schedule K-1 (Form 1120S). These instructions are available, separately from Schedule K-1, at most IRS offices. **Note:** Instructions pertinent only to line items reported on Schedule K-1 may be prepared and given to each shareholder in lieu of the instructions printed by IRS.

General Instructions

The corporation is liable for taxes on lines 25a, b, and c, page 1, Form 1120S. Shareholders are liable for income tax on their share of the corporation's income (reduced by any taxes paid by the corporation on income) and must include their share of the income on their tax return whether or not it is distributed to them. Unlike partnership income, S corporation income reported to shareholders on Schedule K-1 is **not** self-employment income and is not subject to self-employment tax.

The total distributive share items (column (b)) of all Schedules K-1 should equal the amount reported on the same line of Schedule K. Lines 1 through 15 of Schedule K correspond to lines 1 through 15 of Schedule K-1. Other lines do not correspond, but instructions will explain the differences.

Substitute Forms

You do not need IRS approval to use a substitute Schedule K-1 if it is an exact facsimile of the IRS schedule, **or** if it contains only those lines the taxpayer is required to use, and the lines have the same numbers and titles and are in the same order as on the comparable IRS Schedule K-1. In either case, your substitute schedule must include the OMB number, and (1) the Shareholder's Instructions for Schedule K-1 (Form 1120S) or (2) instructions pertinent only to the items reported on Schedule K-1 (Form 1120S) may be prepared and given to each shareholder in lieu of the complete Instructions for Schedule K-1 (Form 1120S).

Other substitute Schedules K-1 require approval. You may apply for approval of a substitute form by writing to: Internal Revenue Service, Attention D:R:R, 1111 Constitution Avenue, NW, Washington, DC 20224.

You may be subject to a penalty if you file a substitute Schedule K-1 that does not conform to the specifications of Rev. Proc. 85-3, 1985-1 C.B. 459.

Shareholder's Distributive Share Items

Items of income, loss, deductions, etc., are allocated to a shareholder on a daily basis, according to the number of shares of stock held by the shareholder on each day during the tax year of the corporation. See item A in the **Line-by-Line Instructions.**

A transferee shareholder (rather than the transferor) is considered to be the owner of stock on the day it is transferred.

Special rule—If a shareholder terminates his or her interest in a corporation during the tax year, the corporation, with the concurrence of all shareholders (including the one whose interest is terminated), may elect to allocate income and expenses, etc., as if the corporation's tax year consisted of 2 tax years, the first of which ends on the date of the shareholder's termination. To make the election, the corporation must file a statement of election with the return for the tax year of election and attach a statement of consent signed by all shareholders. If the election is made, write "Section 1377(a)(2) Election Made" at the top of each Schedule K-1. See section 1377(a)(2) and temporary regulations section 18.1377-1 for details.

Specific Instructions
(Schedule K only)

Enter the total distributive amount for each applicable item listed.

Note: *Calendar year filers do not have to complete certain lines on Schedule K. Completion of the lines is optional because the amounts for these lines appear elsewhere on Form 1120S or on other IRS forms or IRS schedules attached to Form 1120S. Although you do not have to complete the optional lines on Schedule K, you do have to complete these lines on Schedule K-1 (Form 1120S). The optional lines are:*

Line 1a. Ordinary income (loss).

Line 3. Net short-term capital gain (loss).

Line 4. Net long-term capital gain (loss).

Line 5. Net gain (loss) under section 1231 (other than due to casualty or theft).

Note: Lines 3, 4, and 5 are not optional if the corporation is subject to the capital gains tax or the tax on excess net passive income

Line 10a. Jobs credit.

Line 11 Other credits (If the other credits appear elsewhere on an IRS Form or Schedule that is attached to Form 1120S).

(Schedule K-1 only)

On each Schedule K-1, enter the names, addresses, and identifying numbers of the shareholder and corporation; all corporations complete items A, B, and C; only FY corporations complete item D through G; and enter the shareholder's distributive share of each item. Schedule K-1 must be prepared and given to each shareholder on or before the day on which Form 1120S is filed.

Note: *Space has been provided below line 19 (Supplemental Schedules) of Schedule K-1 for you to provide information to shareholders. This space, if sufficient, should be used in place of any applicable schedule required for lines 6, 8, 9, 10c, 10d, 11, 12g, 14c, 14d, 14f, 14g, 17, or other amounts not shown in lines 1a through 18 of Schedule K-1. Please be sure to identify the applicable line number next to the information entered below line 19*

Line-by-Line Instructions

Item A (Schedule K-1 only).—If there was no change in shareholders or in the relative interest in stock the shareholders owned during the tax year, enter the percentage of total stock owned by each shareholder during the tax year. For example, if shareholders X and Y each owned 50% for the entire tax year, enter 50% in item A for each shareholder. Each shareholder's distributive share items (lines 1-19 of Schedule K-1) are figured by multiplying the annual amount on the corresponding line of Schedule K by the percentage in A.

If there was a change in stock ownership during the tax year, each shareholder's percentage of ownership is weighted for the number of days in the tax year that stock was owned. For example, A and B each held 50% for half the tax year and A, B, and C held 40%, 40%, and 20%, respectively, for the remaining half of the tax year. The percentage of ownership for the year for A, B, and C is figured as follows and is then entered in item A.

	a % of total stock owned	b % of tax year held	c (a x b) % of ownership for the year	
A	50% 40	50% 50	25% + 20	45%
B	50 40	50 50	25 + 20	45%
C	20	50	10	10%
Total				100%

If there was a change in stock ownership during the tax year, each shareholder's distributive share items (lines 1–19 of Schedule K-1) are figured on a daily basis, based on the percentage of stock held by the shareholder on each day. See section 1377(a)(1) and (2) for details.

Item B (Schedule K-1 only).—Enter the Internal Revenue Service Center address where the tax return, to which a copy of this K-1 was attached, was or will be filed.

Item C (Schedule K-1 only).—Enter the tax shelter registration number assigned to the corporation by IRS or provided to the corporation by other pass-through entities.

FY Corporations Only

Items D through G (Schedule K-1 Only)

Items D–G are only completed by 1986-87 FY corporations. The information provided by items D–G will be used by shareholders to complete their 1987 tax returns.

Item D.—Check the Yes or No box in item D to indicate that the shareholder (for which the Schedule K-1 is completed) did or did not materially participate in the trade or business activity(ies) for which income or loss is reported on line 1a, or a credit(s) related to the activity(ies) is reported on line 11 of Schedule K-1. In general, a taxpayer is treated as materially participating in an activity only if the taxpayer is involved in the operations of the activity on a regular, continuous, and substantial basis. See section 469(h) and related regulations for other details.

If no income or loss is reported on line 1a, do not complete item D.

If income or loss from more than one activity is reported on line 1a, the corporation must complete item D for each line 1a activity. If income or loss from more than one activity is reported on line 1b, it must also complete item E for each line 1b activity. It must also provide the dates requested in item G for each activity. The determination of what constitutes a separate activity is intended to be made in a realistic economic sense. The items D, E, and G information for each activity must be shown separately in the Supplemental Schedules space for line 19, or on an attached schedule if more space is needed.

Item E.—Check the Yes or No box in item E to indicate that the shareholder did or did not actively participate in the rental real estate activity(ies) for which income or loss is reported on line 1b or for which a credit(s) is reported on line 10b, 10c, or 10d of Schedule K-1. Generally, a shareholder is not considered to actively participate in a rental real estate activity if, at any time during the year (or shorter relevant period), the interest of the shareholder and the shareholder's spouse in the activity is less than 10% (by value) of all interests in an activity. For purposes of applying the less than 10% test, separate buildings are treated as separate rental real estate activities unless the degree of integration of the building and other relevant factors indicate they should be treated as parts of a larger activity (for example, an integrated shopping center).

If no income or loss is reported on line 1b, do not complete item E.

If the shareholder owns a 10% or more interest in the corporation, the shareholder will be considered to actively participate in an activity so long as he or she participates, for example, in the making of management decisions or arranging for others to provide services (such as repairs), in a significant and bona fide sense. The material participation standards of regular, continuous, and substantial involvement in operations are not required.

Active participation in a rental real estate activity is not required for the shareholder to take the low-income housing and rehabilitation investment tax credits. The low-income housing credit is reported on line 10b, and qualified rehabilitation expenditures are reported on an attachment for line 10c of Schedule K-1.

The limitations on passive activity losses do not apply to losses of a qualified investor from a qualified low-income housing project for any tax year in the relief period. See section 502 of the Tax Reform Act of 1986 for a definition of qualified investor, qualified low-income housing project, and the relief period. The low-income housing credit may not be taken for any qualified low-income housing project for which losses are allowed by reason of the exception provided in Act section 502. Report these losses on line 6 of Schedules K and K-1.

Items F and G.—Generally, passive activity limitations on losses and credits are phased in between 1987 and 1990. However, the phase-in provisions only apply to losses and credits attributable to pre-enactment interests. Generally, a pre-enactment interest means stock in the corporation held on October 22, 1986, and at all times thereafter. However, stock acquired after October 22, 1986, pursuant to a binding written contract in effect on October 22, 1986, is considered acquired on that date

Except as stated above, ownership interest attributable to stock acquired after October 22, 1986, is not pre-enactment interest. Accordingly, passive activity losses and credits attributable to ownership interest acquired after October 22, 1986, do not qualify for the phase-in provisions

Complete item F for each shareholder who had a stock ownership increase after October 22, 1986, and received distributive share items of income, loss, deductions, or credits attributable to any passive activity started before October 23, 1986. Enter in item F the shareholder's weighted percentage increase in stock ownership after October 22, 1986, based on the number of days in the tax year the increased stock ownership was held. For example, a shareholder held a 20% stock ownership on October 22, 1986, and increased his or her ownership to 60% on December 18, 1986, and the 60% was held until tax year end, February 28, 1987. The 40% increase (60% - 20% = 40%) is weighted by 20% (73 days held divided by 365 in tax year = 20%) and the percentage for item F would be 8% (40% X 20% = 8%).

If a shareholder disposed of stock after October 22, 1986, and later purchased additional stock, thereby restoring his or her basis, the percentage increase for purposes of item F is figured on the difference between the percentage of ownership immediately after the disposition and the percentage of ownership immediately after the later purchase.

If an activity is acquired or started by the corporation after October 22, 1986, the phase-in rule generally does not apply regardless of when the shareholder acquires his or her stock. However, an activity commencing after October 22, 1986, is considered as being conducted on October 22, 1986, if the property used in the activity is acquired pursuant to a

Page 8

binding written contract in effect on August 16, 1986, or construction of such property began on or before that date. See section 469(l) for other details.

Line 1a (Calendar Year Corporations Only).—Enter ordinary income (loss) from line 24, page 1. If line 24 is a loss, enter the shareholder's full share of the loss. Enter the loss without reference to the adjusted basis of the shareholder's stock in the corporation (section 1366(d)) or the shareholder's amount at risk (section 465). Line 1a should reflect the total ordinary income (loss) from all business operations, including section 465 at-risk activities and income (loss) from other activities.

If the corporation is involved in more than one business activity and has a section 465 at-risk activity loss(es), the corporation must show section 465 loss(es) separately. This separate reporting is to assist the shareholder in determining the allowable loss to claim on his or her tax return.

Lines 1a–1d (FY Corporations Only)

Lines 1a.—Enter amount from line 24, page 1. Enter the income or loss without reference to (1) shareholders' basis in the corporation (section 1366(d)), (2) shareholders' section 465 at-risk limitations, or (3) shareholders' section 469 passive activity limitations.

If the corporation is involved in more than one business activity, the corporation must show in the Supplemental Schedules space for line 19 of Schedule K-1, or on an attached schedule if more space is needed, the income or loss separately for:

a. Section 465 at-risk activities. (For losses after 1986, new subsection 465(b)(6)(E) extends the at-risk limitations to the activity of holding real property (except mineral property).)

b. Section 469 passive activities.

The separate statement must show for each activity: (1) the line 1a income or loss and (2) all properly allocable items of income and expense reported on lines 3 through 19 of Schedule K-1.

Separate statements are also required for lines 1b and 1c if income or loss from more than one activity is reported on these lines.

Also, if the corporation is involved in only one passive activity and line 3, 4, or 5 of Schedule K-1 contains (1) gain or loss attributable to the passive activity and (2) portfolio gain or loss, the corporation must show the gain or loss attributable to the passive activity separately in the Supplemental Schedules space for line 19, or on an attached schedule if more space is needed.

Line 1b.—Enter any gain or loss from rental real estate activities of the corporation. Do not report on line 1b (for shareholders that are qualified investors) certain loss(es) from a qualified low-income housing project. Report such loss(es) on line 6 of Schedule K-1 and attach a statement identifying the loss. See Item E above and section 502 of the Act for definitions and other information on qualified low-income housing projects. **Note:** The gain from a qualified project is reported on line 1b for all shareholders, and the gain or loss for all nonqualified investor shareholders and all nonqualified projects is also reported on line 1b.

Line 1c.—Enter income or loss from rental activities other than that reported on line 1b (or line 6 as explained in line 1b above).

Line 1d.—Enter portfolio income. See the instructions for "Page 1 Changes" at the beginning of the Specific Instructions for an explanation of portfolio income.

Line 2.—Enter the qualifying dividends received from other domestic corporations for which each shareholder is entitled to an exclusion under section 116. The investment companies will tell the S corporation what part, if any, of the dividends qualify for the exclusion. (See the instructions for Form 1120S, page 1, line 4.)

Line 5.—Enter net gain (loss) under section 1231. Do not include net gains or losses from involuntary conversions due to casualties or thefts on this line. Instead, report them on line 6.

Note: If there was a gain (loss) from a casualty or theft to property not used in a trade or business or used for income producing purposes, do not complete Form 4684 for this type of casualty or theft. Instead, provide each shareholder with the needed information to complete their own Form 4684 for their portion of this casualty or theft.

Line 6.—Enter any other items of income or loss not included on lines 1–5, such as:

a. Wagering gains and losses (section 165(d)).

b. Recoveries of bad debts, prior taxes, or delinquency amounts (section 111).

c. Any gain or loss where the corporation was a trader or dealer in section 1256 contracts or property related to such contracts. See sections 1256(f) and 1374(c)(4).

d. Net gain (loss) from involuntary conversions due to casualty or theft.

e. Loss(es) from qualified low-income housing projects for shareholders that are qualified investors.

f. Income or loss from a working interest in any oil or gas property as defined in section 469(c)(3). See "Page 1 Changes (FY Corporations Only)" at the beginning of the Specific Instructions.

Line 7.—Enter the total amount of charitable contributions paid by the corporation during its tax year. Attach an itemized list that separately shows the corporation's charitable contributions subject to the 50%, 30%, and 20% limitations.

If the corporation contributes property other than cash and the aggregate amount of the claimed value exceeds $500, **Form 8283**, Noncash Charitable Contributions, must be completed and attached to Form 1120S. The corporation must give a copy of its Form 8283 to every shareholder if the value of an item or group of similar items of contributed property exceeds $5,000 even though the amount allocated to each shareholder is $5,000 or less. For property that does not meet the $5,000 filing requirement, the corporation does not have to furnish the shareholders with its Form 8283. However, the corporation must provide shareholders with their share of fair market value for property valued between $500 and $5,000 in order for individual shareholders to complete their own Form 8283. See the Instructions for Form 8283 for more information.

If the corporation made a qualified conservation contribution under section 170(h), also include the fair market value of the underlying property before and after the donation, the type of legal interest contributed, and describe the conservation purpose furthered by the donation. Give a copy of this information to each shareholder.

Line 8.—A 1986 calendar year corporation (FY corporations see below) may elect to expense part of the cost (up to $5,000) of recovery property that qualifies for investment credit that the corporation purchased this year for use in its trade or business. The corporation may not deduct the section 179 expense, but should report the expense separately on Schedules K and K-1, line 8.

The corporation must specify the item(s) of section 179 property which it elects to treat as an expense and the portion of the cost of each item which is being treated as an expense. Do this on Form 4562 and on a schedule attached to Schedule K-1. Generally, any election made under section 179 may not be revoked except with the consent of the Commissioner of IRS.

FY Corporations.—Generally, for section 179 property placed in service after 1986, the amount the corporation may elect to expense was increased from $5,000 to $10,000. However, the $10,000 limit may be reduced by other factors. See Instructions for new Form 4562A, Part I, for details. The corporation must provide each shareholder with the necessary information so that he or she can complete Part I of his or her Form 4562A.

Depreciation, amortization, or investment credit may not be taken on any amount for which a deduction is allowed under section 179.

Line 9.—Enter any other deductions not included on lines 7 and 8, such as:

a. Amounts (other than investment interest required to be reported on lines 13a (2) and 13a(3) of Schedules K and K-1, and the portion of line 13a(1) of Schedules K and K-1 deductible under section 162) paid by the corporation that would be itemized deductions on any of the shareholder's income tax returns if they were paid directly by a shareholder for the same purpose. These amounts include, but are not limited to, expenses under section 212 for the production of income other than from the corporation's trade or business.

b. Any penalty on early withdrawal of savings because the corporation withdrew funds from its time savings deposit before its maturity.

c. Soil and water conservation expenditures (section 175).

d. Expenditures paid or incurred for the removal of architectural and transportation barriers to the elderly and handicapped which the corporation has elected to treat as a current expense. Do not deduct these expenditures on page 1 of Form 1120S. See section 190.

If there was a gain (loss) from a casualty or theft to property not used in a trade or business or for income producing purposes, provide each shareholder with the needed information to complete **Form 4684,** Casualties and Thefts.

Page 9

148

Credits

Line 10a.—Enter on line 10a of Schedule K the jobs credit computed by the corporation that is not attributable to a passive activity. If the corporation has a jobs credit for a nonpassive activity and a passive activity, separate computations may have to be made by each shareholder to determine the credit for each. Enter on line 10d or 11 the jobs credit attributable to passive activities. The jobs credit is figured on Form 5884 and the form(s) is attached to Form 1120S. See Form 5884 for details on how the jobs credit was extended and modified for qualified employees hired after 1985.

Enter each shareholder's share of the jobs credit on lines 10a, 10d, or 11 of Schedule K-1.

Line 10b (FY Corporations Only).—Enter on line 10b the low-income housing credit figured by the corporation. The credit is figured at the corporate level on Form 8586 and the form is attached to Form 1120S. The credit is based on qualified expenditures made after 12-31-86. See Form 8586 for other details on the credit.

The credit is not allowed for any qualified low-income housing projects for which losses are allowed by reason of the exception in section 502 of the Tax Reform Act of 1986. See section 502 of the Act and the instructions for Item E of Schedule K-1 for more information.

Line 10c (FY Corporations Only).—Do not enter an amount on line 10c of Schedules K and K-1. Instead, for line 10c of Schedule K, complete the applicable lines of Form 3468 that apply to qualified rehabilitation expenditures for property related to rental real estate activities of the corporation for which income or loss is reported on line 1b of Schedule K. See Form 3468 for details on qualified rehabilitation expenditures. Attach Form 3468 to Form 1120S.

For line 10c of Schedule K-1, show in the Supplemental Schedules space for line 19 of Schedule K-1, or on an attached statement if more space is needed, a listing of the shareholder's distributive share of the corporation's qualified rehabilitation expenditures for property related to rental real estate activities for which income or loss is reported on line 1b of Schedule K-1.

Note: *Qualified rehabilitation expenditures for property that is not related to rental real estate activities must be listed separately as follows: (1) If the expenditures relate to passive activities for which income or loss is reported on lines 1a or 1c of Schedule K-1, show these expenditures separately in a schedule for line 11 of Schedule K-1. (2) If the expenditures relate to nonpassive activities for which income or loss is reported on line 1a of Schedule K-1, show the expenditures with other investment credit property listed for line 17 of Schedule K-1.*

Line 10d (FY Corporations Only).—Show on line 10d of Schedule K, or list separately on an attached statement if more than one credit is involved, all other credits (other than credits for line 10b or 10c) related to rental real estate activities. These credits may include any type credit listed in the line 11 instruction.

Show on line 10d of Schedule K-1, or list separately in the Supplemental Schedules space for line 19 of Schedule K-1 if more than one credit is involved, the shareholder's distributive share of all other credits (other than credits for line 10b or 10c) related to rental real estate activities. These credits may include any type credit listed in the line 11 instruction.

Line 11.—Show on line 11 of Schedule K, or list separately if more than one credit is involved, all other credits (other than credits or expenditures shown or listed for lines 10a through 10d of Schedule K or on Form 3468 attached to Schedule k). Show on line 11 of Schedule K-1, or in the Supplemental Schedules space for line 19 if more than one credit is involved, each shareholder's distributive share of all other credits (other than credits or expenditures shown or listed for lines 10a through 10d and 17 of Schedule K-1). See the listing below for types of credits or other information that could be involved.

If both passive activity and nonpassive activity credits are reported for line 11 of Schedules K and K-1, list the credits separately. Identify the passive activity (i.e., line 1a or 1c) to which any passive activity credit relates. Include any investment credit property related to passive activites in the listing for line 11. Include investment credit property related to nonpassive activities separately in a listing for line 17 of Schedule K-1.

The following credits are also figured at the corporate level and then apportioned to persons who are shareholders of the corporation in accordance with stock ownership:

1. Credit for alcohol used as fuel. Complete and attach **Form 6478**, Credit for Alcohol Used as Fuel, to Form 1120S.
2. Orphan drug credit and credit for increasing research activities. Complete and attach **Form 6765,** Credit for Increasing Research Activities (or for claiming the orphan drug credit), to Form 1120S.
3. Nonconventional source fuel credit.
4. Unused regular investment credit from cooperatives.
5. Unused energy investment credit from cooperatives.
6. Credit for backup withholding on dividends, interest, or patronage dividends.

The nonconventional source fuel credit is figured by the corporation on a separate schedule prepared by the corporation. This computation schedule must also be attached to Form 1120S. See section 29 for computation provisions and other special rules for figuring this credit.

If the corporation is a member of a cooperative that passes an unused regular investment credit or unused energy investment credit through to its members, these credits are in turn passed through to the corporation's shareholders.

If the corporation has only one of the above 6 credits, enter the amount of the credit in the amount column of line 11 and identify the type of credit in the space to the left of the amount. If the corporation has more than one credit, enter the total credits on line 11 and identify and list the amount(s) of the credits on an attached schedule.

Tax Preference and Adjustment Items

Lines 12a through 12g.—Enter items of income and deductions that are tax preference or adjustment items. See **Form 6251**, Alternative Minimum Tax Computation, and **Publication 909**, Alternative Minimum Tax, to determine the amounts to enter and for other information.

Do not include as a tax preference item any qualified expenditures to which an election under section 58(i) may apply.

Note: *The Act revised, deleted, or relocated provisions in sections 55 through 58 that provide for computation of the alternative minimum tax. New and revised provisions are in new sections 55 through 59. Generally, the changes are effective for tax years beginning after 1986, but the changes do affect the 1986-87 FY corporations and the information that must be reported to shareholders to allow them to figure the alternative minimum tax for their 1987 tax years. See instructions for lines 12a, b, c, and g below for details.*

Lines 12a and 12b.—Figure the preference items for lines 12a and 12b based only on property placed in service before 1987.

If the corporation elects to use the new depreciation provisions (new Form 4562A) for property placed in service after July 31, 1986, and before January 1, 1987, see the Instructions for Form 4562A for information on figuring the lines 12a and 12b preferences for this property.

Line 12c.—FY corporations figure the adjustment item for line 12c based only on property placed in service after December 31, 1986. Generally, accelerated depreciation on real property placed in service after 1986 is the excess of the tax depreciation taken over alternative depreciation. See section 168 for a definition of alternative depreciation. Generally, accelerated depreciation on personal property placed in service after 1986 is the excess of the tax depreciation taken over the 150% declining balance method. The adjustment applies to leased personal property and to personal property which is not leased. See the instructions for Form 4562A for more information.

Line 12d.—Do not include any depletion on oil and gas wells. The shareholders must compute their depletion deduction separately under section 613A.

In the case of mines, wells, and other natural deposits, other than oil and gas wells, enter the amount by which the deduction for depletion under section 611 (including percentage depletion for geothermal deposits) is more than the adjusted basis of such property at the end of the tax year. Figure the adjusted basis without regard to the depletion deduction and figure the excess separately for each property.

Lines 12e(1) and 12e(2).—Generally, the amounts to be entered on these lines are not the total corporation income or deductions for oil, gas, and geothermal properties. Generally, they are only the income and deductions included on page 1 Form 1120S, that are used to figure the amount on line 24, page 1, Form 1120S

If there are any items of income or deductions for oil, gas, and geothermal properties included in the amounts that are required to be passed through separately to the shareholders on Schedule K-1, give each shareholder a schedule for the line on which the income or deduction is included and which shows the amount of income or deductions included in the total amount for that line. Do not include any of these direct pass-through amounts on lines 12e(1) or 12e(2). The shareholder is told in the Shareholder's Instructions for Schedule K-1 (Form 1120S) to adjust the amounts on lines 12e(1) and 12e(2) for any other income or deductions from oil, gas, or geothermal properties included in lines 1c through 9 and 19 of Schedule K-1 in order to determine the total income or deductions from oil, gas, and geothermal properties for the corporation.

Figure the amount for lines 12e(1) and 12e(2) separately for oil and gas properties which are not geothermal deposits and for all properties which are geothermal deposits.

Give the shareholders a schedule that shows the separate amounts that are included in the computation of the amounts on lines 12e(1) and 12e(2).

Line 12e(1).—Enter the aggregate amount of gross income (within the meaning of section 613(a)) from all oil, gas, and geothermal properties received or accrued during the tax year that was included on page 1, Form 1120S.

Line 12e(2). — Enter the amount of any deductions allocable to oil, gas, and geothermal properties reduced by the excess intangible drilling costs that were included on page 1, Form 1120S, on properties for which the corporation made an election to expense intangible drilling costs in tax years beginning before January 1, 1983. Do not include nonproductive well costs, or the amounts shown on lines 16a, 16b, 17a, and 17b, page 1, Form 1120S. Instead, use the amounts on lines 16c and 17c, page 1, Form 1120S.

Figure excess intangible drilling costs as follows: From the allowable intangible drilling and development costs (except for costs in drilling a nonproductive well), subtract the amount that would have been allowable if the corporation had capitalized these costs and either amortized them over the 120 months that started when production began, or treated them according to any election the corporation made under section 57(d)(2).

See section 57(a)(11) for more information.

Lines 12f(1) and 12f(2). Qualified Investment Income and Expenses.—Enter the corporation's qualified investment income and expenses from all sources that were included on page 1, Form 1120S. However, do not include as qualified investment expense the amounts shown on lines 16a, 16b, 17a, and 17b, page 1, Form 1120S. Instead, use the amounts on lines 16c and 17c, page 1, Form 1120S. See Form 6251 to determine the amounts to enter.

If there are any items of qualified investment income or expenses included in the amounts that are required to be passed through separately to the shareholders on Schedule K-1, give each shareholder a schedule for the line on which the qualified investment income or expense is included

which shows the amount of qualified investment income or expense included in the total amount for that line. Do not include any of these direct pass-through amounts on lines 12f(1) or 12f(2). The shareholder is told in the Shareholder's Instructions for Schedule K-1 (Form 1120S) to adjust the amounts on lines 12f(1) and 12f(2) for any other qualified investment income or expenses included in lines 2 through 9 and line 19 in order to determine the total qualified investment income or expense for the corporation.

Generally, investment income is gross income from interest, nonqualifying dividends, rents and royalties, and any other amount treated as ordinary income under sections 1245, 1250, and 1254 that is reported on page 1, Form 1120S.

Generally, investment expenses are those expenses allowable against the production of investment income provided they are allowed in figuring a shareholder's adjusted gross income and not includible as a tax preference item.

Note: *For the calendar year, if a shareholder does not actively participate in the management of the corporation, qualified investment income and expenses include income and expenses from the corporation's trade or business. See section 55(e)(8).*

Line 12g.—Attach a schedule which shows each shareholder's share of:

● Amortization of certified pollution control facilities. Enter the amount by which the amortization the corporation took for 1986 is more than the depreciation deduction otherwise allowable.

● Reserves for losses on bad debts of financial institutions. Enter the corporation's share of the excess of the addition to the reserve for bad debts over the reasonable addition to the reserve for bad debts that would have been allowable if the corporation had maintained the bad debt reserve for all tax years based on actual experience.

● Any other applicable tax preference items not shown on lines 12a through 12f.

FY corporations attach a schedule which shows each shareholder's share of the preference items discussed in the line 12g instructions above **and** the following preference and adjustment items:

● Completed contract method of accounting for long-term contracts.—Use of the percentage of completion method is required for minimum tax purposes. See section 56(a)(3) and the 1987 Form 6251 for more information.

● Installment method of accounting.—Applies to use of installment method for dealer sales and sales of trade or business or rental property where the purchase price exceeds $150,000. See section 56(a)(6) and the 1987 Form 6251 for more information.

● Charitable contributions of appreciated property.—Provide shareholders with their distributive share of the amount of the difference between the fair market value of capital gain property donated by the corporation to a charitable organization after August 15, 1986, and the corporation's adjusted basis in the donated property. See section 57(a)(6).

● Losses from passive farming activities.—No loss from any tax shelter

farm activity is allowed for minimum tax purposes. See section 58(a) and the 1987 Form 6251 for information on this adjustment item.

● Passive activity loss.—Provide shareholders with any needed information (in addition to the information given in items D through G and on lines 1a through 1c of Schedule K-1) to figure this adjustment item. See section 58(b) for more information.

Investment Interest
(FY Corporations Only)

Effective for tax years beginning after 1986, section 163 limitations on investment interest are revised. Thus, the information on investment interest that the 1986-87 FY corporation reports to its shareholders for their use in preparing their 1987 tax returns must take into account certain changes made to section 163. See new subsection 163(d)(4) for a definition of investment income and investment expenses. Special attention must be given to section 163(d)(4)(D), which states that investment income and expenses do not include income and expenses used in figuring the income or loss of a passive activity. Where the corporation has a trade or business passive activity in which some shareholders materially participate and other shareholders do not, the reporting of investment income and expenses may be different for each shareholder.

Lines 13a through 13c(2).—Enter the interest on investment indebtedness, items of investment income and expenses, and gains and losses from the sale or exchange of investment property on these lines as applicable.

The interest expense reported on line 13a(1) may also be included on page 1, Form 1120S, line 16c, or Schedules K and K-1, line 9. However, the interest expense reported on line 13a(2) and 13a(3) must not appear elsewhere on the return other than on lines 16a and 16b, page 1, Form 1120S. The income and expenses included on lines 13b and 13c are reported on Form 1120S and Schedule K-1. For example, interest income included on line 13b is reported on Form 1120S, line 4.

For more information, see **Form 4952**, Investment Interest Expense Deduction.

Line 13a(1).—Enter investment interest expense from all sources on debts created before December 17, 1969, from a specific item of property for a specified term. Also include debts in existence after December 16, 1969, if a binding contract was in effect on that date.

Line 13a(2).—Enter investment interest expense from all sources, from a specific item of property for a specified term, and from debts incurred before September 11, 1975, but after December 16, 1969, that is included on line 16b, page 1, Form 1120S. Also include interest on obligations incurred after September 10, 1975, but subject to a written contract or commitment in effect on September 11, 1975, that is included on line 16b, page 1, Form 1120S.

Line 13a(3).—Enter investment interest expense from all sources from obligations incurred after September 10, 1975, that is included on line 16b, page 1, Form 1120S.

Do not include those obligations for which a binding contract was in effect on September 11, 1975.

Note: *The corporation must have an amount on line 16b of page 1, Form 1120S, in order to have an amount shown on either line 13a(2) or 13a(3).*

Line 13b(1).—Enter the corporation's investment income from all sources that was included on page 1, Form 1120S.

Investment income includes the following that are includible in gross income on page 1, Form 1120S: interest, nonqualifying dividends, rents from net lease property, royalties, and amounts recaptured as ordinary income from the sale or exchange of investment property subject to sections 1245, 1250, and 1254 provisions. Investment income generally does not include any amounts connected with a trade or business. See section 163(d)(3).

Caution: The amount to be entered on this line is not the total corporate investment income. It is only the investment income included on page 1, Form 1120S, that is used to figure the amount on line 24, page 1, Form 1120S.

If there are any items of investment income included in the amounts that are required to be passed through separately to the shareholders on Schedule K-1, give each shareholder a schedule showing the amount of investment income and the line for which such income is included. Do not include any of these direct pass-through amounts on line 13b(1) of Schedules K and K-1. The shareholder is told in the Shareholder's Instructions for Schedule K-1 (Form 1120S) to adjust the amount on line 13b(1) for any other investment income included in lines 1d through 9 to determine the total investment income for this corporation.

Line 13b(2).—Enter the corporation's investment expenses from all sources that were included on page 1, Form 1120S.

Note: The amount to be entered on this line is not the total corporate investment expenses. It is only the investment expenses included on page 1, Form 1120S, that are used to figure the amount on line 24, page 1, Form 1120S.

Investment expenses are those deductions directly connected with the production of investment income. Interest is not included in investment expenses for this purpose. Depreciation is limited to the amount figured using the straight-line method. Depletion is limited to an amount based on cost. Investment expenses generally do not include any amounts connected with a trade or business. See section 163(d)(3).

If there are any items of investment expense included in the amounts that are required to be passed through separately to the shareholders on Schedule K-1, give each shareholder a schedule for the line on which the investment expense is included which shows the amount of investment expenses included in the total amount for that line. Do not include any of these direct pass-through amounts on line 13b(2). The shareholder is told in the Shareholder's Instructions for Schedule K-1 (Form 1120S) to adjust the amount on line 13b(2) for any other

investment expenses included on lines 1d through 9 to determine the total investment expenses for this corporation.

Lines 13c(1) and (2).—Enter the corporation's income and expenses from net lease property if the expenses for each property subject to a net lease, allowable under sections 162, 163 (without any reduction for the limitations of section 163(d)), 164(a)(1) and (2), and 212, are more than the income produced by this property. Do not include the income or expenses for any property if the income exceeds the expenses.

For a definition of net lease property, see Form 4952.

Foreign Taxes

Lines 14a through 14g.—In addition to the Instructions below, see **Form 1116,** Computation of Foreign Tax Credit—Individual, Fiduciary, or Nonresident Alien Individual, and the related instructions.

Note: *FY corporations must provide their shareholders with information (in addition to lines 14a through 14g information) needed to comply with revised tax law provisions regarding the computation of the foreign tax credit for tax years beginning after 1986. See revised section 904(d) for details.*

Line 14a.—Enter the type of income earned as follows:

● Nonbusiness (section 904(d)) interest income

● Qualified dividends from an IC-DISC or former DISC

● Qualified dividends from a FSC or former FSC

● All other income from sources outside the U.S. (including income from sources in U.S. possessions)

If, for the country or U.S. possession shown on line 14b, the corporation had more than one type of income, enter "More than one type" and attach a schedule for each type of income for lines 14b through 14g.

Line 14b.—Enter the name of the foreign country or U.S. possession. If, for the type of income shown on line 14a, the corporation had income from, or paid taxes to, more than one foreign country or U.S. possession, enter "More than one foreign country or U.S. possession" and attach a schedule for each country for lines 14a and 14c through 14g.

Line 14c.—Enter in U.S. dollars the total gross income from sources outside the U.S. Attach a schedule that shows each type of income as follows:

● Dividends

● Gross rents and royalties

● Foreign source capital gain net income

● Wages, salaries, and other employee compensation

● Business or profession

● Gross income from trust and estates

● Other (including interest) (specify)

Line 14d.—Enter in U.S. dollars the total applicable deductions and losses. Attach a schedule that shows each type of deduction or loss as follows:

● Expenses directly allocable to business or profession

● Depreciation and depletion directly allocable to rent and royalty income

● Repairs and other expenses directly allocable to rent and royalty income

● Other expenses directly allocable to specific income items (specify)

● Pro rata share of all other deductions not directly allocable to specific items of income

● Losses from foreign sources

Line 14e.—Enter in U.S. dollars the total foreign taxes (described in section 901) that were accrued by the corporation or paid to foreign countries or U.S. possessions. Attach a schedule that shows the date(s) the taxes were paid or accrued, and the amount in both foreign currency and in U.S. dollars, as follows:

● Taxes withheld at source on dividends

● Taxes withheld at source on rents and royalties

● Other foreign taxes paid or accrued

Line 14f.—Enter in U.S. dollars the total reduction in taxes available for credit. Attach a schedule that shows separately the:

● Reduction for foreign mineral income

● Reduction for failure to furnish returns required under section 6038

● Reduction for taxes attributable to boycott operations (section 908)

● Reduction for foreign oil and gas extraction income (section 907(a))

● Reduction for any other items (specify)

Line 14g.—Enter in U.S. dollars any items not covered in lines 14c, 14d, 14e, and 14f.

Line 15 (Schedule K-1).—Enter total distributions made to each shareholder other than dividends reported on line 17 of Schedule K. Noncash distributions of appreciated property are valued at fair market value. See Schedules L and M instructions for ordering rules on distributions.

Line 17 (Schedule K).—Enter total dividends paid to shareholders from accumulated earnings and profits contained in retained earnings (line 26 of Schedule L). Report these dividends to shareholders on Form 1099-DIV. Do not report them on Schedule K-1.

Property Eligible for Investment Credit

Generally, for property placed in service after 1985, the regular investment credit has been repealed. See the Instructions for **Form 3468,** Computation of Investment Credit, for exceptions and other details.

Complete the applicable parts of Form 3468 for property that continues to qualify for the regular investment credit and for the energy investment credit. Attach Form 3468 to Form 1120S.

Line 17 (Schedule K-1).—Show in the Supplemental Schedules space for line 19 of Schedule K-1, or on an attached schedule if more space is needed, each shareholder's share of the corporation's investment in property that:

(1) Is attributable to activities that are not passive activities, and

(2) Continues to qualify for the regular investment credit. This property includes certain transition property, qualified timber property, qualified progress expenditure property, and qualified rehabilitation expenditures. Also show the corporation's investment

in business energy property (used in passive activities) that qualifies for the business energy investment credit.

The corporation must reduce the basis of regular and energy credit property by any credit allowable for the property. See section 48(q) and **Publication 572,** Investment Credit, regarding adjustments to be made to the basis of investment credit property as well as the shareholders' adjusted basis in stock of the corporation.

Property Subject to Recapture of Investment Credit

Line 18 (Schedule K-1).—Complete line 18 when regular or energy investment credit property is disposed of, ceases to qualify, or if there is a decrease in the business percentage before the end of the "life-years category" or "recovery period" assigned. For more information, see Form 4255, Publication 572, and section 48(q).

The corporation itself is liable for investment credit recapture in certain cases. See instructions for line 25c, page 1, Form 1120S, for details.

Other Items

Line 16 (Schedule K).—Attach a statement to Schedule K to report the corporation's total income, expenditures, or other information for items a through j of the line 19 instruction below.

Line 19 (Schedule K-1).—Enter in the Supplemental Schedules space for line 19 of Schedule K-1, or on an attached schedule if more space is needed, each shareholder's share of any information asked for on lines 6, 8, 9, 10c, 10d, 11, 12g, 14c, 14d, 14f, 14g, 17, and items **a** through **j** below. Please identify the applicable line number next to the information entered in the Supplemental Schedules space. Show income or gains as a positive number. Show losses with the number in parentheses.

a. Tax-exempt income realized by the corporation. Corporations should report tax-exempt interest separately to assist shareholders in figuring the taxable portion (if any) of their social security or railroad retirement benefits.

b. Nondeductible expenses incurred by the corporation.

c. Taxes paid on undistributed capital gains by a regulated investment company. As a shareholder of a regulated investment company, the corporation will receive notice on **Form 2439,** Notice to Shareholder of Undistributed Long-Term Capital Gains, that the company paid tax on undistributed capital gains.

d. Gross income and other information relating to oil and gas well properties that are reported to shareholders to allow them to figure the depletion deduction for oil and gas well properties. See section 613A(c)(13) for details.
The corporation cannot deduct depletion on oil and gas wells. The shareholders must determine the allowable amount to report on his or her return. See Publication 535 for more information.

e. Recapture of section 179 expense deduction. Enter the amount that was originally passed through and the corporation's tax year in which it was passed through. Tell the shareholder if the recapture amount was caused by the

disposition of the recovery property. See section 179(d)(10) for more information. Do not include this amount on line 8, page 1, Form 1120S.

f. Total qualified expenditures (and the period paid or incurred during the tax year) to which an election under section 58(i) applies. Do not report these expenditures as tax preference items on line 12 of Schedules K and K-1.

g. Intangible drilling costs under section 263(c). See Publication 535 to determine the amount to pass through to each shareholder.

h. Deduction and recapture of certain mining exploration expenditures paid or incurred (section 617).

i. Any information or statements the corporation is required to furnish to shareholders to allow them to comply with requirements under section 6111 (registration of tax shelters) or 6661 (substantial understatement of tax).

j. Any other information the shareholders need to prepare their tax returns.

Schedules L and M

Note: *Lines 23 through 27 of Schedule L were revised for 1986.*
The balance sheets must agree with your books and records. Include certificates of deposit as cash on line 1 of Schedule L. The following rules apply in determining the balances of lines 23 through 27 of Schedule L and amounts used in figuring lines 1 through 9 of Schedule M.

If Schedule L, column (c), amounts for lines 23, 24, or 25 are not the same as corresponding amounts on line 9 of Schedule M, attach a schedule explaining any differences. For example, the balance of the accumulated adjustments account (line 23) may differ if Schedule L reflects straight-line depreciation and some other method is used for purposes of line 2 of Schedule M. You may show your explanation below Schedule M if there is sufficient space.

Note: *Schedule M does not provide for a reconciliation of book income to tax return income. However, you may want to make your own separate reconciliation of book income or (loss) to tax return income or (loss). Make sure that all items of income, loss, and deductions reported on page 1, Form 1120S, and on Schedule K of Form 1120S, are used in figuring lines 2, 3, 5, 6, and 7 of Schedule M.*

Line 23.—The "accumulated adjustments account" (AAA) is to be maintained by all S corporations. At the end of the tax year, if the corporation **does not have accumulated earnings and profits (E&P),** the AAA is determined by taking into account all items of income, loss, and deductions for the tax year (including nontaxable income and nondeductible losses and expenses). See section 1368 for other details. After the year-end income and expense adjustments are made, the account is reduced by distributions made during the tax year. See the Distributions instruction below for distribution rules.

At the end of the tax year, if the corporation **has accumulated E&P,** the AAA is determined by taking into account the taxable income, deductible losses and expenses, and nondeductible losses and expenses for the tax year. Adjustments for

nontaxable income are made to the other adjustments account as explained in the Line 24 instruction below. See section 1368. After the year-end income and expense adjustments are made, the account is reduced by distributions made during the tax year. See the Distributions instruction below for distribution rules.
Note: *The AAA may have a negative balance at year end. See section 1368(e).*

Line 24.—The "other adjustments" account is maintained only by corporations that **have** accumulated E&P at year end. The account is adjusted for tax-exempt income (and related expenses) of the corporation. See section 1368. After adjusting for tax-exempt income, the account is reduced for any distributions made during the year. See the Distributions instructions below.

Line 25.—The "shareholders' undistributed taxable income previously taxed" account, also called previously taxed income (PTI), is only maintained if the corporation had a balance in this account at the start of its 1986 tax year. If there is a beginning balance for the 1986 tax year, no adjustments are made to the account except to reduce the account for distributions made under section 1375(d) (as in effect before the enactment of the Subchapter S Revision Act of 1982). See Distributions instruction below for the order of distributions from the account.

Each shareholder's right to nontaxable distributions from PTI is personal and cannot be transferred to another person. The corporation is required to keep records of each shareholder's net share of PTI. See regulations section 1.1375-4(d) for more information.

Line 26.—Enter retained earnings other than that reported on lines 23, 24, and 25. Other retained earnings include the appropriated and unappropriated retained earnings accumulated in prior years when the S corporation was a C corporation (section 1361(a)(2)) or a small business corporation prior to 1983 (section 1371 of prior law). Generally, the S corporation has a balance on line 26 only if it had ending balances in appropriated or unappropriated retained earnings prior to 1986 (lines 23 and 24 of Schedule L of the 1985 Form 1120S or Form 1120).

If the corporation maintained separate accounts for appropriated and unappropriated retained earnings, it may want to continue such accounting for purposes of preparing its financial balance sheet. Also, if the corporation converts to C corporation status in a subsequent year, it will be required to report its retained earnings on separate lines of Schedule L of Form 1120.

If line 26 has a beginning balance for 1986, and the account contains accumulated earnings and profits (E&P), the only adjustments made to accumulated E&P are:
(1) reductions for dividend distributions,
(2) adjustments for redemptions, liquidations, reorganizations, etc., and
(3) reductions for section 47 recapture tax for which the corporation is liable.

See Distributions instruction below regarding distributions from retained earnings and section 1371(c) for other details.

Page 13

Check the box below line 26 if the corporation was a C corporation in a prior year(s) and has subchapter C earnings and profits (E&P) at the close of its 1986 tax year. For this purpose, "subchapter C E&P" means E&P of any corporation for any tax year when it was not an S corporation. See sections 1362(d)(3)(B) and 312 for other details. If the corporation has subchapter C E&P, it may be liable for tax imposed on excess net passive income. See instructions for line 25a, page 1, of Form 1120S for details on this tax.

Line 27.—Combine lines 23 through 26, column (a) and column (c), and enter the totals in line 27, column (b) and column (d) In most cases, the totals should equal the beginning and ending balances of the corporation's retained earnings shown in it's general ledger. If line 27, column (d), does not agree with the corporation's books, attach a schedule explaining the differences. **Note:** The schedule asked for at the top of Schedule M, Form 1120S, will usually explain any net differences. If so, an additional schedule is not required.

Distributions
Generally, property distributions (including cash) are applied to reduce balance sheet equity accounts in the following order:

a. Reduce AAA. If distributions during the tax year exceed the AAA at the close of the tax year, the AAA is allocated pro rata to each distribution made during the tax year. See section 1368(c).
b. Reduce shareholders' PTI account for any section 1375(d) (as in effect before January 1, 1983) distributions.
c. Reduce retained earnings accounts to the extent of accumulated E&P.
d. Reduce the other adjustments account.
e. Reduce any remaining shareholders' equity accounts.

If a section 1368(e)(3) election is made, distributions are made from the retained earnings account before the AAA. If the corporation has PTI and wants to make distributions from retained earnings before PTI, the election under regulations section 1.1375-4(c) must be made. In the case of either election, after all accumulated earnings and profits in the retained earnings are distributed, the above general order of distributions applies except that item c is eliminated.

Changes Made by the Act

1986 Calendar Year Changes
Investment Credit
Generally, for property placed in service after 1985, the regular investment credit has been repealed. See **Form 3468,** Computation of Investment Credit, for exceptions and other details. The business energy investment tax credit for solar, geothermal, ocean thermal, biomass, and wind property has been extended for tax years after 1985. See Form 3468 for details.

Targeted Jobs Credit
The jobs credit for hiring members of certain targeted groups has been extended and modified. For employees hired after 1985, a credit is allowed only for "first-year

wages" paid to a qualified employee. See **Form 5884,** Jobs Credit, for other information.

Research Credit
The tax credit for increasing research has been extended for 3 more years, and the manner of computing the credit was revised. Additionally, the credit was made a part of the general business tax credit. See **Form 6765,** Credit for Increasing Research Activities (or claiming the orphan drug credit), for more information.

Long-Term Contracts
For long-term contracts entered into after February 28, 1986, all costs (including research and experimental costs attributable to the contract) must be allocated to the contract as set forth in section 451. Expenses for unsuccessful bids and proposals and marketing, selling, and advertising expenses are not considered attributable to long-term contracts. Production period interest expenses attributable to long-term contracts are to be capitalized under the rules of new section 263A. For exceptions, definitions, and other information, see new section 460.

Deduction for Removing Barriers to the Handicapped
The election to deduct expenses for the removal of architectural barriers to the handicapped and elderly, scheduled to expire at the end of 1985, was permanently extended.

Penalty for Failure To Furnish Statements
The maximum penalty for failure to furnish copies of Schedule K-1 to shareholders has been increased. The maximum amount that can be imposed in any calendar year is increased from $50,000 to $100,000. If a Schedule K-1 given to a shareholder does not include all of the information required to be shown or includes incorrect information, an additional penalty of $5 for each Schedule K-1 may be imposed. See sections 6722 and 6723 for details.

1986–87 FY Changes
Passive Activity Limitations
New Code section 469, added by the Act, provides for limitations on losses and credits from passive activities. Generally, a passive activity is any activity of the S corporation which involves the conduct of any trade or business in which a shareholder does not materially participate (nonparticipating shareholder) or any rental activity. A passive activity does not include any working interest in oil or gas property as defined in section 469(c)(3). Certain portfolio or investment income (section 469(e)(1)) is excluded from passive activity income or loss.

The passive activity limitations apply to each nonparticipating shareholder's share of any loss or credit attributable to a passive activity which involves the conduct of any trade or business and to all shareholders' shares of losses and credits from rental activities. The limits first apply to passive activity losses and credits of 1986–87 FY corporations that will be claimed on the shareholders' 1987 Form 1040 or Form 1041.

See the General Instructions for "Passive Activity Provisions"; the Specific Instructions for "Page 1 Changes (FY Corporations Only)"; instructions for items D, E, F, and G of Schedule K-1; and the instructions for lines 1a, 1b, and 1c of Schedules K and K-1 for details on how passive activity income or loss is figured on Form 1120S and how the income or loss and related information is reported to shareholders.

Tax Preference Items
The 1986 Tax Act made many changes to the alternative minimum tax provisions affecting shareholders of the S corporation. Generally, the changes are effective for the shareholder's tax year beginning after December 31, 1986. Accordingly, 1986-87 fiscal year corporations with tax years ending in 1987 must furnish information on the following new or revised preference items:

a. Accelerated depreciation (ACRS) on real or personal property placed in service after 1986.
b. Completed contract method of accounting for long-term contracts.
c. Installment method of accounting.
d. Charitable contributions of appreciated property.
e. Losses from passive farming activities.
f. Passive activity losses.

See Instructions for Schedules K and K-1 for details on each of the above items.

Depreciation and Section 179 Deduction
The rules for figuring depreciation have been substantially changed for property placed in service after 1986. The new system provides specific methods for each class of assets. Corporations may also elect these new provisions for property placed in service after July 31, 1986. Additionally, the section 179 deduction is increased to $10,000 for property placed in service after 1986. See **Form 4562A,** Depreciation of Property Placed in Service After December 31, 1986, for other details.

New Low-Income Housing Credit
A new low-income housing credit applies to certain buildings placed in service after 1986. The credit is figured at the corporate level and then passed through to shareholders on a pro rata basis. See **Form 8586,** Low-Income Housing Credit, for details.

Foreign Intangible Drilling, Exploration, and Development Costs
Generally, foreign intangible drilling, exploration, and development costs paid or incurred after 1986 must either be added to the corporation's basis for cost depletion purposes or be deducted ratably over a 10-year period. See sections 263(i), 616(d), and 617(h) for exceptions and other details.

Trademark and Trade Name Expenditures
Generally, trademark and trade name expenditures made after 1986 will no longer be amortizable.

Gain or Loss on Liquidation Distributions
Generally, corporations will recognize gain or loss on liquidation distributions of their property as if they had sold the property at its fair market value. See sections 336 and 337.

Changes in Corporate Tax Rates

Effective July 1, 1987, the corporate tax rates under section 11 will change. Effective January 1, 1987, the alternative tax rate under section 1201 will change. Because of these changes, the computation of excess net passive income tax and the income tax on capital gains (lines 25a and 25b, page 1, Form 1120S) will also change for FY 1986-87 filers. See the instructions for line 25a of page 1, Form 1120S, and Schedule D (Form 1120S) for details.

1987 Tax Year Changes

All S Corporations Must Have Permitted Tax Year

For tax years beginning after 1986, the Act deletes section 1378(c) that permitted an existing S corporation to have or retain a tax year that is not a permitted tax year until such time as the corporation had a more than 50% change in ownership. After 1986, for all S corporations, a permitted year will be a tax year ending December 31 or a tax period for which the S corporation establishes a business purpose. The IRS plans to publish a Revenue Ruling and a Revenue Procedure in early 1987 to provide guidance to S corporations in determining what is a business purpose under section 1378(b)(2) and in making any necessary change in tax year required by the Act.

After 1986, if an S corporation has a tax year that is not a permitted tax year, it must change to a permitted tax year for its first tax year beginning after 1986. For example, an S corporation with a tax year beginning July 1, 1987, and ending June 30, 1988, for which it cannot establish a business purpose must change to a tax year endnng December 31 for its first tax year beginning in 1987. To make the change, it must file a short year return for the period July 1, 1987, to December 31, 1987.

Generally, a shareholder is allowed to report income for any short tax year that results from the change in the corporate tax year ratably over each of the first four tax years beginning after December 31, 1986.

Accounting Provision Changes

The Act made several changes that affect the way in which income and expenses are reported by the S corporation. These changes have different effective dates. The changes include the following:

● **Certain Costs Required To Be Capitalized.**—New section 263A requires that certain costs incurred in the production of real and intangible property by the corporation, or costs incurred when property is acquired for resale, be capitalized or included in inventory costs rather than deducted. Generally, the changes affecting inventory are effective for tax years beginning after 1986. The changes affecting capitalization are effective for costs incurred after 1986 in tax years ending after 1986. See section 263A for details.

● **Reserve Method for Bad Debts.**—For tax years beginning after 1986, only certain financial institutions will be able to use the reserve method for figuring their bad debt deduction. All other taxpayers must use the specific charge-off method for figuring their bad debt deduction. All corporations not entitled to use the reserve method must include in income any amount remaining in the reserve as income ratably over a 4-year period. See section 166 for other details.

● **LIFO Inventory.**—For tax years beginning after 1986, S corporations whose average gross receipts for the 3 preceding tax years do not exceed $5 million can elect to use a simplified method of determining dollar value LIFO inventory values. See section 474 for other details.

● **Installment Method.**—Effective for sales after 1986, the use of the installment method is not allowed for sales of personal property under a revolving credit plan and for sales of certain publicly traded property. Also, the use of the installment method is limited for certain sales of S corporations that regularly sell real or personal property. The limitations apply to sales of business or rental property if the selling price exceeds $150,000. See new section 453C for how the limitations are figured and other details.

● **Long-term Contracts.**—New section 460 provides rules for accounting for long-term contracts entered into after February 28, 1986. See section 460 for details.

Deductible Expenses for Meals and Entertainment

For tax years beginning after 1986, many changes were made to the tax law that defines and provides for computation of expenses that may be deducted for meals and entertainment. Generally, the amount deductible for meals and entertainment expenses is limited to 80% of allowable expenses. To qualify as an allowable expense, meals must not be lavish or extravagant; a bona fide business discussion must precede or take place directly following the meal; and a corporate employee must be present at the meal. If the corporation claims a deduction for unallowable meal expenses, it may have to pay a penalty. See new section 274 for details.

Minimum Tax

Effective for tax years beginning after 1986 the minimum tax no longer applies to the S corporation and the new alternative minimum tax does not apply to the S corporation.

Tax on Built-in Gain

Effective for tax years beginning after 1986 (but only in cases where the first tax year for which the corporation is an S corporation begins after 1986), section 1374 is amended to provide for a tax on certain built-in gains that are recognized within 10 years after the corporation is an S corporation. See section 1374 for definitions, limitations, and other details.

Codes for Principal Business Activity

These industry titles and definitions are based, in general, on the Standard Industrial Classification System authorized by Regulatory and Statistical Analysis Division, Office of Information and Regulatory Affairs, Office of Management and Budget, to classify enterprises by type of activity in which they are engaged.

Using the list below, enter on page 1, under B, the code number for the specific industry group from which the largest percentage of "total

receipts" is derived. "Total receipts" means the total of: gross receipts on line 1a, page 1; all other income on lines 4 through 8, page 1; and income (receipts only) on lines 1b, 1c, and 1d of Schedule K.

On page 2, under H, state the principal business activity and principal product or service that account for the largest percentage of total receipts. For example, if the principal

business activity is "Grain mill products," the principal product or service may be "Cereal preparations."

If, as its principal business activity, the corporation (1) purchases raw materials, (2) subcontracts out for labor to make a finished product from the raw materials, and (3) retains title to the goods, the corporation is considered to be a manufacturer and must enter one of the codes (2010-3998) under "Manufacturing."

Agriculture, Forestry, and Fishing
Code
0400	Agricultural production.
0600	Agricultural services (except veterinarians), forestry, fishing, hunting, and trapping.

Mining
Metal mining:
1010	Iron ores.
1070	Copper, lead and zinc, gold and silver ores.
1098	Other metal mining.
1150	Coal mining.

Oil and gas extraction:
1330	Crude petroleum, natural gas, and natural gas liquids
1380	Oil and gas field services.

Nonmetallic minerals, except fuels:
1430	Dimension, crushed and broken stone; sand and gravel
1498	Other nonmetallic minerals, except fuels.

Construction
General building contractors and operative builders:
1510	General building contractors.
1531	Operative builders.
1600	Heavy construction contractors.

Special trade contractors:
1711	Plumbing, heating, and air conditioning.
1731	Electrical work
1798	Other special trade contractors

Manufacturing
Food and kindred products:
2010	Meat products
2020	Dairy products.
2030	Preserved fruits and vegetables
2040	Grain mill products
2050	Bakery products.
2060	Sugar and confectionery products
2081	Malt liquors and malt
2088	Alcoholic beverages, except malt liquors and malt
2089	Bottled soft drinks, and flavorings
2096	Other food and kindred products.
2100	Tobacco manufacturers.

Textile mill products:
2228	Weaving mills and textile finishing.
2250	Knitting mills.
2298	Other textile mill products

Apparel and other textile products:
2315	Men's and boys' clothing.
2345	Women's and children's clothing.
2388	Other apparel and accessories
2390	Miscellaneous fabricated textile products

Lumber and wood products:
2415	Logging, sawmills, and planing mills
2430	Millwork, plywood, and related products.
2498	Other wood products, including wood buildings and mobile homes
2500	Furniture and fixtures.

Paper and allied products:
2625	Pulp, paper, and board mills
2699	Other paper products

Printing and publishing:
2710	Newspapers
2720	Periodicals
2735	Books, greeting cards, and miscellaneous publishing.
2799	Commercial and other printing, and printing trade services

Code
Chemicals and allied products:
2815	Industrial chemicals, plastics materials and synthetics.
2830	Drugs
2840	Soap, cleaners, and toilet goods.
2850	Paints and allied products
2898	Agricultural and other chemical products

Petroleum refining and related industries (including those integrated with extraction):
2910	Petroleum refining (including integrated).
2998	Other petroleum and coal products.

Rubber and misc. plastics products:
3050	Rubber products, plastics footwear, hose, and belting.
3070	Misc. plastics products.

Leather and leather products:
3140	Footwear, except rubber
3198	Other leather and leather products.

Stone, clay, and glass products:
3225	Glass products.
3240	Cement, hydraulic
3270	Concrete, gypsum, and plaster products
3298	Other nonmetallic mineral products.

Primary metal industries:
3370	Ferrous metal industries; misc primary metal products.
3380	Nonferrous metal industries.

Fabricated metal products:
3410	Metal cans and shipping containers.
3428	Cutlery, hand tools, and hardware; screw machine products, bolts, and similar products.
3430	Plumbing and heating, except electric and warm air
3440	Fabricated structural metal products.
3460	Metal forgings and stampings.
3470	Coating, engraving, and allied services
3480	Ordnance and accessories, except vehicles and guided missiles.
3490	Misc fabricated metal products.

Machinery, except electrical:
3520	Farm machinery
3530	Construction and related machinery
3540	Metalworking machinery
3550	Special industry machinery
3560	General industrial machinery
3570	Office, computing, and accounting machines.
3598	Other machinery except electrical

Electrical and electronic equipment:
3630	Household appliances
3665	Radio, television, and communication equipment
3670	Electronic components and accessories
3698	Other electrical equipment
3710	Motor vehicles and equipment

Transportation equipment, except motor vehicles:
3725	Aircraft, guided missiles and parts.
3730	Ship and boat building and repairing
3798	Other transportation equipment, except motor vehicles

Instruments and related products:
3815	Scientific instruments and measuring devices; watches and clocks
3845	Optical, medical, and ophthalmic goods
3860	Photographic equipment and supplies
3998	Other manufacturing products.

Transportation and Public Utilities
Code
Transportation:
4000	Railroad transportation.
4100	Local and interurban passenger transit.
4200	Trucking and warehousing.
4400	Water transportation.
4500	Transportation by air
4600	Pipe lines, except natural gas.
4700	Miscellaneous transportation services.

Communication:
4825	Telephone, telegraph, and other communication services.
4830	Radio and television broadcasting.

Electric, gas, and sanitary services:
4910	Electric services.
4920	Gas production and distribution
4930	Combination utility services.
4990	Water supply and other sanitary services.

Wholesale Trade
Durable:
5008	Machinery, equipment, and supplies.
5010	Motor vehicles and automotive equipment.
5020	Furniture and home furnishings.
5030	Lumber and construction materials.
5040	Sporting, recreational, photographic, and hobby goods, toys and supplies.
5050	Metals and minerals, except petroleum and scrap.
5060	Electrical goods.
5070	Hardware, plumbing and heating equipment and supplies.
5098	Other durable goods

Nondurable:
5110	Paper and paper products
5129	Drugs, drug proprietaries, and druggists' sundries.
5130	Apparel, piece goods, and notions
5140	Groceries and related products.
5150	Farm-product raw materials.
5160	Chemicals and allied products.
5170	Petroleum and petroleum products.
5180	Alcoholic beverages.
5190	Misc nondurable goods.

Retail Trade
Building materials, garden supplies, and mobile home dealers:
5220	Building materials dealers.
5251	Hardware stores.
5265	Garden supplies and mobile home dealers.
5300	General merchandise stores.

Food stores:
5410	Grocery stores
5490	Other food stores

Automotive dealers and service stations:
5515	Motor vehicle dealers.
5541	Gasoline service stations.
5598	Other automotive dealers.
5600	Apparel and accessory stores.
5700	Furniture and home furnishings stores.
5800	Eating and drinking places.

Misc. retail stores:
5912	Drug stores and proprietary stores
5921	Liquor stores
5995	Other retail stores.

Finance, Insurance, and Real Estate
Code
Banking:
6030	Mutual savings banks
6060	Bank holding companies
6090	Banks, except mutual savings banks and bank holding companies

Credit agencies other than banks:
6120	Savings and loan associations.
6140	Personal credit institutions
6150	Business credit institutions
6199	Other credit agencies.

Security, commodity brokers and services:
6210	Security brokers, dealers, and flotation companies
6299	Commodity contracts brokers and dealers; security and commodity exchanges; and allied services.

Insurance:
6355	Life Insurance
6356	Mutual insurance, except life or marine and certain fire or flood insurance companies.
6359	Other insurance companies.
6411	Insurance agents, brokers, and service

Real estate:
6511	Real estate operators and lessors of buildings.
6516	Lessors of mining, oil, and similar property
6518	Lessors of railroad property and other real property
6530	Condominium management and cooperative housing associations
6550	Subdividers and developers
6599	Other real estate

Holding and other investment companies, except bank holding companies:
6742	Regulated investment companies
6743	Real estate investment trusts
6744	Small business investment companies
6749	Other holding and investment companies except bank holding companies

Services
7000	Hotels and other lodging places.
7200	Personal services.

Business services:
7310	Advertising.
7389	Business services, except advertising

Auto repair; miscellaneous repair services:
7500	Auto repair and services
7600	Misc repair services

Amusement and recreation services:
7812	Motion picture production, distribution, and services
7830	Motion picture theaters
7900	Amusement and recreation services, except motion pictures

Other services:
8015	Offices of physicians, including osteopathic physicians
8021	Offices of dentists
8040	Offices of other health practitioners
8050	Nursing and personal care facilities
8060	Hospitals.
8071	Medical laboratories
8099	Other medical services
8111	Legal services
8200	Educational services
8300	Social services
8600	Membership organizations
8911	Architectural and engineering services.
8930	Accounting, auditing, and bookkeeping.
8980	Miscellaneous services (including veterinarians)

U.S. GOVERNMENT PRINTING OFFICE : 1987 O - 493-200

Form **1120S**	**U.S. Income Tax Return for an S Corporation**	OMB No. 1545-0130
Department of the Treasury Internal Revenue Service	For the calendar year 1986 or tax year beginning _____, 1986, ending _____, 19____ ▶ For Paperwork Reduction Act Notice, see page 1 of the instructions.	**1986**

A Date of election as an S corporation	Use IRS label. Other-wise, please print or type.	Name	C Employer identification number
		Number and street	D Date incorporated
B Business Code No. (see Specific Instructions)		City or town, state, and ZIP code	E Total assets (see Specific Instructions) Dollars / Cents

F. Check applicable boxes: (1) ☐ Final return (2) ☐ Change in address (3) ☐ Amended return $

1986-87 fiscal year corporations see Specific Instructions before completing page 1.

Income

1a	Gross receipts or sales _____ b Less returns and allowances _____ Balance ▶	1c	
2	Cost of goods sold and/or operations (Schedule A, line 7).	2	
3	Gross profit (subtract line 2 from line 1c)	3	
4	Taxable interest and nonqualifying dividends	4	
5	Gross rents	5	
6	Gross royalties	6	
7	Net gain or (loss) from Form 4797, line 17, Part II	7	
8	Other income (see instructions—attach schedule)	8	
9	TOTAL income (loss)—Combine lines 3 through 8 and enter here ▶	9	

Deductions

10	Compensation of officers	10	
11a	Salaries and wages _____ b Less jobs credit _____ Balance ▶	11c	
12	Repairs	12	
13	Bad debts (see instructions)	13	
14	Rents	14	
15	Taxes	15	
16a	Total deductible interest expense not claimed elsewhere on return (see instructions)	16a	
b	Interest expense required to be passed through to shareholders on Schedule K-1, lines 9, 13a(2), and 13a(3)	16b	
c	Subtract line 16b from line 16a	16c	
17a	Depreciation from Form 4562 (attach Form 4562)	17a	
b	Depreciation claimed on Schedule A and elsewhere on return	17b	
c	Subtract line 17b from line 17a	17c	
18	Depletion (**Do not deduct oil and gas depletion.** See instructions)	18	
19	Advertising	19	
20	Pension, profit-sharing, etc. plans	20	
21	Employee benefit programs	21	
22	Other deductions (attach schedule)	22	
23	TOTAL deductions—Add lines 10 through 22 and enter here ▶	23	
24	Ordinary income (loss)—Subtract line 23 from line 9	24	

Tax and Payments

25	Tax:		
a	Excess net passive income tax (attach schedule)	25a	
b	Tax from Schedule D (Form 1120S), Part IV	25b	
c	Add lines 25a and 25b	25c	
26	Payments:		
a	Tax deposited with Form 7004	26a	
b	Credit for Federal tax on gasoline and special fuels (attach Form 4136)	26b	
c	Add lines 26a and 26b	26c	
27	**TAX DUE** (subtract line 26c from line 25c). See instructions for Paying the Tax ▶	27	
28	**OVERPAYMENT** (subtract line 25c from line 26c)	28	

Please Sign Here

Under penalties of perjury, I declare that I have examined this return, including accompanying schedules and statements, and to the best of my knowledge and belief, it is true, correct, and complete. Declaration of preparer (other than taxpayer) is based on all information of which preparer has any knowledge.

▶ Signature of officer   Date   ▶ Title

Paid Preparer's Use Only

Preparer's signature ▶	Date	Check if self-employed ▶ ☐	Preparer's social security number
Firm's name (or yours, if self-employed) and address ▶		E.I. No. ▶	
		ZIP code ▶	

Form **1120S** (1986)

Schedule A Cost of Goods Sold and/or Operations (See instructions for Schedule A)

		1		
1	Inventory at beginning of year	1		
2	Purchases	2		
3	Cost of labor	3		
4	Other costs (attach schedule)	4		
5	Total—Add lines 1 through 4	5		
6	Inventory at end of year	6		
7	Cost of goods sold and/or operations—Subtract line 6 from line 5. Enter here and on line 2, page 1	7		

8a Check all methods used for valuing closing inventory:

(i) ☐ Cost

(ii) ☐ Lower of cost or market as described in Regulations section 1.471-4 (see instructions)

(iii) ☐ Writedown of "subnormal" goods as described in Regulations section 1.471-2(c) (see instructions)

(iv) ☐ Other (Specify method used and attach explanation) ▶ _____

b Check this box if the LIFO inventory method was adopted this tax year for any goods (if checked, attach Form 970) . . . . . ☐

c If the LIFO inventory method was used for this tax year, enter percentage (or amounts) of closing inventory computed under LIFO . . . . **8c** | _____

d If you are engaged in manufacturing, did you value your inventory using the full absorption method (Regulations section 1.471-11)? . . . . ☐ Yes ☐ No

e Was there any change in determining quantities, cost, or valuations between opening and closing inventory? . . . . ☐ Yes ☐ No
If "Yes," attach explanation.

Additional Information Required

		Yes	No
G	Did you at the end of the tax year own, directly or indirectly, 50% or more of the voting stock of a domestic corporation? (For rules of attribution, see section 267(c).)		
	If "Yes," attach a schedule showing:		
	(1) Name, address, and employer identification number;		
	(2) Percentage owned;		
	(3) Highest amount owed by you to such corporation during the year; and		
	(4) Highest amount owed to you by such corporation during the year.		
	(Note: For purposes of G(3) and G(4), "highest amount owed" includes loans and accounts receivable/payable.)		
H	Refer to the listing of Business Activity Codes at the end of the Instructions for Form 1120S and state your principal: Business activity ▶ _____; Product or service ▶ _____		
I	Were you a member of a controlled group subject to the provisions of section 1561?		
J	Did you claim a deduction for expenses connected with:		
	(1) Entertainment facilities (boat, resort, ranch, etc.)?		
	(2) Living accommodations (except for employees on business)?		
	(3) Employees attending conventions or meetings outside the North American area? (See section 274(h).)		
	(4) Employees' families at conventions or meetings?		
	If "Yes," were any of these conventions or meetings outside the North American area? (See section 274(h).)		
	(5) Employee or family vacations not reported on Form W-2?		
K	At any time during the tax year, did you have an interest in or a signature or other authority over a financial account in a foreign country (such as a bank account, securities account, or other financial account)? (See instructions for exceptions and filing requirements for form TD F 90-22.1.)		
	If "Yes," write the name of the foreign country ▶ _____		
L	Were you the grantor of, or transferor to, a foreign trust which existed during the current tax year, whether or not you have any beneficial interest in it? If "Yes," you may have to file Forms 3520, 3520-A, or 926		
M	During this tax year did you maintain any part of your accounting/tax records on a computerized system?		
N	Check method of accounting: **(1)** ☐ Cash **(2)** ☐ Accrual **(3)** ☐ Other (specify) ▶ _____		
O	Check this box if the S corporation has filed or is required to file Form 8264. Application for Registration of a Tax Shelter . . . . ▶ ☐		
P	Check this box if the corporation issued publicly offered debt instruments with original issue discount . . . . . ▶ ☐ If so, the corporation may have to file Form 8281.		

Schedule K	Shareholders' Share of Income, Credits, Deductions, etc. (See Instructions.)			
	(a) Distributive share items		(b) Total amount	

Income (Losses) and Deductions

1a	Ordinary income (loss) (page 1, line 24) *	**1a**		
b	Income (loss) from rental real estate activity(ies) (FY corporations only)	**1b**		
c	Income (loss) from other rental activity(ies) (FY corporations only)	**1c**		
d	Portfolio income not reported elsewhere on Schedule K (FY corporations only)	**1d**		
2	Dividends qualifying for the exclusion	**2**		
3	Net short-term capital gain (loss) (Schedule D (Form 1120S)) *	**3**		
4	Net long-term capital gain (loss) (Schedule D (Form 1120S)) *	**4**		
5	Net gain (loss) under section 1231 (other than due to casualty or theft) *	**5**		
6	Other income (loss) (attach schedule)	**6**		
7	Charitable contributions	**7**		
8	Section 179 expense deduction (FY corporations attach schedule)	**8**		
9	Other deductions (attach schedule)	**9**		

Credits

10a	Jobs credit *	**10a**		
b	Low-income housing credit (FY corporations only)	**10b**		
c	Qualified rehabilitation expenditures related to rental real estate activity(ies) (FY corporations only) (attach schedule)		/////	
d	Other credits related to rental real estate activity(ies) other than on line 10b and 10c (FY corporations only) (attach schedule)	**10d**		
11	Other credits (attach schedule) *	**11**		

Tax Preference and Adjustment Items

12a	Accelerated depreciation on nonrecovery real property or 15, 18, or 19-year real property placed in service before 1-1-87	**12a**		
b	Accelerated depreciation on leased personal property or leased recovery property, other than 15, 18, or 19-year real property, placed in service before 1-1-87	**12b**		
c	Accelerated depreciation on property placed in service after 12-31-86 (FY corporations only)	**12c**		
d	Depletion (other than oil and gas)	**12d**		
e	**(1)** Gross income from oil, gas, or geothermal properties	**12e(1)**		
	(2) Gross deductions allocable to oil, gas, or geothermal properties	**12e(2)**		
f	**(1)** Qualified investment income included on page 1, Form 1120S	**12f(1)**		
	(2) Qualified investment expenses included on page 1, Form 1120S	**12f(2)**		
g	Other items (attach schedule)	**12g**		

Investment Interest

13a	Interest expense on: **(1)** Investment debts incurred before 12-17-69	**13a(1)**		
	(2) Investment debts incurred before 9-11-75 but after 12-16-69	**13a(2)**		
	(3) Investment debts incurred after 9-10-75	**13a(3)**		
b	**(1)** Investment income included on page 1, Form 1120S	**13b(1)**		
	(2) Investment expenses included on page 1, Form 1120S	**13b(2)**		
c	**(1)** Income from "net lease property"	**13c(1)**		
	(2) Expenses from "net lease property"	**13c(2)**		
d	Excess of net long-term capital gain over net short-term capital loss from investment property	**13d**		

Foreign Taxes

14a	Type of income		/////	
b	Name of foreign country or U.S. possession		/////	
c	Total gross income from sources outside the U.S. (attach schedule)	**14c**		
d	Total applicable deductions and losses (attach schedule)	**14d**		
e	Total foreign taxes (check one): ▶ ☐ Paid ☐ Accrued	**14e**		
f	Reduction in taxes available for credit (attach schedule)	**14f**		
g	Other (attach schedule)	**14g**		

Other Items

15	Total property distributions (including cash) other than dividend distributions reported on line 17	**15**		
16	Other items and amounts not included in lines 1 through 15 that are required to be reported separately to shareholders (attach schedule).		/////	
17	Total dividend distributions paid from accumulated earnings and profits contained in other retained earnings (line 26 of Schedule L)	**17**		

* Calendar year filers are not required to complete lines 1a, 10a, and 11. Completion of these lines is optional because the amounts which would appear in column (b) appear elsewhere on Form 1120S or on other IRS forms or schedules which are attached to Form 1120S. See Specific Instructions for Schedules K and K-1.

Schedule L — Balance Sheets

Assets	Beginning of tax year		End of tax year	
	(a)	(b)	(c)	(d)
1 Cash				
2 Trade notes and accounts receivable				
a Less allowance for bad debts				
3 Inventories				
4 Federal and state government obligations				
5 Other current assets (attach schedule)				
6 Loans to shareholders				
7 Mortgage and real estate loans				
8 Other investments (attach schedule)				
9 Buildings and other depreciable assets				
a Less accumulated depreciation				
10 Depletable assets				
a Less accumulated depletion				
11 Land (net of any amortization)				
12 Intangible assets (amortizable only)				
a Less accumulated amortization				
13 Other assets (attach schedule)				
14 Total assets				
Liabilities and Shareholders' Equity				
15 Accounts payable				
16 Mortgages, notes, bonds payable in less than 1 year				
17 Other current liabilities (attach schedule)				
18 Loans from shareholders				
19 Mortgages, notes, bonds payable in 1 year or more				
20 Other liabilities (attach schedule)				
21 Capital stock				
22 Paid-in or capital surplus				
23 Accumulated adjustments account				
24 Other adjustments account				
25 Shareholders' undistributed taxable income previously taxed				
26 Other retained earnings (see instructions). Check this box if the corporation has subchapter C earnings and profits at the close of the tax year ▶ ☐ (see instructions)				
27 Total retained earnings per books—Combine amounts on lines 23 through 26, columns (a) and (c) (see instructions)				
28 Less cost of treasury stock		( )		( )
29 Total liabilities and shareholders' equity				

Schedule M — Analysis of Accumulated Adjustments Account, Other Adjustments Account, and Shareholders' Undistributed Taxable Income Previously Taxed (If Schedule L, column (c), amounts for lines 23, 24, or 25 are not the same as corresponding amounts on line 9 of Schedule M, attach a schedule explaining any differences. See instructions.)

	Accumulated adjustments account	Other adjustments account	Shareholders' undistributed taxable income previously taxed
1 Balance at beginning of year			
2 Ordinary income from page 1, line 24			
3 Other additions			
4 Total of lines 1, 2, and 3			
5 Distributions other than dividend distributions			
6 Loss from page 1, line 24			
7 Other reductions			
8 Add lines 5, 6, and 7			
9 Balance at end of tax year—Subtract line 8 from line 4			

19**86**

Department of the Treasury
Internal Revenue Service

Instructions for Form 4562

Depreciation and Amortization

(Section references are to the Internal Revenue Code, unless otherwise noted.)

Paperwork Reduction Act Notice

We ask for this information to carry out the Internal Revenue laws of the United States. We need it to ensure that taxpayers are complying with these laws and to allow us to figure and collect the right amount of tax. You are required to give us this information.

Items You Should Note

● Recent legislation changed the method of figuring your allowable deduction for depreciation of property placed in service after 12/31/86. However, you may elect to use that method for property placed in service after 7/31/86. The deduction for depreciation of certain property, such as automobiles and real estate, will be less under the new system. New rules will also apply to the section 179 expense deduction. Figure your allowable deduction for depreciation using the new method on Form 4562A and enter your allowable deduction on the 1986 Form 4562, Part I, line 9. For "listed property" placed in service after December 31, 1986, see the instructions to Form 4562A.

● Line 4h is new. This is to be used for real property that has a recovery period of 19 years.

● All taxpayers claiming a deduction for any listed property (such as automobiles, computers, and property used for purposes of entertainment, recreation and amusement) are required to complete Part III on page 2, regardless of when such property was placed in service.

● As an alternative to depreciation, self-employed individuals may elect to use the standard mileage allowance. For more information, see **Publication 917,** Business Use of a Car.

● All details of depreciation should be retained as part of your permanent books and records. See **Publication 534,** Depreciation, for example of how to keep depreciation records.

Purpose of Form

Use Form 4562 to claim this year's deduction for depreciation and amortization, to make the election to expense recovery property, and to provide information concerning the business use of automobiles and other listed property.

In using this form, a taxpayer should prepare and submit a separate Form 4562 for each business or activity in the return.

For more information about depreciation, the election to expense newly acquired recovery property, and leased listed property, see **Publication 534,** Depreciation and **Publication 917,** Business Use of a Car. For more information about amortization (including depreciation/amortization of leasehold expenses), see **Publication 535,** Business Expenses.

Line-by-Line Instructions

Caution: These instructions do not reflect the new rules and limits for property placed in service after December 31, 1986. See Form 4562A and Publication 534 for details.

Part I.—Depreciation

Depreciation is an amount you can deduct each year for assets, except land, you acquire to use in your business or hold to produce income. (Land is never depreciable.) Depreciation starts when you first start using the property in your business. It ends when you take the property out of service, deduct all of your depreciable cost, or no longer use the property in your business. However, except for 15, 18, or 19-year real property, or low income housing, no depreciation deduction is allowed in the year the property is disposed of.

Complete Section A of Part III on page 2, instead of Part I, for depreciation of all listed property, regardless of when such property was placed in service.

If any "listed property" placed in service after June 18, 1984, was used more than 50% in a trade or business in the year it was placed in service, and used 50% or less in a later year, part of the depreciation, Section 179 deduction, and investment credit will have to be recaptured in the later year. Figure the amount of depreciation and Section 179 deduction to be recaptured on **Form 4797,** Gains and Losses From Sales or Exchanges of Assets Used in a Trade or Business and Involuntary Conversions. Figure the amount of investment credit to be recaptured on **Form 4255,** Recapture of Investment Credit.

Assets you place in service after December 31, 1980, are depreciated using the Accelerated Cost Recovery System (ACRS). These assets are called "recovery property." You may be able to elect to expense up to $5,000 of certain recovery property in Section A. Show your depreciation for recovery property in Section B. If you have an asset that is nonrecovery property, show your depreciation in Section C.

Section A.—Election to Expense Recovery Property.—You may choose to expense part of the cost of depreciable personal property used in your trade or business and certain other property described in Publication 534. To do so, you must have purchased (as defined in section 179(d)(2)) the property and placed it in service during the 1986 tax year. If you take this deduction, the amount on which you figure your depreciation or amortization deduction and your investment tax credit, if any, must be reduced by the amount you deduct as a section 179 expense.

Note: *The following do not qualify as section 179 property: (1) property that is used 50% or less in your trade or business; and (2) property held for the production of income (section 212 property).*

An estate or trust may not elect to expense recovery property. A partnership or S corporation may choose to expense and pass through to its partners or shareholders a maximum of $5,000. Partners or shareholders add their share of the partnership or S corporation amount to their own section 179 expense they choose to take, and deduct the combined amount up to the $5,000 (or $2,500 for married taxpayers filing separately) limit for each taxpayer. See Publication 534 for more information.

Line 1.—

*Column (a).—*Enter the class of recovery property (that is, 3-year, 5-year, etc.) for which you make the election and a brief description of the item.

*Column (b).—*Enter the property's cost. Omit any undepreciated basis on assets you traded in. For information about basis, see **Publication 551,** Basis of Assets.

*Column (c).—*Enter the part of the cost you choose to expense. You can choose to expense part of the cost of an asset and depreciate the rest of it.

*Line 2.—*If you choose to claim a section 179 expense deduction for automobiles and other listed property, complete Section A, Part III. See "Limitations for automobiles" under Section A, Part III.

*Line 3.—*Enter the column (c) total, up to $5,000 ($2,500 for married taxpayers filing separately). Partnerships and S corporations should carry the line 3 amount to their Schedules K and K-1.

Section B.—Depreciation of Recovery Property.—

Note: *Lines 4a through 4h should be completed for assets, other than automobiles and other listed property, placed in service only during the tax year beginning in 1986.*

*Column (a).—*Two factors determine the class of property: whether the property is section 1245 or section 1250 class property; and what midpoint class life (if any) would have applied to it on January 1, 1981, if the asset depreciation range (ADR) system had been elected. The midpoint class lives are listed in the asset guideline period column of the table for depreciation in the back of Publication 534.

In each recovery class, except 15, 18, or 19-year real property, list as one item all new and used property you placed in service in 1986. However, you must list separately:

● Property used mainly outside the United States.

● Retirement-replacement-betterment property.

● Property financed by tax-exempt obligations.

● Property not predominantly used in a qualified business use.

In the 15, 18, and 19-year real property classes, group property by the depreciation method elected and the month and year you placed it in service.

Attach additional sheets, if necessary.

*Column (b).—*For lines 4e through 4h, enter the month and year you placed the property in service.

*Column (c).—*Enter the basis for depreciation of the assets you placed in service in the current tax year. To find the basis for depreciation, multiply the cost or other basis of the property by the percent of business use. From that result, subtract any section 179 expense, and one-half of investment credit taken, if applicable, (unless you took the reduced credit.)

Column (d).—Enter the recovery period you are using. This is usually the class of property itself (that is, 3-year, 5-year, etc.); but you may instead elect an alternate percentage figured by using the straight-line method over one of the following periods.

For—	You may choose:
3-year property	3, 5, or 12 years
5-year property	5, 12, or 25 years
10-year property	10, 25, or 35 years
15-year public utility property or 15-year real property	15, 35, or 45 years
18-year real property	18, 35, or 45 years
19-year real property	19, 35, or 45 years
Low-income housing	15, 35, or 45 years

Also, for certain assets (described in column (e), below) you may be required to use a specified recovery period.

Column (e).—For property for which you are using the prescribed percentages (described in Section B, lines 4a through 4h below), enter "PRE." If you elect an alternate percentage, as described above in column (d) instructions, enter "SL." If the asset is used mainly outside the United States, enter "FP" and see section 168(f)(2). If the asset is retirement-replacement-betterment property, enter "RRB" and see section 168(f)(3). If the asset is property financed by tax-exempt obligations, enter "TEO" and see section 168(f)(12). For property leased to tax-exempt entities, see section 168(j).

Column (f).—Unless you use an alternate percentage, or a special percentage required for certain types of property (as described above in column (e) instructions), multiply the amount in column (c) by the applicable percentage, from the line instructions below, and enter the result in column (f). If you use an alternate percentage, use the percentage based on the recovery period you chose. Except for 15, 18, and 19-year real property, and low-income housing, and property requiring a special percentage (as described above), use the same alternate percentage for all property in the same class that you place in service in the same year.

If you elect an alternate percentage, do not figure depreciation by the number of months the property was in use; instead use the half-year convention by dividing the result explained in the instructions for column (d) by 2, for the first and last year of depreciating the property, but before the year of disposition. However, for 15, 18, and 19-year real property, and low income housing , you can elect an alternate percentage on a property-by-property basis, and the half-year convention does not apply.

Section B, Line 4a—3-year property.— Includes section 1245 class property that:

• Has a class life of 4 years or less, or

• Is used for research and experimentation, or

• Is a race horse more than 2 years old when you place it in service, or any other horse that is more than 12 years old when you place it in service.

An example of 3-year property is: machinery and equipment used in connection with research and experiments.

The percentages prescribed for these assets are:

1st year	25%
2nd year	38%
3rd year	37%

Line 4b—5-year property.—Includes section 1245 class property that is not assigned to one of the other recovery classes.

Examples of 5-year property are: machinery; office furniture; and single purpose agricultural and horticultural structures (other than a building and its structural components).

The percentages prescribed for these assets are:

1st year	15%
2nd year	22%
3rd through 5th year	21%

Line 4c—10-year property.—Includes: public utility property (except 3-year property or section 1250 class property) that has a class life of more than 18 years and no more than 25 years; section 1250 class property that has a class life of 12.5 years or less; manufactured homes; railroad tank cars; and qualified coal utilization property which would otherwise be 15-year public utility property. However, under a special rule for theme parks, etc., a building and its structural components shall not be treated as having a class life of 12.5 years or less by reason of any use other than the use for which that building was originally placed in service.

The percentages prescribed for these assets are:

1st year	8%
2nd year	14%
3rd year	12%
4th through 6th year	10%
7th through 10th year	9%

Line 4d—15-year public utility property.—Public utility property (except 3-year property or section 1250 property) that has a class life of more than 25 years.

The percentages prescribed for these assets are:

1st year	5%
2nd year	10%
3rd year	9%
4th year	8%
5th and 6th year	7%
7th through 15th year	6%

Line 4e—Low-income housing.— Property described in clause (i), (ii), (iii), or (iv) of section 1250 (a)(1)(B).

Different percentages apply to low-income housing than to 15, 18, or 19-year real property. The percentage to use each year depends on the month you placed the property in service during the tax year. Publication 534 gives complete percentage tables for low-income housing and the optional write-off periods.

For qualified rehabilitated buildings, see section 48(g).

Line 4f—15-year real property.— Section 1250 property that does not have a class life of 12.5 years or less. Applies to property placed in service before March 16, 1984, unless under construction or subject to a binding contract before March 16, 1984, and placed in service before January 1, 1987.

Line 4g—18-year real property.— Section 1250 class property that does not have a class life of 12.5 years or less. Applies to property that is placed in service after March 15, 1984, and before May 9, 1985, unless under construction or subject to a binding contract before May 9, 1985, and placed in service before January 1, 1987. Enter property grouped by the depreciation method elected and the month and year you placed it in service. The percentages to be used depend on the month of your tax year in which the property was placed in service. The chart above for line 4g shows the percentages prescribed for the first three years.

Line 4f. 15-year real property.—(mid-month convention)

Year	\multicolumn{12}{c}{Use the column for the month of taxable year placed in service}
	1	2	3	4	5	6	7	8	9	10	11	12
1st	12%	11%	10%	9%	8%	7%	6%	5%	4%	3%	2%	1%
2nd	10%	10%	11%	11%	11%	11%	11%	11%	11%	11%	11%	12%
3rd	9%	9%	9%	9%	10%	10%	10%	10%	10%	10%	10%	10%
4th	8%	8%	8%	8%	8%	8%	9%	9%	9%	9%	9%	9%
5th	7%	7%	7%	7%	7%	7%	8%	8%	8%	8%	8%	8%
6th	6%	6%	6%	6%	7%	7%	7%	7%	7%	7%	7%	7%

Line 4g. 18-year real property.—(mid-month convention)

Year	\multicolumn{12}{c}{Use the column for the month of taxable year placed in service}
	1	2	3	4	5	6	7	8	9	10	11	12
1st	9%	9%	8%	7%	6%	5%	4%	4%	3%	2%	1%	0.4%
2nd	9%	9%	9%	9%	9%	9%	9%	9%	9%	10%	10%	10%
3rd	8%	8%	8%	8%	8%	8%	8%	8%	9%	9%	9%	9%

Line 4h. 19-year real property.—(mid-month convention)

Year	\multicolumn{12}{c}{Use the column for the month of taxable year placed in service}
	1	2	3	4	5	6	7	8	9	10	11	12
1st	8.8%	8.1%	7.3%	6.5%	5.8%	5.0%	4.2%	3.5%	2.7%	1.9%	1.1%	0.4%
2nd	8.4%	8.5%	8.5%	8.6%	8.7%	8.8%	8.8%	8.9%	9.0%	9.0%	9.1%	9.2%
3rd	7.6%	7.7%	7.7%	7.8%	7.9%	7.9%	8.0%	8.1%	8.1%	8.2%	8.3%	8.3%

Line 4h—19-year real property.— Section 1250 property that does not have a class life of 12.5 years or less placed in service after May 8, 1985, and not under construction or subject to a binding contract before May 9, 1985. The chart above for line 4h shows the percentages prescribed for the first three years.

Capital improvements made to buildings placed in service prior to 1981 can qualify as recovery property.

Capital improvements will qualify as 15, 18, or 19-year real property, depending on when the improvements were placed in service. Such improvements are to be treated as though they were separate buildings.

Include in lines 4f, 4g or 4h only the amount of capital expenditures for improvements that were placed in service in your taxable year beginning in 1986.

Section B, Line 6.—Enter the amount of your ACRS deduction for recovery property, other than automobiles and other listed property, placed in service prior to January 1, 1986. This amount is obtained by multiplying the applicable percentage by the basis for depreciation for each of the prior years for each class of property. DO NOT include any amounts deducted in lines 4a through 5.

The basis and amounts claimed for depreciation in prior years should be part of your permanent books and records. **No attachment is necessary.**

Section C.—Depreciation of Nonrecovery Property.—Use Section C for property, other than automobiles and other listed property, you do not amortize, expense, or use ACRS to depreciate. This includes:
● Property placed in service before January 1, 1981;
● Certain public utility property, which does not meet certain normalization requirements;
● Certain property acquired from related persons;
● Property acquired in certain nonrecognition transactions; and
● Certain sound recordings, movies, and videotapes.

Section C, Line 7.—Report property that you elect, under section 168(e)(2), to depreciate by the units-of-production method or any other method not based on a term of years. If you use the retirement-replacement-betterment method, see section 168(f)(3).

On a separate sheet, attach: (1) a description of the property and what depreciation method you elect that excludes the property from ACRS; and (2) the depreciable basis (cost or other basis reduced, if applicable, by salvage value, half the investment credit, and the section 179 expense).

Enter the depreciation deduction for the property in column (f).

Section C, Line 8.— Enter the total amount of depreciation attributable to assets, other than automobiles and other listed property, acquired before January 1, 1981 (pre-ACRS), or property that cannot otherwise be depreciated under ACRS. This amount should be calculated from your permanent books and records. **No attachment is necessary.** For a sample worksheet, see Publication 534.

Include any amounts attributable to the Class Life Asset Depreciation Range

(CLADR) system. If you previously elected the CLADR system, you must continue to use it to depreciate assets left in your vintage accounts. You must continue to meet recordkeeping requirements.

If you elect CLADR for assets that do not qualify for ACRS (see sections 168(e)(1) and (4)), attach a statement that specifies the items that still apply to those listed in Regulations section 1.167(a)-11(f)(2).

Part II.—Amortization

Each year you may elect to deduct part of certain capital expenses over a fixed period. If you amortize property, the part you amortize does not qualify for the election to expense recovery property or depreciation.

Line 1.—Complete line 1 only for property placed in service during your tax year beginning in 1986.

Column (a).—Describe the property you are amortizing. Amortizable property includes:
● Pollution control facilities (section 169, limited by section 291 for corporations).
● Bond premiums (section 171).
● Expenses paid before January 1, 1982, for child-care facilities (section 188).
● Amounts paid for research or experiments (section 174), or for a trademark or trade name (section 177).
● Business start-up expenditures (section 195).
● Qualified forestation and reforestation costs (section 194).
● Organizational expenses for a corporation (section 248) or partnership (section 709).
● Certain railroad property (section 185).
● Construction period interest and taxes on real property (for exceptions, see section 189).
● Certain rehabilitation expenses of historic structures made before January 1, 1982 (section 191 (as before repeal)).
● Optional write-off of certain tax preferences over the period specified in section 58(i).

Column (b).—Enter the date you acquired or completed the property or spent the amount you are amortizing.

Column (c).—Enter the total amount you are amortizing. See the applicable Code section for limits on the amortizable amount.

Column (d).—Enter the Code section under which you amortize the property.

Attach any other information the Code and Regulations may require in order to make a valid election. For additional information, see Publication 535.

Line 2.—Enter the amount of amortization attributable to property placed in service before 1986.

Part III.— Automobiles and Other Listed Property

All taxpayers claiming any type of deduction for automobiles and other listed property, regardless of the tax year such property was placed in service, must provide the information requested in Part III. Listed property includes, but is not limited to:
● Passenger automobiles weighing 6,000 pounds or less.
● Any other property used as a means of transportation if the nature of the property lends itself to personal use, such as motorcycles, pick-up trucks, etc.

● Any property of a type generally used for purposes of entertainment, recreation, or amusement (such as photographic, phonographic, communication, and video recording equipment.)
● Computers or peripheral equipment.

Listed property does not include photographic, phonographic, communication, or video equipment used exclusively in a taxpayer's trade or business or regular business establishment. It also does not include any computer or peripheral equipment used exclusively at a regular business establishment and owned or leased by the person operating such establishment.

Listed property does not include an ambulance, hearse, or a vehicle used for transporting persons or property for hire.

Section A.—Depreciation

Column (a).—List on a property by property basis all of your listed property in the following order:
(1) Automobiles and other vehicles ;
(2) Other listed property (computers and peripheral equipment ,etc.);

In column (a), list the make and model of automobiles, and give a general description of listed property.

If you have more than five vehicles used 100% in your trade or business, you may group them by tax year. Otherwise, list all vehicles separately.

Column (b).—Enter the date the property was placed in service. This is the date you first start using the property for any purpose, whether personal or business.

Column (c).—Enter the percentage of business use. For automobiles and other "vehicles," this is determined by dividing the number of miles the vehicle is driven for purposes of a trade or business during the year by the total number of miles the vehicle is driven for any purpose. For vehicles used by non-more than 5% owner employees, treat the vehicles as being used 100% in your trade or business, if the value of personal use is included in the employees' gross income or the employee reimburses the employer for the personal use.

If the employer reports the amount of personal use of the vehicle in the employee's gross income, and withholds the appropriate taxes, for purposes of this form, the employer is to enter "100%" for the percentage of business use. For more information see Publication 917. For listed property (such as computers or video equipment), allocate the use on a basis of the most appropriate unit of time the property is actually used. See Temp. Regs. 1.280F-6T.

If you have property that is used solely for personal use that is converted to business use during the tax year, figure the percent of business use only for the number of months the property is used in your business. Multiply that percentage by the number of months the property is used in your business, and divide the result by 12.

Column (d).—Enter the property's actual cost. For leased property, enter the lease payment for the year.

Column (e). — Multiply column (d) by the percentage in column (c). From that result, subtract any section 179 expense and one-half of investment credit taken, if applicable (unless you took the reduced credit).

Column (f). — Enter the method of figuring your depreciation deduction. If you are using the prescribed percentages presented in Part I, Section B, enter "PRE." If you elect an alternate percentage, or if the business percentage is 50% or less, enter "S/L."

Also, enter your recovery period. See the instructions to Part I, Section B, Column (d) for property used more than 50% in your trade or business. For property used 50% or less in your trade or business, enter 5 years for 3-year property (automobiles, etc.), 12 years for 5-year property (computers, etc.), and 25 years for 10-year property.

Column (g). — If column (c) shows more than 50% use in a trade or business, multiply column (e) by the applicable percentages given in the instructions for Section B. Treat automobiles as 3-year property and computers as 5-year property.

If column (c) shows 50% or less use in a trade or business, and the property was placed in service after June 18, 1984, you must figure column (g) by using the straight line method with the following percentages:

	3-year property	5-year property	10-year property
1st year	10%	4%	2%
2nd year	20%	9%	4%
3rd year	20%	9%	4%

For property used 50% or less in a qualified trade or business, no section 179 expense deduction is allowed.

Enter zero, if the property was disposed of during the year.

Limitations for automobiles. — When calculating your depreciation plus section 179 expense deduction for automobiles for the first tax year in the recovery period, your deduction is limited to $3,200.

For succeeding tax years the deduction is limited to $6,000 if placed in service after June 18, 1984, but before January 1, 1985; $6,200 if placed in service after December 31, 1984 and before April 3, 1985; and $4,800 if placed in service after April 2, 1985.

Note: *These limitations are further reduced when the percentage of business use (column (c)) is less than 100%. For* example, *if an automobile is placed in service in 1986, and is used 60 percent for business, then the first year depreciation plus section 179 expense deduction is limited to 60 percent of $3,200, which is $1,920.*

For leased automobiles see Publication 917 and Temporary Regulations 1.280F-5T, for amounts to be included in gross income.

Column (h). — Enter the amount you choose to expense for property used more than 50% in a qualified business use, (subject to limitations noted above).

Section B. — Information Regarding Use of Vehicles —

The information requested in Questions 1 through 7 is to be completed for each vehicle identified in Section A.

Employees are to provide their employers with the information requested in Questions 1 through 7 for each automobile or vehicle provided for his or her use.

Employers providing more than five vehicles to their employees, who are not more than 5% owners or related persons, are not required to complete Questions 1 through 7 for such vehicles. Instead, they are to obtain this information from their employees, check "Yes" to Question 11, and retain the information received as part of their permanent records.

Section C. — Questions For Employers Who Provide Vehicles For Use By Employees

For employers providing vehicles to their employees, a written policy statement regarding the use of such vehicles, if initiated and kept by the employer, will relieve the employee of keeping a separate set of records for substantiation requirements.

There are two types of written policy statements that will satisfy the employer's substantiation requirements under section 274(d). The first type which prohibits personal use, including commuting, must meet the following conditions:

● The vehicle is owned or leased by the employer and is provided to one or more employees for use in connection with the employer's trade or business;

● When the vehicle is not used in the employer's trade or business, it is kept on the employer's business premises, unless it is temporarily located elsewhere, for example, for maintenance or because of a mechanical failure;

● No employee using the vehicle lives at the employer's business premises;

● No employee may use the vehicle for personal purposes, other than de minimis personal use (such as a stop for lunch between two business deliveries); and

● The employer reasonably believes that, other than de minimis use, no employee uses the vehicle for any personal purpose.

The second type prohibits personal use, except for commuting. This is NOT available if the employee using the vehicle for commuting is an officer, director, or 1% or more owner. This type of written policy statement must meet the following conditions:

● The vehicle is owned or leased by the employer and is provided to one or more employees for use in connection with the employer's trade or business and is used in the employer's trade or business;

● For bona fide noncompensatory business reasons, the employer requires the employee to commute to and/or from work in the vehicle;

● The employer establishes a written policy under which the employee may not use the vehicle for personal purposes, other than commuting or de minimis personal use (such as a stop for a personal errand between a business delivery and the employee's home);

● The employer reasonably believes that, except for de minimis use, the employee does not use the vehicle for any personal purpose other than commuting; and

● The employer accounts for the commuting use by including an appropriate amount in the employee's gross income.

For both written policy statements there must be evidence that would enable the IRS to determine whether the use of the vehicle meets the conditions stated above.

An employer may establish the business and personal use of each vehicle in the fleet according to a probability sampling method developed by the employer in accordance with Regulation section 1.274-7(f).

An automobile is considered to have qualified demonstration use if the employer maintains a written policy statement prohibiting its use by individuals other than full-time automobile salesmen, prohibiting its use for personal vacation trips, prohibiting storage of personal possessions in the automobile, and limiting the total mileage outside the salesmen's normal working hours.

Form **4562**

Department of the Treasury
Internal Revenue Service (0)

Depreciation and Amortization

▶ **See separate instructions.**
▶ **Attach this form to your return.**

OMB No. 1545-0172

1986

Attachment
Sequence No. **67**

Name(s) as shown on return

Identifying number

Business or activity to which this form relates

Part I **Depreciation** (Do not use this part for automobiles, certain other vehicles, computers, and property used for entertainment, recreation, or amusement. Instead, use Part III.)
See instructions under Items You Should Note for new rules for certain assets placed in service after July 31, 1986.

Section A.—Election To Expense Recovery Property (Section 179)

(a) Class of property	(b) Cost	(c) Expense deduction
1		

2 Listed property—Enter total from Part III, Section A, column (h). . . . .

3 Total (see instructions for limitations). (Partnerships or S corporations—see the Schedule K and Schedule K-1 Instructions of Form 1065 or 1120S) . . . .

Section B.—Depreciation of Recovery Property

(a) Class of property	(b) Date placed in service	(c) Basis for depreciation (Business use only—see instructions)	(d) Recovery period	(e) Method of figuring depreciation	(f) Deduction
4 Accelerated Cost Recovery System (ACRS) (see instructions): *For assets placed in service **ONLY** during tax year beginning in 1986*				/////	/////
a 3-year property	/////				
b 5-year property	/////				
c 10-year property	/////				
d 15-year public utility property	/////				
e Low-income housing					
f 15-year real property					
g 18-year real property					
h 19-year real property					

5 Listed property—Enter total from Part III, Section A, column (g). . . . .

6 ACRS deduction for assets placed in service prior to 1986 (see instructions)

Section C.—Depreciation of Nonrecovery Property

7 Property subject to section 168(e)(2) election (see instructions) . . . .

8 Other depreciation (see instructions) . . . .

Section D.—Summary

9 Depreciation from Form 4562A (see instructions) . . . .

10 Total (add deductions on lines 3 through 9). Enter here and on the Depreciation line of your return (Partnerships and S corporations—Do NOT include any amounts entered on line 3.) . . . .

Part II **Amortization**

(a) Description of property	(b) Date acquired	(c) Cost or other basis	(d) Code section	(e) Amortization period or percentage	(f) Amortization for this year
1 Amortization for property placed in service **only** during tax year beginning in 1986			/////	/////	/////
2 Amortization for property placed in service prior to 1986					

3 Total. Enter here and on Other Deductions or Other Expenses line of your return . . . .

See Paperwork Reduction Act Notice on page 1 of the separate instructions.

Form **4562** (1986)

164

Part III **Automobiles, Certain Other Vehicles, Computers, and Property Used for Entertainment, Recreation, or Amusement (Listed Property).**

If you are using the standard mileage rate or deducting vehicle lease expense, complete columns (a) through (d) of Section A, all of Section B, and Section C if applicable.

Section A.—Depreciation (If automobiles and other listed property placed in service after June 18, 1984, are used 50% or less in a trade or business, the Section 179 deduction is not allowed and depreciation must be taken using the straight line method over 5 years. For other limitations, see instructions.)

Do you have evidence to support the business use claimed? ☐ **Yes** ☐ **No**   If yes, is the evidence written? ☐ **Yes** ☐ **No**

(a) Type of property (list vehicles first)	(b) Date placed in service	(c) Business use percentage (%)	(d) Cost or other basis (see instructions for leased property)	(e) Basis for depreciation (Business use only—see instructions)	(f) Depreciation method and recovery period	(g) Depreciation deduction	(h) Section 179 expense

Total (Enter here and on line 2, page 1.) . . . .

Total (Enter here and on line 5, page 1.) . . . .

Section B.—Information Regarding Use of Vehicles

Complete this section as follows, if you deduct expenses for vehicles:

- *Always complete this section for vehicles used by a sole proprietor, partner, or other more than 5% owner or related person.*
- *If you provided vehicles to employees, first answer the questions in Section C to see if you meet an exception to completing this section for those items.*

	Vehicle 1		Vehicle 2		Vehicle 3		Vehicle 4		Vehicle 5		Vehicle 6	
1 Total miles driven during the year . . .												
2 Total business miles driven during the year												
3 Total commuting miles driven during the year.												
4 Total other personal (noncommuting) miles driven												
	Yes	No	Yes	No	Yes	No	Yes	No	Yes	No	Yes	No
5 Was the vehicle available for personal use during off-duty hours?												
6 Was the vehicle used primarily by a more than 5% owner or related person? . . .												
7 Is another vehicle available for personal use?.												

Section C.—Questions for Employers Who Provide Vehicles for Use by Employees.

(Answer these questions to determine if you meet an exception to completing Section B. **Note:** Section B must always be completed for vehicles used by sole proprietors, partners, or other more than 5% owners or related persons.)

	Yes	No
8 Do you maintain a written policy statement that prohibits all personal use of vehicles, including commuting, by your employees?		
9 Do you maintain a written policy statement that prohibits personal use of vehicles, except commuting, by your employees? (See instructions for vehicles used by corporate officers, directors, or 1% or more owners.)		
10 Do you treat all use of vehicles by employees as personal use?		
11 Do you provide more than five vehicles to your employees and retain the information received from your employees concerning the use of the vehicles?.		
12 Do you meet the requirements concerning fleet vehicles or qualified automobile demonstration use (see instructions)?		

Note: *If your answer to 8, 9, 10, 11, or 12 is "Yes," you need not complete Section B for the covered vehicles.*

☆ U.S. Government Printing Office: 1986—493-238 23-0916750

Shareholder's Instructions for Schedule K-1 (Form 1120S)

Shareholder's Share of Income, Credits, Deductions, etc.

(For Shareholder's Use Only)

(Section references are to the Internal Revenue Code, unless otherwise noted.)

Changes You Should Note
Changes to Schedule K-1

The Tax Reform Act of 1986 (Act) made many tax law changes that affect the S corporation and its shareholders. Only a few changes apply to shareholders in preparing their 1986 individual tax returns. Most changes take place after 1986 and are applicable to shareholders preparing their 1987 individual tax returns.

Changes to Schedule K-1 that, if applicable, affect shareholders filing 1986 or 1987 tax returns are:

(1) The schedule for investment credit property was deleted. See the investment credit highlight below.

(2) A new line 19, Supplemental Schedules, was added to provide for information which before was shown on attachments to Schedule K-1.

Changes to Schedule K-1 that primarily affect shareholders filing 1987 returns are listed below:

(1) New items D, E, F, and G at top of Schedule K-1. Shareholders filing 1986 calendar year and 1986-87 FY tax returns should ignore these items.

(2) New lines 1b, 1c, and 1d; lines 10b, 10c, and 10d; and line 12c. Shareholders filing 1986–87 FY tax returns report income, loss, or credits from these lines, however, the passive activity limitations explained below do not apply.

(3) Instructions for lines 6, 8, 12g, and 19 refer to attached schedules which contain certain information to be used by shareholders filing 1987 returns.

Passive Activity Limitations

If the S corporation's tax year ends in 1987, new passive activity limitations may apply to losses reported on lines 1a, 1b, and 1c, and credits reported on lines 10b, 10c, 10d, and 11 of Schedule K-1. When applicable, the passive activity limitations are applied after the limitations on losses for a shareholder's basis in stock and debt and the shareholder's at-risk amount. See the instruction for Passive Activity Limitations in the instructions for "Lines 1a Through 1d" to determine if the limitations apply to your share of loss(es) or credit(s) reported on Schedule K-1.

Investment Credit

Except for certain limited properties, the regular investment tax credit was repealed for property placed in service after 1985. When applicable, the corporation will show in the Supplemental Schedules space for line 19 of Schedule K-1, or on an attached statement if more space is needed, your share of investment credit property that continues to qualify for the credit. See the instructions for line 10c, 10d, or 11 for investment credit property attributable to passive activities and the instructions for line 17 for property attributable to nonpassive activities for more information.

Purpose of Schedule K-1

The corporation uses Schedule K-1 (Form 1120S) to report to you your share of the corporation's income (reduced by any tax the corporation paid on the income), credits, deductions, etc. Please keep it for your records.

Although the corporation is subject to a capital gains tax and an excess net passive income tax, you, the shareholder, are liable for the income tax on your share of the corporation's income, whether or not distributed, and you must include your share on your tax return. **Your distributive share of S corporation income is not self-employment income and it is not subject to self-employment tax.**

You, as a shareholder, should use these instructions to help you report the items shown on Schedule K-1 on your tax return.

Where "(attach schedule)" appears next to lines 6, 8, 9, 10c, 10d, 11, 12g, 14c, 14d, 14f, 14g, and 17 it means the information for these lines (if applicable) will be shown in the "Supplemental Schedules" space below line 19 of Schedule K-1, or if additional space was needed, the corporation will have attached a statement to Schedule K-1 to show the information for the line item.

The notation "(see instructions for Schedule K-1)" in item F at the top of Schedule K-1 is directed to the corporation. You, as a shareholder, should ignore this notation.

Schedule K-1 does not show the amount of actual dividend distributions the corporation paid to you. The corporation must report to you such amounts totaling $10 or more during the calendar year on Form 1099-DIV. You report actual dividend distributions on Schedule B (Form 1040).

General Instructions

Basis in Corporate Stock.—You are responsible for maintaining records to show the computation of your basis in stock of the corporation. Schedule K-1 provides you with information to help you make the computation at the end of each corporate tax year. Your basis in stock is adjusted as follows (this list is not all-inclusive):

Increased for:

(1) All income (including tax-exempt income) reported on Schedule K-1. Note: Taxable income must be reported on your tax return for it to increase your basis.

(2) The excess of the deduction for depletion over the basis of the property subject to depletion.

Decreased for:

(1) Property distributions made by the corporation (excluding dividend distributions reported on Form 1099-DIV and distributions in excess of basis) reported on Schedule K-1, line 15.

(2) All losses and deductions (including nondeductible expenses) reported on Schedule K-1.

Inconsistent Treatment of Items Shown on This Schedule K-1 (and Any Attached Schedule or Similar Statements).—You must treat corporate items on your return consistent with the way the corporation treated the items on its filed return. See sections 6242, 6243, and 6244 for more information.

If your treatment on your original or amended return is (or may be) inconsistent with the corporation's treatment, or if the corporation has not filed a return, you must file **Form 8082**, Notice of Inconsistent Treatment or Amended Return, with your original or amended return to identify and explain the inconsistency (or noting that a corporate return has not been filed).

If you are required to file Form 8082 but fail to do so, you may be subject to the negligence penalty under section 6653(a). This penalty is in addition to any tax that results from making your amount or treatment of the item consistent with that shown on the corporation's return. Any deficiency that results from making the amounts consistent may be assessed immediately.

Errors.—If you believe the corporation has made an error on your Schedule K-1, notify the corporation and ask for a corrected Schedule K-1. Do not change any items on your copy. Be sure that the corporation sends a copy of the corrected Schedule K-1 to the IRS. See above instructions on inconsistent treatment of items on Schedule K-1.

Tax Shelters.—If you receive a copy of **Form 8271**, Investor Reporting of Tax Shelter Registration Number, or if your S corporation is involved in a tax shelter, see the instructions for Form 8271 for the information you are required to furnish the Internal Revenue Service. Attach the completed forms to your income tax return. The tax shelter registration number can be found in item C at the top of your Schedule K-1.

Windfall Profit Tax.—If you are a producer of domestic crude oil, your corporation will inform you of your income tax deduction for windfall profit tax on **Form 6248**, Annual Information Return of Windfall Profit Tax, and not on this Schedule K-1. In addition, generally, you must determine if you are entitled to a refund of overpaid windfall profit tax. See **Form 6249**, Computation of Overpaid Windfall Profit Tax. You will not be notified of any overpayment on this Schedule K-1.

International Boycotts.—Every S corporation that had operations in, or related to, a boycotting country, company, or national of a country, must file **Form 5713**, International Boycott Report. If the corporation did not cooperate with an international boycott and notifies you of that fact, you do not have to file Form 5713 unless you had other boycotting operations.

If the corporation cooperated with an international boycott, it must give you a copy of the Form 5713 that it filed. You also must file Form 5713 to report the activities of the corporation and any other boycott operations of your own. You may lose certain tax benefits if the corporation participated in, or cooperated with, an international boycott. Please see Form 5713 and the instructions for more information.

Elections.—Generally, the corporation decides how to figure taxable income from its operations. For example, it chooses the accounting method and depreciation methods it will use.

However, certain elections are made by you separately on your income tax return and not by the corporation. These elections are made under:

● Section 901 (foreign tax credit);
● Section 617 (deduction and recapture of certain mining exploration expenditures);
● Section 57(c) (net leases);
● Section 163(d)(6) (limitation on interest on investment indebtedness); and
● You may make an election under section 58(i) (new section 59(e) after 1986) to deduct ratably, over the period of time specified in section 58(i), certain qualified expenditures. For more information see the instructions for line 19, item g.

Additional Information.—For more information on the treatment of S corporation income, credits, deductions, etc., see **Publication 589**, Tax Information on S Corporations, **Publication 535**, Business Expenses, **Publication 536**, Net Operating Losses and the At-Risk Limits, and **Publication 550**, Investment Income and Expenses.

Specific Instructions

Name, Address, and Identifying Number.—Your name, address, and identifying number, the corporation's name, address, and identifying number, and items A and B should have been entered. If the corporation is involved in a tax shelter, item C will be completed.

If the corporation's tax year ends after 1986, it completes items D, E, F, and G, if applicable. This information is used by shareholders to complete their 1987 individual tax returns.

Lines 1a Through 19
If you are an individual shareholder, take the amounts shown in column (b) and enter them on the appropriate lines of your tax return. If you are an estate or trust, report the amounts shown in column (b) as instructed on **Form 1041**, U.S. Fiduciary Income Tax Return.

Note: *The line number references in column (c) are to forms in use for tax years beginning in 1986. If you are a calendar year shareholder in a fiscal year 1986–87 corporation, enter these amounts on the corresponding lines of the tax form in use for 1987.*

Caution: *If you have losses, deductions, credits, etc., from a prior year that were not deductible or useable because of certain limitations, such as the at-risk rules, they may be taken into account in determining your income, loss, etc., for this year. However, do not combine the prior year amounts with any amounts shown on this Schedule K-1 to get a net figure to report on your return. Instead, report the amounts on your return on a year-by-year basis.*

If you have amounts, other than line 1a, to report on Schedule E (Form 1040), enter each item on a separate line of Part II of Schedule E, column (e) or (f), whichever applies. Enter any deduction items in column (e).

Lines 1a–1d
The amounts shown on lines 1a through 1d are your share of the S corporation's income or loss(es) for its tax year. For shareholders of 1986 calendar year corporations, only line 1a income or loss will be reported. For shareholders of 1986-87 fiscal year corporations, income or losses may be reported on all lines 1a through 1d. Separate reporting for each line (if applicable) is made to facilitate your determination of passive activity limitations that apply to losses reported on your 1987 individual tax return. See explanation of **Passive Activity Limitations** below.

The amounts shown on lines 1a through 1d reflect your share of ordinary income or loss from all corporate business operations without reference to limitations on losses or adjustments that may be required by you because of: (1) your adjusted basis in stock and debt of the corporation, (2) the amount you are at risk as determined under section 465, or (3) the passive activity limitations of section 469. Details on these provisions are given on page 3.

Aggregate Losses and Deductions Limited to Basis In Stock and Debt
Generally, your deduction for your share of aggregate losses and deductions reported on Schedule K-1 is limited to your basis in stock and debt of the corporation. Your basis in stock is figured at year end. See Basis in Corporate Stock in the General Instructions. Your basis in loans made to the corporation is the balance the corporation now owes you less any reduction for losses in a prior year. See the instructions for line 16. Any loss not allowed for the tax year because of this limitation is available for indefinite carryover, limited to your basis in stock and debt in each subsequent tax year. See section 1366(d) for details.

At-Risk Limitations
Generally, if you have (1) a loss from any activity carried on as a trade or business or for the production of income by the corporation, and (2) amounts in the activity for which you are not at risk, you will have to complete **Form 6198**, Computation of Deductible Loss From an Activity Described

in Section 465(c), to figure the allowable loss to report on your return.

Section 465(c)(3)(D) which provided for an exclusion from at-risk provisions for losses attributable to the holding of certain real property was repealed. Generally, the repeal applies to losses incurred after 1986, for property placed in service after 1986. However, in the case of an interest in an S corporation acquired after 1986, the at-risk provisions apply to losses incurred after December 31, 1986, that are attributable to real property placed in service by the S corporation on, before, or after January 1, 1986.

Generally, your deductible loss from each activity for the tax year is limited to the amount you are at risk for the activity at the end of the corporation's tax year, or the amount of the loss, whichever is less. You are not at risk for the following:

a. Your basis in stock of the corporation or basis in loans you made to the corporation if the cash or other property used to purchase the stock or make the loans was from a source covered by nonrecourse indebtedness (except for qualified nonrecourse financing defined in section 465(b)(6)) or protected against loss by a guarantee, stop-loss agreement, or other similar arrangement, or that is covered by indebtedness from a person who has an interest in the activity or from a related person to a person (other than the taxpayer) having such an interest, other than a creditor.

b. Any cash or property contributed to a corporate activity, or your interest in the corporate activity, that is covered by nonrecourse indebtedness (except for qualified nonrecourse financing defined in section 465(b)(6)) or protected against loss by a guarantee, stop-loss agreement, or other similar arrangement, or that is covered by indebtedness from a person who has an interest in such activity or from a related person to a person (other than the taxpayer) having such an interest, other than a creditor.

Any loss from a section 465 activity not allowed for this tax year will be treated as a deduction allocable to the activity in the next tax year.

Note: *If the corporation sells or otherwise disposes of (1) an asset used in the activity to which the at-risk rules apply or (2) any part of its interest in such an activity (or if you sell or dispose of your interest), you must combine the gain or loss on the sale or disposition with the profit or loss from the activity to determine the net profit or loss from the activity. If this is a net loss, it may be limited because of the at-risk rules.*

To help you complete Form 6198, if required, the corporation should tell you your share of the total pre-1976 loss(es) from a section 465(c)(1) activity (i.e., films or video tapes, leasing section 1245 property, farm, or oil and gas property) for which there existed a corresponding amount of nonrecourse liability at the end of the year in which the loss(es) occurred. In addition, you should get a separate statement of income, expenses, etc., for each activity from the corporation.

Page 2

Passive Activity Limitations

Passive activity limitations of section 469 apply to any loss reported on line 1a and any credit on line 11 attributable to the line 1a activity if question D of Schedule K-1 is checked **"No."**

The section 469 limitations **also** apply to any rental real estate activity loss on line 1b and any other rental loss on line 1c and any credits related to these activities. If question E on Schedule K-1 is checked "Yes," line 1b loss(es) and the deduction equivalent of any credits on line 10b, c, or d that are related to line 1b activities are generally allowed up to $25,000. (Active participation in an activity is not required for the low-income housing credit or the rehabilitation investment credit to qualify for the $25,000 allowance.) The deduction equivalent of credits is the amount which (if allowed as a deduction) would reduce tax liability by an amount equal to such credits. Generally, the $25,000 allowance is phased out when a shareholder's adjusted gross income exceeds $100,000 ($200,000 in the case of the low-income housing and rehabilitation credits). The $25,000 allowance does not apply to losses on line 1c.

Section 469 Computation.—The limitations of section 469 are figured at the shareholder level. To figure the limitations, the applicable income and loss(es) on lines 1a, 1b, 1c, and other related passive activity income, loss, and deductions reported on Schedule K-1 are combined with other passive activity income and loss(es) from other sources to determine if the shareholder has an overall passive activity loss. The portion of such loss attributable to rental real estate activities (including the deduction equivalent) may be taken under the $25,000 allowance described above. The remaining overall loss is disallowed to the extent of the phase-in rules discussed below. The remaining credits from line 10b, 10c, 10d, or 11 are combined with passive activity credits from other sources and are limited to the tax liability attributable to all passive activities. For 1987, the disallowance is phased in to the extent the overall loss (or portion thereof) or credits are attributable to pre-enactment interest.

Phase-in Provisions.—Generally, phase-in relief is provided for any loss or credit attributable to your pre-enactment interest in a passive activity. Generally, your pre-enactment interest means any interest (stock ownership) held by you on October 22, 1986, for passive activities acquired or started by the corporation before October 23, 1986. Generally, paragraphs A through D below explain when the the phase-in provisions are applicable and how they are applied.

A. If item F of Schedule K-1 is not completed (i.e., you did not increase your stock ownership after October 22, 1986), you do not have to make the paragraph B computation below. In this case, any loss attributable to any activity started before October 23, 1986, is phased in in accordance with paragraph C below. You also do not have to make the computation for any income or loss attributable to activities started after October 22, 1986. The phase-in relief provisions do not apply to these losses as stated in paragraph D below.

B. If item F of Schedule K-1 is completed, use the percentages in items A and F of Schedule K-1 to figure what portion of your distributive share of income, loss, credits, or deductions related to each passive activity is attributable to pre-enactment interest in the corporation (step 3 below) and is not attributable to pre-enactment interest (step 2 below). The computation is made for passive activities started before October 23, 1986. The computation is made as follows:

1) Divide your distributive share of each item of income or loss (line 1a, 1b, or 1c); income or deductions (lines 5 through 9); or credits (lines 10b, 10c, 10d, or 11) attributable to a passive activity by the decimal equivalent (e.g., 50% = .50) of the percentage shown in item A of Schedule K-1. Use this amount for figuring step 2 but for no other purpose.

2) Multiply the step 1 amount by the decimal equivalent of the percentage shown in item F of Schedule K-1. This amount is the portion of your distributive share item used in step 1 that **is not attributable** to your pre-enactment interest in the corporation. See paragraph D below for treatment of this loss.

3) Subtract the amount figured in step 2 from your full distributive share item. This is the portion of your distributive share item that **is attributable** to your pre-enactment interest in the corporation. See paragraph C below for treatment of this loss.

C. If the overall loss or credit(s) (net of amounts allowable against up to $25,000 of nonpassive income) is attributable to pre-enactment interest, the loss or credit is not allowed to the extent of the phase-in percentage for the tax year. Phase-in provisions apply to tax years 1987 through 1990. The phase-in percentage is 35% for 1987 (60% for 1988, 80% for 1989, and 90% for 1990). For example, if your section 469 computation results in an overall loss of $1,000 for 1987, the phase-in provisions specify that $350 is disallowed ($1,000 × 35%) and the remaining $650 is allowed. The $350 would be available for carryover to future years.

D. To the extent the overall loss or credit(s) (net of amounts allowable against up to $25,000 of nonpassive income) is not attributable to pre-enactment interest, the phase-in provisions do not apply and the loss or credit(s) is fully disallowed. The disallowed loss or credit(s) are available for carryover to future years.

Line 1a Income or Loss

1986 Form 1040 Filers.—If you are reporting line 1a income or loss on your 1986 tax return, report the income or loss in Schedule E, Part II, column (e) or (f), of the 1986 Form 1040.

1987 Form 1040 Filers.—If you are reporting line 1a income or loss on your 1987 tax return, and question D of Schedule K-1 is checked **"Yes,"** report the income or loss in Schedule E of the 1987 Form 1040.

If you are reporting line 1a income or loss on your 1987 tax return and question D of Schedule K-1 is checked **"No,"** you must make a section 469 computation as explained above. The 1987 Instructions for Form 1040 will tell how and where to report any gain or any allowed loss shown in the computation.

Lines 1b and 1c Income or Loss

FY 1986–87 Form 1040 Filers.—If you are reporting line 1b or 1c income or loss on your 1986–87 tax return, report the income or loss in Schedule E, Part II, column (e) or (f), of the 1986 Form 1040.

1987 Form 1040 Filers.—If you are reporting line 1b or 1c income or loss on your 1987 tax return, you must make a section 469 computation as explained above. The 1987 Instructions for Form 1040 will tell how and where to report any gain or any allowed loss shown in the computation.

Line 1d Income or Loss

FY 1986–87 or 1987 Form 1040 Filers.—If you are reporting line 1d income or loss on your 1986–87 tax return, report it separately in Schedule E, Part II, column (e) or (f) of the 1986 Form 1040. Report the line 1d income or loss in the same manner when reporting it on your 1987 tax return.

Additional Information for Lines 1a through 1c.

If gain or loss from more than one trade or business activity is reported on line 1a, or gain or loss from more than one rental activity is reported on line 1b (or 1c), the corporation will provide the following information for each activity. The information will be identified and shown separately in the Supplemental Schedules space for line 19 of Schedule K-1, or on an attached statement if more space is needed.

(1) Losses from at-risk activities. See At-Risk Limitations on page 2 for details on figuring the limitations on losses from at-risk activities.

(2) Items D, E, and G Information. If applicable, items D and E of Schedule K-1 must be completed for each activity, and the start-up dates referenced in item G must be shown for each activity. See Passive Activity Limitations above for details on how this information is used.

(3) Distributive share items of income or loss; income or deductions; and credit(s) on lines 3 through 19 of Schedule K-1, that are attributable to each passive activity. You must combine the line 1a, 1b, or 1c income or loss with the other applicable income and expense items to determine the combined income or loss for the activity. See instructions above for details on Passive Activity Limitations.

Also, if the corporation is involved in only one passive activity for either line 1a, 1b, or 1c and line 5 of Schedule K-1 contains (1) income or loss attributable to the passive activity and (2) portfolio gain or loss, the corporation will separately identify the line 5 gain or loss that is applicable to the passive activity. The passive activity income or loss on line 1a, 1b, or 1c must be combined with the line 5 gain or loss and other items of income, loss, or deductions on Schedule K-1 that are attributable to the passive activity to determine the combined gain or loss for the passive activity.

Note: For 1987, estates and trusts are also subject to the section 469 limitations. Accordingly, shareholders that are estates or trusts report income or loss from lines 1a, 1b, and 1c, and credits on 10b, 10c, 10d, or line 11 on their 1987 Form 1041 after applying the section 469 limitations.

Line 5—Net Gain (Loss) Under Section 1231 (Other Than Due to Casualty or Theft).—The amount on this line is to be entered on line 1, column (g) or (h),

Page 3

whichever is applicable, of **Form 4797,** Gains and Losses From Sales or Exchanges of Assets Used in a Trade or Business and Involuntary Conversions. You do not have to complete the information called for on columns (b) through (f) of Form 4797. Write "From Schedule K–1 (Form 1120S)" across these columns.

Line 6—Other Income (Loss).—Amounts on this line are other items of income, gain, or loss not included on lines 1 through 5 such as:

a. Wagering gains and losses (section 165(d)).

b. Recoveries of bad debts, prior taxes, or delinquency amounts (section 111).

c. Gain or loss from section 1256 contracts where the corporation itself was a trader or dealer in section 1256 contracts. This income (or loss) is treated as a gain (or loss) from the sale or exchange of a capital asset. See section 1256(f) and 1402(i).

d. Net gain (loss) from involuntary conversions due to casualty or theft. The corporation will give you a schedule that shows the amounts to be reported in Section B of **Form 4684,** Casualties and Thefts. If there was a gain (or loss) from a casualty or theft to property not used in a trade or business or for income-producing purposes, you will be notified by the corporation. You must complete Form 4684 for the type of casualty or theft based on the information the corporation provides.

e. Loss(es) from qualified low-income housing projects for shareholders that are qualified investors.

f. Income or loss from a working interest in any oil or gas property as defined in section 469(c)(3).

The corporation should give you a description and the amount of your share of each of these items.

Line 7—Charitable Contributions.—The corporation will give you a schedule that shows which contributions it made were subject to the 50%, 30%, and 20% limitations. For further information, see the Form 1040 Instructions.

If property other than cash is contributed, and the fair market value of one item or group of similar items of property exceeds $5,000, the corporation is required to file **Form 8283,** Noncash Charitable Contributions, and give you a copy to attach to your tax return. Do not deduct the amount shown on Form 8283. It is the corporation's contribution. You should deduct the amount shown on line 7, Schedule K-1.

If the corporation provides you with information that the contribution was property other than cash and does not give you a Form 8283, see the Instructions for Form 8283 for filing requirements. A Form 8283 does not have to be filed unless the total claimed value of all contributed items of property exceeds $500.

Line 8—Section 179 Expense Deduction.—The amount on line 8 is your share of the corporation's section 179 expense deduction attributable to property placed in service before January 1, 1987. The corporation will show separately your share of the corporation's section 179

Page 4

expense deductions for property placed in service after 1986, with other information you need to complete Part I of Form 4562A, Depreciation of Property Placed in Service After December 31, 1986. The deductions and information will be shown in the Supplemental Schedules space for line 19 of Schedule K-1, or on an attached statement if more space is needed. See the instructions for Form 4562, Form 4562A, and Schedule E (Form 1040) for more information.

Line 9. Other Deductions.—Amounts on this line are other deductions not included on lines 7 and 8, such as:

a. Itemized deductions (Form 1040 filers enter on Schedule A (Form 1040)). If there was a gain (loss) from a casualty or theft to property not used in a trade or business or for income-producing purposes, you will be notified by the corporation. You must complete Form 4684 for the type of casualty or theft based on the information the corporation provides.

b. Any penalty on early withdrawal of savings.

c. Soil and water conservation expenditures (section 175).

d. Expenditures for the removal of architectural and transportation barriers to the elderly and handicapped which the corporation has elected to treat as a current expense. The expenses are limited by section 190.

The corporation should give you a description and the amount of your share of each of these items.

Line 10a.—If applicable, your distributive share of the corporation's jobs credit related to nonpassive activities is shown on line 10a. Any jobs credit related to a passive activity is reported on line 10d or line 11. Enter the jobs credit on Form 5884, Jobs Credit, to figure the credit you are allowed for the tax year.

Line 10b.—Your distributive share of the S corporation's low-income housing credit(s) attributable to rental real estate activity(ies) is shown on line 10b. If you are claiming the credit for a tax year beginning after 1986, the passive activity limitations of section 469 may limit the amount of credit you are allowed to take for your tax year. You must make a section 469 computation as explained in the instructions for Passive Activity Limitations on page 3 to determine if the credit is limited. After the section 469 computation, any allowable credit is entered on Form **8586,** Low-Income Housing Credit, to determine the credit allowed for the year.

Line 10c.—If applicable, your distributive share of qualified rehabilitation expenditures for property related to rental real estate activities will be shown and identified as line 10c expenditures in the Supplemental Schedules space for line 19 of Schedule K-1, or on an attached statement if more space is needed. All other information you need to figure your investment credit for these expenditures will also be shown. If you are claiming the investment credit for these expenditures for any tax year beginning after 1986, the passive activity limitations of section 469 may limit the credit you are allowed for the

tax year. You must make a section 469 computation as explained in the instructions for Passive Activity Limitations on page 3 to determine if the credit is limited. After the section 469 computation, any allowable credit is entered on Form 3468, Computation of Investment Credit, to determine your allowed credit for the tax year. **Note:** See instructions for lines 11 and 17 below for information on qualified rehabilitation expenditures for property related to other type passive activities and nonpassive activities.

Line 10d.—If applicable, your distributive share of any other credit (other than on line 10b or 10c) related to rental real estate activities will be shown on line 10d. If more than one credit is involved, the credits will be shown and identified as line 10d credits in the Supplemental Schedules space for line 19 of Schedule K-1, or on an attached statement if more space is needed. If the corporation has more than one rental real estate activity, each activity will be separately identified with any credit(s) of the activity, and other information needed to figure the passive activity limitations when the credit is claimed for tax years beginning after 1986. See the instructions for Passive Activity Limitations on page 3 for details. The credits for line 10d could include the jobs credit; any type credit listed in the instructions for line 11 below; or regular or energy investment credit property.

Line 11. Other Credits.—If applicable, your distributive share of any other credit (other than on lines 10a through 10d and any investment credit property listed for line 17) will be shown on line 11. Line 11 credits may include credits related to passive or nonpassive activities. If more than one credit is reported, or if investment credit property related to passive activities is involved, the credits or property will be shown and identified as line 11 credits or property in the Supplemental Schedules space for line 19 of Schedule K-1, or on an attached schedule if more space is needed. If the corporation has more than one trade or business activity for which income or loss is reported on line 1a, and one or more of the activities is passive, any credit(s) related to the passive activity(ies) will be identified with the passive activity(ies). Also, if a credit relates to a rental activity reported on line 1c, the credit will be identified with the line 1c activity. If you are claiming any passive activity credit(s) for tax years beginning after 1986, the passive activity limitations of section 469 may limit the credit you are allowed for your tax year. You must make a section 469 computation as explained in the instructions for Passive Activity Limitations on page 3 to determine the amount of credit you may claim.

Line 11 credits include the following:

a. Jobs credit related to a passive activity for which income or loss is reported on line 1a or 1c.

b. Investment credit property related to passive activities for which income or loss is reported on line 1a or 1c.

c. Credit for backup withholding on dividends, interest income, and other types of income (see Form 1040 instructions on backup withholding under Total Federal Income Tax Withheld).

d. Credit for alcohol used as fuel. Enter this credit on **Form 6478**, Credit for Alcohol Used as Fuel.

e. Nonconventional source fuel credit. Enter this credit on a schedule you prepare yourself to determine the allowed credit to take on your tax return. See section 29 for rules on how to figure the credit.

f. Unused credits from cooperatives.

g. Credit for increasing research activities and the orphan drug credit (enter these credits on **Form 6765**, Credit for Increasing Research Activities).

Tax Preference and Adjustment Items

1987 Filers.—The Act made many changes to the alternative minimum tax provisions. Generally, the changes are effective for tax years beginning after 1986. Lines 12a through 12g were revised to reflect the applicable changes. New line 12c was added to Schedule K-1 and line 12g instructions were expanded to provide for the following new preference and adjustment items: (1) completed contract method of accounting for long term contracts, (2) installment method of accounting, (3) losses from passive farming activities, (4) charitable contributions of appreciated property, and (5) information on passive activity losses. The corporation will list items (1) through (5) and any other preference items not listed in lines 12a through 12f of Schedule K-1 in the Supplemental Schedules space for line 19 of Schedule K-1, or on an attached schedule if more space is needed. Note: The line 12c amount and items (1) through (5) are used to complete the 1987 Form 6251 when required.

Lines 12f(1) and (2)—Qualified Investment Income and Qualified Investment Expenses.—Use the amount on these lines to determine the amount to enter on line 2e(2) of the **Form 6251**, Alternative Minimum Tax Computation.

Caution: *The amounts on lines 12f(1) and 12f(2) include only qualified investment income and expenses included in line 1a of Schedule K-1. Section 55(e)(5) defines qualified investment income and expenses. The corporation will show any qualified investment income and expenses included in lines 1d through 9 of Schedule K-1 in the Supplemental Schedules space for line 19 of Schedule K-1, or on an attached statement if more space is needed.*

You will have to adjust lines 12f(1) and (2) for any other qualified investment income or qualified investment expenses included in lines 1d through 9 and dividends reported to you on Form 1099-DIV, to determine the total qualified investment income and total qualified investment expenses for this corporation.

To determine the amount to enter on line 2e(2) of Form 6251, add to the amount shown on lines 12f(1) and (2), the qualified investment income and qualified investment expenses from all other sources, including any qualified investment income and qualified investment expenses shown on lines 1d through 9 of this Schedule K-1, and enter the result (but not less than zero) on line 2e(2) of Form 6251.

Investment Interest

The Act made several changes to section 163(d) which provides for limitations on investment interest. Generally, the changes are effective for tax years beginning after 1986. If you are completing **Form 4952**, Investment Interest Expense Deduction, for your 1987 tax year, use the information the corporation reports to you on lines 13a through 13d, and the amount of any investment income and expenses included in lines 1d through 9 of Schedule K-1 that the corporation reports to you in the Supplemental Schedules space for line 19 of Schedule K-1, or on an attached schedule if more space is needed. Also, if you are allowed any passive activity loss under the phase-in rules of section 469(l), you must reduce your investment income by this loss. See section 163(d)(4)(E) for details.

Line 13—Investment Interest.—If the corporation paid or accrued interest on debts it incurred to buy or hold investment property, the amount of interest you can deduct may be limited. The corporation should have entered the interest on investment indebtedness; items of investment income and expenses; and gains and losses from the sale or exchange of investment property.

For more information see Publication 550 and Form 4952.

Note: *Generally, if your total investment interest expense including investment interest expenses from all other sources (including carryovers, etc.) is less than $10,000 ($5,000 if married filing separately), you do not need to get Form 4952. Instead, you may enter the amounts of investment interest expense directly on Schedule A (Form 1040). The corporation will tell you if any of the amounts should be reported on Schedule E (Form 1040).*

Lines 13b(1) and (2)— Investment Income and Investment Expenses.—Use the amounts on these lines to determine the amount to enter on line 2 or 10a of Form 4952.

Caution: *The amounts on lines 13b(1) and 13b(2) include only investment income and expenses included in line 1a of Schedule K-1. The corporation will show any investment income and expenses included in lines 1d through 9 of Schedule K-1 in the Supplemental Schedules space for line 19 of Schedule K-1, or on an attached statement if more space is needed.*

To determine the amount to enter on Form 4952, add to the amount on lines 13b(1) and (2) the investment income and investment expenses from all other sources including any investment income and investment expenses reported to you in the Supplemental Schedules space for line 19 as explained above.

Lines 13c(1) and (2)—Income and Expenses From Net Lease Property.—Use the amounts on these lines to determine the net amount to enter on lines 11 and 19 of Form 4952.

Line 15.—Reduce your basis in stock of the corporation by the distributions on line 15. If these distributions exceed your basis in stock, the excess is treated as gain from the sale or exchange of property.

Line 16.—If the line 16 payments are made on indebtedness with a reduced basis, the repayments result in income to you to the extent the repayments are more than the adjusted basis of the loan. See section 1367(b)(2) for information on reduction in basis of a loan and restoration in basis of a loan with a reduced basis. See Revenue Ruling 64-162, 1964-1 (Part 1) C.B. 304 and Revenue Ruling 68-537, 1968-2 C.B. 372 for other information.

Line 17—Property Eligible for Investment Credit.—Except for certain limited properties, the regular investment tax credit has been repealed for property placed in service after 1985. Except for investment credit property related to passive activities, the corporation will list as line 17 property your distributive share of the corporation's investment in property that continues to qualify for the regular and energy investment credit in the Supplemental Schedules space for line 19 of Schedule K-1, or on an attached statement if more space is needed. This property includes certain transition property, qualified progress expenditures, qualified rehabilitation expenditures, and energy property.

If regular or energy investment credit property was placed in service for a passive activity, this property will be listed as line 10c, 10d, or 11 property in the Supplemental Schedules space for line 19 of Schedule K-1.

You can claim a tax credit based on your pro rata share of all investment in regular and energy investment credit property by filing **Form 3468**. (For more information, see Form 3468 and the related instructions.)

Line 18— Property Subject to Recapture of Investment Credit.—When investment credit property is disposed of, ceases to qualify, or there is a decrease in the percentage of business use before the end of the "life-years category" or "recovery period" assigned, you will be notified. You may have to recapture (pay back) the investment credit taken in prior years. Use the information on line 18 to figure your recapture tax on **Form 4255**, Recapture of Investment Credit. See the Form 3468 on which you took the original credit for other information you need to complete Form 4255.

You may also need Form 4255 if you disposed of more than one-third of your interest in the corporation. See **Publication 572**, Investment Credit, for more information.

Line 19—Supplemental Schedules.—If applicable, the corporation has listed in line 19, Supplemental Schedule, at the bottom of Schedule K-1, page 2, or if additional space was needed, on an attached statement to Schedule K-1, your distributive share of the following:

a. Information for lines 6, 8, 9, 10c, 10d, 11, 12g, 14c, 14d, 14f, 14g, and 17 of Schedule K-1.

b. Tax-exempt income realized by the corporation. Generally, this income is not reported on your 1986 tax return, but does increase your basis in stock of the corporation. Tax-exempt interest earned by the corporation is stated separately for the following reasons:

Page 5

(1) If applicable, to assist you in figuring the taxable portion of your social security or railroad retirement benefits. See instructions for Form 1040 for details.

(2) For tax years beginning after 1986, if you are required to file a tax return, you must report on your return as an item of information the amount of tax-exempt interest received or accrued during the tax year. See section 6012(d).

c. Nondeductible expenses realized by the corporation. These expenses are not deducted on your tax return but decrease your basis in stock.

d. Taxes paid on undistributed capital gains by a regulated investment company. (Form 1040 filers enter your share of these taxes on line 62 of Form 1040, and add the words "from Form 1120S." Also reduce your basis in stock of the S corporation by this tax.)

e. Gross income from oil and gas well property, share of production for the tax year, etc., needed to figure your depletion deduction for oil and gas wells. The corporation should also allocate to you a proportionate share of the adjusted basis of each corporate oil or gas property. The allocation of the basis of each property is made as specified in section 613A(c)(13). See Publication 535 for how to figure your depletion deduction. Also reduce your basis in stock by this deduction (section 1367(a)(2)(E)).

f. Recapture of expense deduction for recovery property (section 179). The corporation will tell you if the recapture of expense deduction for recovery property was caused by the disposition of property.

The recapture amount is limited to the deduction you took in a prior year. You will have to look at your prior year return(s) to determine the amount that you previously deducted. See Form 4797 for additional information.

g. Total qualified expenditures, and the applicable period paid or incurred during the tax year, to which an election under section 58(i) (new section 59(e) after 1986) applies.

You may either deduct the total amount of these expenditures or you may make an election under section 58(i) to deduct them ratably over the period of time specified in section 58(i). If you choose to make the election under section 58(i), the expenditures will not be classified as tax preference items and thus will not be subject to the alternative minimum tax. Make the election on Form 4562.

If you choose not to make the election, deduct the section 58(i) expenditures in full on your return (subject to any other limitations, such as the at-risk or basis limitations).

If intangible drilling costs or certain mining expenditures are passed through

to you, see items h and i before making an election to deduct them under section 58(i).

h. Intangible drilling costs which may be deducted under section 263. See Publication 535 for more information. You may choose to deduct these costs under section 263 or under section 58(i) (new section 59(e) after 1986), but not both.

i. Deduction and recapture of certain mining expenditures paid or incurred (section 617). You may choose to deduct section 617 expenditures under section 617 or 58(i) (new section 59(e) after 1986), but not both.

j. Any information or statements you need to comply with requirements under section 6111 (registration of tax shelters) or 6661 (substantial understatement of tax liability).

k. Gross farming and fishing income. If you are an individual shareholder, enter this income on Schedule E (Form 1040), Part IV, line 37. Do not report this income elsewhere on Form 1040.

If you are a shareholder that is an estate or trust, report this income to your beneficiaries on Schedule K-1 (Form 1041). Do not report it elsewhere on Form 1041.

l. Any other information you may need to file with your individual tax return that is not shown elsewhere on Schedule K-1.

Shareholder's Share of Income, Credits, Deductions, etc.

For calendar year 1986 or tax year

beginning _____ 1986, and ending _____ 19 ___

(Complete a separate Schedule K-1 for each shareholder—see Instructions)

OMB No. 1545-0130

1986

Shareholder's identifying number ▶ | Corporation's identifying number ▶

Shareholder's name, address, and ZIP code | Corporation's name, address, and ZIP code

A Shareholder's percentage of stock ownership for tax year . . . . ▶ _____ %

B Internal Revenue Service Center where corporation filed its return ▶

C Tax shelter registration number (see Instructions) . . . . ▶

D Did the shareholder materially participate in the trade or business activity(ies) for which income or loss (or credit(s)) is reported on line 1a, 6, or 9 or line 11 below? . . . . ☐ Yes ☐ No

E Did the shareholder actively participate in the rental real estate activity(ies) for which income or loss (or credit(s)) is reported on line 1b, 6, or 9 or line 10b, c, or d below? . . . . ☐ Yes ☐ No

F If (1) question D is checked "No" or income or loss is reported on line 1b or 1c and (2) the shareholder had acquisition(s) of corporate stock after 10/22/86, check here ▶ ☐ and enter the shareholder's weighted percentage increase in stock ownership after 10/22/86 (see instructions for Schedule K-1) . . . . ▶ _____ %

G If question D is checked "No" and any activity referred to in question D was started or acquired by the corporation after 10/22/86, check here ▶ ☐ and enter the date of start-up or acquisition in the date space on line 1a. Also, if an activity for which income or loss is reported on line 1b or 1c was started after 10/22/86, check the box and enter the start-up date in the date space on line 1b or 1c.

Caution: *Refer to attached Instructions for Schedule K-1 before entering information from Schedule K-1 on your tax return.*

	(a) Distributive share items	**(b)** Amount	**(c)** 1986 1040 filers enter the amount in column (b) on:
Income (Losses) and Deductions	**1a** Ordinary income (loss). Date: _____		Sch. E, Part II, col. (e) or (f)
	b Income or loss from rental real estate activity(ies). Date: _____		⎫ See Shareholder's Instructions for Schedule K-1 (Form 1120S)
	c Income or loss from rental activity(ies) other than line 1b above. Date: _____		
	d Portfolio income not reported elsewhere on Schedule K-1		⎭
	2 Dividends qualifying for the exclusion		Sch. B, Part II, line 4
	3 Net short-term capital gain (loss)		Sch. D, line 5, col. (f) or (g)
	4 Net long-term capital gain (loss)		Sch. D, line 12, col. (f) or (g)
	5 Net gain (loss) under section 1231 (other than due to casualty or theft) .		Form 4797, line 1
	6 Other income (loss) (attach schedule)		(Enter on applicable line of your return)
	7 Charitable contributions		See Form 1040 Instructions
	8 Section 179 expense deduction (attach schedule) . . .		See Shareholder's Instructions for Schedule K-1 (Form 1120S)
	9 Other deductions (attach schedule)		(Enter on applicable line of your return)
Credits	**10a** Jobs credit		Form 5884
	b Low-income housing credit		⎫
	c Qualified rehabilitation expenditures related to rental real estate activity(ies) (attach schedule)	▨▨▨	See Shareholder's Instructions for Schedule K-1 (Form 1120S)
	d Other credits related to rental real estate activity(ies) other than on line 10b and 10c (attach schedule) .		
	11 Other credits (attach schedule)		⎭
Tax Preference and Adjustment Items	**12a** Accelerated depreciation on nonrecovery real property or 15, 18, or 19-year real property placed in service before 1/1/87	▨▨▨	Form 6251, line 4c
	b Accelerated depreciation on leased personal property or leased recovery property, other than 15, 18, 19-year real property, placed in service before 1/1/87 .	▨▨▨	Form 6251, line 4d
	c Accelerated depreciation on property placed in service after 12/31/86 .		See Form 6251 Instructions
	d Depletion (other than oil and gas)		Form 6251, line 4i
	e (1) Gross income from oil, gas, or geothermal properties		⎫ See Form 6251 Instructions
	(2) Gross deductions allocable to oil, gas, or geothermal properties . .		⎭
	f (1) Qualified investment income included on page 1, Form 1120S .		⎫ See Shareholder's Instructions for Schedule K-1 (Form 1120S)
	(2) Qualified investment expenses included on page 1, Form 1120S .		
	g Other items (attach schedule)		⎭

For Paperwork Reduction Act Notice, see page 1 of Instructions for Form 1120S.

Schedule K-1 (Form 1120S) 1986

	(a) Distributive share items	(b) Amount	(c) 1986 1040 filers enter the amount in column (b) on:
Investment Interest	**13a** Interest expense on:		
	(1) Investment debts incurred before 12/17/69		Form 4952, line 1
	(2) Investment debts incurred before 9/11/75 but after 12/16/69 . .		Form 4952, line 15
	(3) Investment debts incurred after 9/10/75 . . .		Form 4952, line 5
	b (1) Investment income included on page 1, Form 1120S		
	(2) Investment expenses included on page 1, Form 1120S		See Shareholder's Instructions for Schedule K-1 (Form 1120S)
	c (1) Income from "net lease property"		
	(2) Expenses from "net lease property"		
	d Excess of net long-term capital gain over net short-term capital loss from investment property		Form 4952, line 20
Foreign Taxes	**14** Type of income ▶		Form 1116, Check boxes
	b Name of foreign country or U.S. possession ▶		Form 1116, Part I
	c Total gross income from sources outside the U.S. (attach schedule) . .		Form 1116, Part I
	d Total applicable deductions and losses (attach schedule)		Form 1116, Part I
	e Total foreign taxes (check one): ▶ ☐ Paid ☐ Accrued .		Form 1116, Part II
	f Reduction in taxes available for credit (attach schedule)		Form 1116, Part III
	g Other (attach schedule)		See Form 1116 Instructions
Other Items	**15** Property distributions (including cash) other than dividend distributions reported to you on Form 1099-DIV		See Shareholder's Instructions for Schedule K-1 (Form 1120S)
	16 Amount of loan repayments for "Loans from Shareholders"		
	17 Property eligible for investment credit (attach schedule)		

		A	B	C	
Property Subject to Recapture of Investment Credit	**18** Properties:				
	a Description of property (State whether recovery or non-recovery property. If recovery property, state whether regular percentage method or section 48(q) election used.) . .				Form 4255, top
	b Date placed in service				Form 4255, line 2
	c Cost or other basis . .				Form 4255, line 3
	d Class of recovery property or original estimated useful life				Form 4255, line 4
	e Date item ceased to be investment credit property . . .				Form 4255, line 8

19 Supplemental information for lines 6, 8, 9, 10c, 10d, 11, 12g, 14c, 14d, 14f, 14g, 17, or other items and amounts not included in lines 1a through 18 that are required to be reported separately to each shareholder (attach additional schedules if more space is needed):

Supplemental Schedules

SCHEDULE D (Form 1120S) Department of the Treasury Internal Revenue Service	Capital Gains and Losses ▶ Attach to your tax return.	OMB No. 1545-0130 1986

Name	Employer identification number

Part I — Short-term Capital Gains and Losses—Assets Held Six Months or Less

(a) Kind of property and description (Example. 100 shares of "Z" Co.)	(b) Date acquired (mo., day, yr.)	(c) Date sold (mo., day, yr.)	(d) Gross sales price	(e) Cost or other basis, plus expense of sale	(f) Gain or (loss) ((d) less (e))
1					

2 Short-term capital gain from installment sales from Form 6252, line 22 or 30 . . . . **2**

3 Unused capital loss carryover (attach computation) . . . . **3** ( )

4 Net short-term capital gain or (loss) (combine lines 1, 2, and 3). Enter here and on line 3 of Schedule K of Form 1120S **4**

Part II — Long-term Capital Gains and Losses—Assets Held More Than Six Months

5					

6 Long-term capital gain from installment sales from Form 6252. line 22 or 30 . . . . **6**

7 Net long-term capital gain or (loss) (combine lines 5 and 6 and enter here). (Reduce this amount by any applicable tax on line 28 below and enter this amount on line 4 of Schedule K of Form 1120S.) . . . **7**

8 Enter section 1231 gain from line 8, Form 4797. (See instructions regarding casualties and thefts and the line 8 amount to be entered on Schedule K of Form 1120S.) **8**

9 Net long-term capital gain or (loss) (combine lines 7 and 8). **9**

Part III — Summary of Schedule D Gains for Tax Computation Purposes

Note: *If the corporation is liable for the excess net passive income tax (line 25a, page 1, Form 1120S), see line 10a instruction before completing line 10a.*

10a Net capital gain—Enter excess of net long-term capital gain (line 9) over net short-term capital loss (line 4). If 10a is more than $25,000, see Instructions for Part IV. If line 10a is $25,000 or less, do not complete Part IV. **10a**

b Fiscal year corporations only—If Part IV applies, enter net capital gain attributable to transactions occurring before 1-1-87. Do not enter more than line 10a . . . **10b**

Part IV — Tax Computation (See Instructions)

11	Taxable income (See instructions for line 25a, page 1, Form 1120S.)	11	
12	Enter tax on line 11 amount (See instructions for computation of tax.)	12	
13	Net capital gain from line 10a	13	
14	$25,000 (statutory minimum).	14	$25,000
15	Subtract line 14 from line 13	15	
16	Calendar year corporations only—Enter 28% of line 15 (Calendar year corporations skip lines 17 through 25 and continue on line 26.)	16	
17	Enter net capital gain from line 10b.	17	
18	Subtract line 17 from line 13	18	
19	(Amount on line 17 ÷ by amount on line 13) × $25,000	19	
20	(Amount on line 18 ÷ by amount on line 13) × $25,000	20	
21	Subtract line 19 from line 17	21	
22	Subtract line 20 from line 18	22	
23	Line 21 × 28%	23	
24	Line 22 × 34%	24	
25	Add lines 23 and 24	25	
26	Calendar year corporations enter smaller of line 12 or 16 } Fiscal year corporations enter smaller of line 12 or 25 }	26	
27	Minimum tax (see instructions)	27	
28	Total tax—Add lines 26 and 27. Enter here and on line 25b, page 1, Form 1120S	28	

For Paperwork Reduction Act Notice, see page 1 of Instructions for Form 1120S.   Schedule D (Form 1120S) 1986

Instructions

(Section references are to the Internal Revenue Code, unless otherwise noted.)

Note: *See the instructions for Form 1120S for tax law changes.*

Purpose of Schedule

Schedule D should be used by corporations to report sales or exchanges of capital assets and gains on distributions to shareholders of appreciated assets that are capital assets (hereafter referred to as distributions).

Sales, exchanges, and distributions of property other than capital assets, including property used in a trade or business, involuntary conversions (other than casualties or thefts), and gain from the disposition of an interest in oil, gas, or geothermal property should be reported on **Form 4797**, Gains and Losses From Sales or Exchanges of Assets Used in a Trade or Business and Involuntary Conversions. See the instructions for Form 4797 for more information. If property is involuntarily converted because of a casualty or theft, use **Form 4684**, Casualties and Thefts.

Parts I and II

Generally, you should report sales and exchanges (including like-kind exchanges) even though there is no gain or loss. Report gain, but not loss, on a distribution. In Part I, report the sale, exchange, or distribution of capital assets held 6 months or less. In Part II, report the sale, exchange, or distribution of capital assets held more than 6 months.

For more information, see **Publication 544**, Sales and Other Dispositions of Assets, and **Publication 589**, Tax Information on S Corporations.

Exchange of like-kind property.—Report the exchange of "like-kind" property on Schedule D or on Form 4797, whichever applies. Report it even though no gain or loss is recognized when you exchange business or investment property for property of "like-kind." For exceptions, see Publication 544.

If you use Schedule D, identify the property you disposed of in column (a). Enter the date you acquired it in column (b), and the date you exchanged it in column (c). Write "like-kind exchange" in column (d). Enter the cost or other basis in column (e). Enter zero in column (f).

Special Rules for the Treatment of Certain Gains and Losses

• **Gain on distributions of appreciated property.**—Except as stated below, gain is recognized by an S corporation on a distribution of appreciated property to shareholders in the same manner as if the property had been sold to the shareholder at its fair market value. Like other capital gains, it is subject to the capital gains tax and is passed through to shareholders.

Exceptions—The above rule does not apply to (1) distributions of property in complete liquidation, and (2) distributions in tax-free reorganizations where gain or loss is not recognized by the distributee shareholders.

• **Gain from installment sales.**—Except as explained below, if you sold property at a gain this year and will receive any payment in a later tax year, you must use the installment method to report your gain. You must file **Form 6252**, Computation of Installment Sale Income, to report the sale and gain as payments are received.

If the corporation wants to elect out of the installment method; it must do the following on a timely filed return (including extensions):

(1) Report the full amount of the sale on Schedule D (Form 1120S).

(2) If you received a note or other obligation and are reporting it at less than face value, state that fact in the margin and enter the face amount of percentage of valuation.

For additional information, get **Publication 537**, Installment Sales.

• **Gains and losses on section 1256 contracts and straddles.**—Use **Form 6781**, Gains and Losses From Section 1256 Contracts and Straddles, to report section 1256 gains and losses. See instructions for Form 6781 for more information.

• **Gain or loss on an option to buy or sell property.**—See section 1234 for the rules that apply to a purchaser or grantor of an option.

• **Gain or loss from a short sale of property.**—Report the gain or loss to the extent that the property used to close the short sale is considered a capital asset in the hands of the taxpayer. A loss from a wash sale of stock or securities or from certain transactions between related persons is not deductible. (Sections 1091 and 267.)

• **Loss from securities that are capital assets that become worthless during the year.**—Except for securities held by a bank, treat the loss as a capital loss as of the last day of the tax year. (See section 582 for the rules on the treatment of securities held by a bank.)

How To Determine the Cost or Other Basis of the Property

In determining gain or loss, the basis of property will generally be its cost (section 1012). The exceptions to the general rule are provided in sections contained in subchapters C, K, O, and P of the Code. For example, if the corporation acquired the property by dividend, liquidation of another corporation, transfer from a shareholder, reorganization, contribution or gift, bequest, bankruptcy, tax-free exchange, involuntary conversion, certain asset acquisitions, or wash sale of stock, see sections 301 (or 1059), 334, 362 (or 358), 1015, 1014, 372 (or 374), 1031, 1033, 1060, and 1091, respectively. Attach an explanation if you use a basis other than actual cash cost of the property.

If you are allowed a charitable contribution deduction because you sold property to a charitable organization, figure the adjusted basis for determining gain from the sale by dividing the amount realized by the fair market value and multiplying that result by the adjusted basis.

Line 8.—If the corporation has a gain from line 8 of Form 4797, enter it on line 8.

If the line 8 gain is from line 8 of Form 4797, and it contains gain from line 21, Section B, of Form 4684 and other gain or loss under section 1231, enter the gain from Form 4684 on a schedule for line 6 of Schedule K and report the portion that is gain or loss under section 1231 (reduced by any capital gains tax applicable to the gain) on line 5 of Schedule K.

Part III—Summary of Schedule D Gains

If the net long-term capital gain is more than the net short-term capital loss, there is a net capital gain. If this gain exceeds $25,000, the corporation may be liable for an income tax on the gain. Answer the questions in the instructions for Part IV, below, to determine if the corporation is liable for income tax on its net capital gain. If the capital gain tax applies, fiscal year (FY) corporations must make a separate computation of net capital gain attributable to transactions occurring before 1987 and enter this gain on line 10b.

Line 10a.—If the corporation is liable for the tax on excess net passive income (line 25a, page 1, Form 1120S), and capital gain income was included in the computation of the tax, the amount to be entered on lines 10a and 10b is figured as follows:

1. Reduce the capital gain income reported on lines 1–2 and 5–8 of Schedule D by the portion of the excess net passive income attributable to such gain.

2. Refigure lines 4 and 9 of Schedule D based on the revised amounts from step 1 above.

3. Enter on lines 10a and 10b the net capital gain (if any) based on revised lines 4 and 9.

See section 1375(c)(2) for more information.

Part IV—Tax Computation

Section 1374 imposes a tax on certain capital gains of an S corporation.

By answering the following questions, you can determine if you are liable for the tax. If your net capital gain is more than $25,000, and you are not liable for the tax, you must answer questions A through D below as your explanation of why you are not liable for the tax.

If answers to questions A, B, and C or questions A, B, and D are "Yes," the tax applies and you must complete Part IV of Schedule D (Form 1120S). Otherwise, you are not liable for the tax.

Note: *Taxable income referred to in questions A and B below is NOT the income figured on line 24, page 1, of Form 1120S. See the instruction for "Taxable income" in the instructions for line 25a, page 1, of Form 1120S.*

A. Is taxable income more than $25,000? . . . . ☐ Yes ☐ No

B. Is net capital gain (line 10a, Part III, Schedule D (Form 1120S)) more than $25,000, and more than 50% of taxable income? . . . . ☐ Yes ☐ No

C. Have you been other than an S corporation at any time during the 3 tax years just before this year or since existence, if less than 4 years? . . . . ☐ Yes ☐ No

D. If the answer to question C is "No," does any long-term capital gain (line 9, Schedule D (Form 1120S)) represent gain from property described in each of items 1, 2, and 3 that follow? . . . ☐ Yes ☐ No

1. Property was acquired during the tax year or within 36 months before the tax year;

2. Property was acquired, directly or indirectly, from a corporation that was not in existence as an S corporation during the tax year or within 36 months before the tax year up to the time of the acquisition; and

3. Property has a substituted basis to you. (A substituted basis is one determined by reference to its basis in the hands of the transferor corporation.)

If the answer to question D is "Yes" and the tax is applicable, multiply the net capital gain from property described in question D (reduced by any excess net passive income attributable to this gain) by 28% (or a combined 28% and 34% may be applicable for FY corporations). See instruction for line 10a and section 1375(c)(2). If this amount is less than the tax figured on line 12, Part IV, enter this amount on line 26, Part IV, and write to the right of the amount, "Substituted basis." Attach the computation of the substituted basis amount to Schedule D. (See section 1374(c)(3).)

For purposes of questions C and D above, a corporation is not considered to be in existence for any tax year before the first tax year in which the corporation has shareholders, acquires assets, or begins business, whichever occurs first.

Line 11.—See Instructions for line 25a, page 1, of Form 1120S regarding computation of taxable income for line 11 of Schedule D. Do **NOT** enter amount from line 24, page 1, Form 1120S.

Line 12.—Figure a regular corporate income tax (section 11 tax) based on the taxable income on line 11 of Schedule D as if the S corporation were a C corporation and enter the tax on line 12. Use the instructions for Schedule J of Form 1120 in the 1986 Instructions for Form 1120 and 1120A, to make your computation. Disregard all references to alternative tax in the Schedule J instructions as the alternative tax is figured on lines 13 through 25 of Schedule D (Form 1120S). Attach your computation of tax to Schedule D (Form 1120S).

Line 27.—S corporations are subject to the minimum tax only for the capital gains item of tax preference and only to the extent that the gains are subject to the tax imposed by section 1374. Corporations having such capital gains of more than $10,000 must attach **Form 4626**, Computation of Minimum Tax—Corporations, to Form 1120S.

Index